W9-BVJ-926

The Failure of Theology in Modern Literature

The Failure of Theology in Modern Literature

JOHN KILLINGER

ABINGDON PRESS — New York — Nashville

THE FAILURE OF THEOLOGY IN MODERN LITERATURE

Library of Congress Catalog Card Number: 63-14595

SET UP, PRINTED, AND BOUND BY THE PARTHENON PRESS, AT NASHVILLE, TENNESSEE, UNITED STATES OF AMERICA

This book is lovingly dedicated to

ERIC

who, while it was being written, would often "tippytoe" at the study door, fumble with the knob, and then burst in like sunshine and music and perfume, all put together in the pleasantest form I think myself likely ever to see

Foreword

THE TITLE OF THIS BOOK IS SHAMELESSLY NEGATIVE. IT HAD ITS ORIGIN on an occasion when I heard Paul Scherer say that every Christian doctrine has its secular counterpart. I wondered if that is true of literature. Could such a statement be documented by the great literary works of our time? This book is my answer. Begun on a negative bias, it never overcame it. At least, not completely. In a way, I am glad it did not, for otherwise it would have ended by coming at the subject by the same route traveled by so many authors writing on the subject of theology and literature. This, dear reader, will at least be different.

Now that the book is finished, my main regret is that so many authors and works have been left unmentioned. Some have been omitted because I simply did not know them. I realize that this is inexcusable. The further I got into the subject, the more I admitted to myself that this is the sort of task that ought to be tackled only by an old man who has read omnivorously since childhood; but I had started, and could not turn back. If it is any satisfaction to the reader, I am sure that I shall mentally rewrite the text a hundred times before I am done—once for each new item I come across through the years that should have been included. But I hasten to lay claim also to that refuge-statement so frequently found in the prefaces of other books of large design: some works are omitted because there has actually not been room to include them. The kind reader will doubtless assign the charge for most omissions to this reason.

To those already familiar with many of the plays and novels mentioned in the book, I humbly apologize for the detail with which I have tried to present them. My reason is twofold. First, I wanted the book to be readable to many people who probably have not had occasion or opportunity to know the material before. These include parish ministers, who, in their harried round of activities, have possibly failed to become acquainted with such things as the plays of T. S. Eliot or the novels of Albert Camus. I hope especially that this group of men will find these chapters stimulating and revealing. Second, I have had in mind from the beginning to make this book a kind of running commentary on writings that are related to the Christian faith, in order that it may be useful as secondary reading matter in college and seminary classes seeking to uncover instances where faith and culture cross lines. Certainly it will in no way substitute for the assiduous study of the primary sources themselves, or for the give-and-take of multilateral discussion in a preceptorial setting. But it may chance to point up a name or a direction of thought that the lecturer, with his specialized task, may have neither the time nor the occasion to introduce.

I wish especially to thank the following persons for their contributions to the book: Paul Scherer, for numerous helpful comments on the manuscript, as well as for the idea that initiated it; President Robert L. Mills and the Trustees of Georgetown College, for the leave of absence from that institution during which most of the manuscript was completed; President James I. McCord and the Trustees of Princeton Theological Seminary, for employment with the leisure for study and writing; my wife Anne, for the pressure of her genial nagging to stop working so hard, without which I should probably never feel really comfortable in my work; and, finally, my students, for their friendly jostling and debate, which have helped more than anything else to crystallize many of the ideas contained herein. Theirs the praise, mine the blame.

JOHN KILLINGER

Contents

1

The Failure of Theology in Modern Literature

JONATHAN EDWARDS ONCE SAID THAT HE WOULD LIKE TO HAVE STUDIED the novels of Richardson in order to improve his own style of writing. Anyone who has read Edwards' remarkable treatise on the *Freedom of the Will* or his briefer and even more appealing *Treatise Concerning the Religious Affections* knows that Edwards really needed no lessons from Richardson—he was one of the purest stylists ever to write in the English language, and one whom contemporary philosophers and theologians might study with great profit. The interesting thing about his comment, though, is the light it sheds upon his completely utilitarian attitude toward the novel—the preacher's study of the novel might help him to improve his style of composition.

To some extent, this attitude is still with us today. One hears it frequently from seminary students, who, realizing somewhat the deficiencies of their own prose, wonder whether a careful reading of Fitzgerald or Hemingway or Katherine Anne Porter might not do marvelous things for their sermons. As a lover of literature in its own right, I cannot but confess that such a callous approach to sensitive writing still tends to stiffen my hackles.

But, by and large, at a more serious level the situation has changed. Real interest is now expressed by both writers and theologians in the achievement of some genuinely dialogical arrangement whereby they may exchange opinions and interpretations regarding God, man, sin, redemption, and other topics vital to both their enterprises. The "borderland" between the two, as Roger Lloyd has called it in his book of that title, is rapidly being populated from both sides, and already boasts such prominent names as T. S. Eliot, W. H. Auden, Allen Tate, Dorothy Sayers, C. S. Lewis, and Charles Williams, from the ranks of the writers, and, from the critics and theologians, Paul Tillich, Roland Frye, Stanley Hopper, Nathan Scott, Preston Roberts, and Amos Wilder.

The first overtures to conversation came from among the poets, particularly those who were under the spell of Eliot's *The Waste Land*. Their concern for the failure of culture led them to consider the disintegration of ecclesiastical authority and theological centrality in the age of the Reformation and Renaissance, and resulted in frequent expressions of regret at the passing of the spiritual unity man had enjoyed in earlier ages.

Then men within the church began to recognize the familiar voices on the outside. As early as 1934, Halford Luccock broke ground with his rambling, book-length study entitled *Contemporary American Literature and Religion*. It was not a great success. As usual, Luccock was more the raconteur and epigrammatist than he was the scholar. But it led the way, and in 1940 Amos Wilder published his significant *Spiritual Aspects of the New Poetry*. Though it was confined mostly to the discussion of verse, it had everything Luccock's exploratory work had lacked—depth, critical insight, and suavity. Serious dialogue had begun.

The correlation of literature and theology began to be seen in a new light. Ministers began turning to literature, not just to improve their homiletic styles and not just for sermon illustrations, but to find in the best contemporary poetry and fiction diagnostic treatments of the malaise of our times, sensitive probings of the needs of man that are not alone social at bottom, but spiritual. As Scott was writing in the late fifties, "The most sensitive interpreters of the Christian faith, in their efforts to speak to the disintegrated consciousness of modern man, are often turning today to this whole body of confessional literature in order to discover a point of entry into the country of the mind inhabited by the men of our time." [1] Even Karl Barth, who is often accused of being incorrigibly set against any dialogue between art and faith, has been willing all along to allow that "God may speak to us through a pagan or an atheist, and in that way give us to understand that the boundary between Church and the profane still and repeatedly takes a course quite different from that which we hitherto thought we saw." [2]

Many of the major colleges and theological seminaries in this country now offer accredited courses in the general area of faith and literature. Several well-known periodicals are either partly or entirely devoted to the publication of articles dealing specifically with Christianity and the arts, and other prominent journals have dedicated special issues to the topic. Nearly a dozen major books on the subject have appeared within the last four or five years. Thoughtful ministers, especially those preaching in or near the university context, have delivered sermons making extensive use of current literary works. I have in mind particularly George Buttrick's Harvard sermon [3] which deals with Camus' *The Fall,* and Ernest Gordon's Princeton sermon [4] based on Steinbeck's novel *The Winter of Our Discontent.* We have come a long way from the attitude of Edwards toward the novels of Richardson.

It is to the credit of most of the critics who approach the faith-literature relationship from the side of theology that they deal almost exclusively with literature that stands on its own merits as literature. They spend little time on religious formula writing, which Samuel H. Miller calls "the irreligious use of religious material." They flock especially to poets Eliot and Auden, to playwrights Sartre and Beckett,

[1] Nathan Scott, Jr., *Modern Literature and the Religious Frontier* (New York: Harper & Row, 1958), p. 46.

[2] *Church Dogmatics I/1,* tr. G. T. Thomson (Edinburgh: T. & T. Clark, 1960), pp. 60-61.

[3] "Expiation," in *Sermons Preached in a University Church* (Nashville: Abingdon Press, 1959), pp. 179-86.

[4] "The Winter of Our Discontent," *Princeton Seminary Bulletin,* XV (January, 1962), 44-47.

and to novelists such as Kafka, Camus, and Faulkner, who may be said to make religious use of apparently irreligious materials. Randall Stewart says of Eliot, for instance, that, more than any other twentieth-century poet writing in English, he "takes us into the heart of the devotional, the liturgical, the sacramental aspects of Christianity." [5] Surely there is a new honesty here in our time, when churchmen accept religious meanings "found in secular guise, unordained except by the authenticity of their utterance." Balaam hears the word of the Lord being spoken from the mouth of the ass.

Just as certainly as we who speak from the side of theology feel that the poets can derive much from a more thorough examination of our science, so the theologians may learn much from the poets. Wordsworth, who in the Preface to the *Lyrical Ballads* defined a poet as "a man speaking to men," went on to say that he is a man "endowed with more lively sensibility, more enthusiasm and tenderness, who has a greater knowledge of human nature, and a more comprehensive soul than are supposed to be common among mankind." In other words, he is the very nervous system of the body of humanity. And therefore theology cannot afford to be out of touch with him. To be so is to be cut off from feeling. Perhaps we do not always like what we feel through the poets, and sometimes call it an abuse of the senses; but whether or not we can reorder the information that is wired to the brain, we cannot forswear it without forswearing life itself.

To most of the best contemporary writers poetry is a spiritual calling. It has all the high seriousness for them that the minister's calling has for him. They feel a sense of mission, even of urgency. Most of them are not in our day, as in a former time, content to depict only the adventurous, the external, the peripheral; they bear to the heart of the matter, to the condition of the human soul. They are become the *ex officio* priests of our generation. And for the Church to ignore them would be for it to ignore the most sensitive impulses from the finest listening posts of our day. As Wallace Stevens has said, both art and religion mediate reality to us, and the supreme virtue here "is humility,

[5] *American Literature and Christian Doctrine* (Baton Rouge: Louisiana State University Press, 1958), p. 132.

for the humble are they that move about the world with the love of the real in their hearts." [6]

It is little wonder, when one compares the lackadaisical attitude toward worship in most churches with the relentless pursuit of mystery in much of the finest modern literature, that many people claim to discover a greater sense of the numinous in the latter than they do in the former. I heard Samuel Miller say once that he had been asked by a young seminarian where in New York City he might attend church and be sure of finding stimulation. Miller confessed that he knew of only one or two such churches and that then he could guarantee the stimulation only if the regular ministers were not out of town. But, he added hesitantly, he did know of at least four or five plays where the student might be reasonably assured of such a galvanizing experience. The lesson is plain. When the Church fails to listen to contemporary art, it usually misses the temper and mood of humanity and loses its opportunity to deal with the needs of man at the point where it might most readily have entered into them. If Eliot's description of the poet in an early essay is correct, that he is the catalyst whose presence transmutes the passions of man into verbal experience,[7] then theology can ill afford to abjure or neglect the dialogical relationship with the arts.

So much for the positive side of such a relationship. Theology must welcome the entente and work for its realization. At the same time, however, theology cannot renounce completely its own nature as creative critic in such a relationship. It can ill afford to become a mere transmitter, only relaying the message of modern literature to men in search of redemption. It has, I am convinced, a solemn responsibility to interpret and editorialize. If it believes in itself *qua* theology, if it is confident of its own authority, then it cannot willingly surrender its hegemony to painting or literature or music or anything else, regardless of how diagnostic of the human situation, or how therapeutic, or even how salutary, that particular form of the fine arts may be. It must always continue to ask hard questions of the creative

[6] *Opus Posthumous,* ed. Samuel F. Morse (New York: Alfred A. Knopf, 1957), p. 238.

[7] "Tradition and the Individual Talent," in *Selected Essays* (New York: Harcourt, Brace & World, 1932), p. 7.

arts. While allowing them their integrity and independence of existence as art, it must still press insistently upon them to "give an answer for the faith" that is in them. It cannot resign the critical function and remain theology. It must judge, or it has nothing at all to say.

This is to test the arts in their responsibility for the truthful, consistent, and coherent representation of the faith, not to disparage their spirituality. It takes for granted that there is a certain distinguishable content to the Christian faith, a peculiar genius about it against which particular works of art may be viewed for a proximate measurement of their fidelity to "the faith once for all delivered to the saints."

I am well aware that the poet, as Charles Glicksberg says, "cannot hope to shadow forth the truth of reality by imprisoning it within some institutional dogma"; that he "must communicate the whole of experience in all its baffling complexity, its irreducible contradictions and irrationalities, its ugliness as well as its grandeur, its boredom and evil as well as its beauty and holiness." [8] This goes almost without saying. But I am not prepared to follow Glicksberg when he says that no poet or novelist or dramatist can be judged by the validity of his *Weltanschauung* and that "only the dogmatic religious-minded critic would venture to grade them according to theological co-ordinates of orthodoxy." [9] Of course we cannot expect of a work of literature the orderliness or systematization that we find in Aquinas' *Summa* or Calvin's *Institutes;* one holds a mirror up to life, and the others a template. But it seems to me that Christianity is fully justified in asking, when it is represented in an artistic fashion, how *well* it is represented. Surely there can be no more crucial question put to modern literature, from the standpoint of Christianity, than that of its fidelity to the full record of the developing theological experience of the Christian faith. Does it represent the totality of the theological enterprise, even as the point of a spear represents the shaft and the force behind it, or only a limited and unconnected aspect of it? Does it drive deep at vital points, uniting them at base with subterraneous passages from other soundings, or does it merely depress the surface with some isolated and weightless instance of similarity to the faith?

[8] *Literature and Religion* (Dallas: Southern Methodist University Press, 1960), pp. 61-62.

[9] *Ibid.,* pp. 3-4.

For after all, as John Dixon has noted, "The artist works in a world where redemption is the key act in the ordering of life"; and "No Christian who takes his work and his faith seriously can go on acting as though the order of the world is one thing and the act of redemption is an act like all others, of relevance only to the individual who might take note of it ." [10] There is a very real basis, from the Christian viewpoint, for asking such a question.

The answer to the question, unfortunately, is not entirely in the affirmative. We have seen exciting things from the pens of some writers —notably Eliot, Auden, Fry, Dorothy Sayers, Charles Williams, and a few others. But on the whole there have not been many works primarily of a literary nature that have at the same time represented adequately the essential mood of the Christian faith. And only a handful of the writings of the authors mentioned could be said to actually represent, with genuine congruence, the total pattern of Christian theology, or even the total impact of it.

Partial borrowings from the Christian mythological structure occur rather frequently in contemporary literature. It is upon the discovery of these, I fear, that we have tended so often to congratulate ourselves for the progress in the dialogical relationship. They glitter like bits of colored glass from the mosaics of Eliot's comparative-religion poetry; they appear in various Christ figures, often in twisted form, as in Faulkner's Benjy or Joe Christmas or in Hemingway's old Santiago; they stand behind the symbols of baptism and the imagery of passion and the language of predestination. But there are few writers indeed who present us with a world view shaped entirely to the world R. W. B. Lewis said he wished to depict—a "world after the Incarnation." As Nathan Scott says, most contemporary writing reminds us rather of "the world *before* the Incarnation, of Aeschylus and Sophocles." [11] Not much of it seems to proceed from a truly Christian *Weltbild.*

Compare the present literary scene with the accomplishment of

[10] "On the Possibility of a Christian Criticism of the Arts," *The Christian Scholar,* XL (December, 1957), 305.

[11] *Modern Literature and the Religious Frontier,* p. 113. Cf. also Roger Hazelton, *New Accents in Contemporary Theology* (New York: Harper & Row, 1960), p. 14: "It is a welcome fact that creative artists no longer go out of their way to avoid the traditional symbols and emphases of Christianity. However, the *rapprochement* is far from being an *entente cordiale.*"

Dante, for example. His *Commedia,* which remains perennially one of the most exciting artistic achievements of all time, is a supreme example of the ability of the Christian poet to combine theology and the creative impulse. In a perfect fusion of theme and method, story and allegory, the threefold panorama of *Inferno, Purgatorio,* and *Paradiso* unfolds before the reader as an incomparable blend of the Italian and the eschatological, the local and the universal, the timely and the timeless. Faith and culture reinforce each other and speak with an almost unbelievable univocalism.

Dante tells us that his apocalypse occurred in the year 1300, when he was halfway to his three score and ten and the world was at the apex of the Middle Ages. Moving with him, we enter swiftly into the Dark Woods, symbolic of evil, and meet the Mantuan poet Vergil, who is to be our guide through the Inferno. Soon we pass through the Gate of Hell, which bears over it the inscription "Abandon all hope, ye that enter," and begin the dreadful descent through the nine circles to the bottom of the pit where Satan roars, immured to the waist in frozen streams.

The first circle is Limbo, where exist those spirits who had not the advantage of Christian baptism because they lived before Christ's era. It is to this circle that Vergil himself belongs, where, he confesses, "without hope we live in desire." Here also are Homer and Plato and Aristotle, "the Master of those that know." The second circle contains the carnal sinners, who are forever swept over by a hellish storm which they in turn answer with blasphemies against the divine power. In the third circle are the epicures and gluttons, rained, hailed, and snowed upon by a vile precipitation, so that the very ground emits a putrid odor.

In the fourth circle are met the prodigals and the avaricious, "the ill-giving and the ill-keeping," rolling great stones in semicircles till they meet, then rolling them back again. In the fifth circle, a marsh of mud, is encountered Filippo Argenti, a man of arrogance and brutality. In the sixth circle, a wide plain covered with burning sepulchers, suffer all the heretics and their followers. Flowing around the seventh circle is a river of blood in which are immersed to varying degrees all who have committed blood violence. In the seventh circle itself are found others guilty of violence—those who have done self-murder, condemned to live as poison-bearing trees, and those who have done violence against God, nature, and art, rained down upon by flakes of fire like "snow in Alps without a wind." In the eighth circle are panderers, seducers, flatterers (appropriately immersed in human excrement), simonists (including several popes), diviners and sorcerers (forced to walk backwards), scoundrels in public office, hypocrites (in gilded leaden coats), thieves, schismatics (including Mahomet), and falsifiers. In the frozen fords of the ninth and final circle dwell the souls of Cain, Antenora, Count Ugolino and Archbishop Ruggieri of Pisa (both traitors), Judas Iscariot, Brutus and Cassius; and, in the midst of such perfidious companions, caught to the breast in the ice and beating his great wings furiously against it, roars the archtraitor Satan himself, a fearful sight with three faces, champing a sinner in each mouth.

"How icy chill and hoarse I then became," writes Dante, "ask not, O Reader! for I write it not, because all speech would fail to tell." [12]

The bitter journey through the concentric circles of hell behind him, and the stars of heaven before him, Dante resumes his narrative in a new tone of gladness. The sun rises to reveal the way of ascent up the Mountain of Purgation, "that second realm, where the human spirit is purged and becomes worthy to ascend to Heaven." There Dante and his guide encounter the souls of late repenters and those who died as children, "innocent babes, bitten by the fangs of death, ere they were exempt from human sin." On the steps of sincerity, contrition, and love, Dante implores admission to purgatory proper; an angel carves on his forehead seven *P*'s, for the seven deadly sins (*peccata*) which are to be purged on the terraces above, and, turning the golden and silver keys which he holds in charge from Peter, admits him. On the seven terraces are seen examples of the seven sins: pride, envy, wrath, sloth, prodigality-avarice, gluttony, lust; and of their opposites: humility, generosity, meekness, right love, right use, abstinence, and chastity. In each case, the virtue corresponding to the vice punished on the terrace is illustrated by an episode drawn from the life of the

[12] Dante, *Inferno,* XXXIII, 8. All references to *The Divine Comedy* are to the Carlyle-Okey-Wicksteed translation, published by E. P. Dutton & Co., Inc., a Temple Classic, and used by permission of E. P. Dutton & J. M. Dent & Sons, Ltd.

Virgin; and in the ascent, at each level, a *P* is erased from Dante's brow by a stroke of the angel's wing.

At last, reaching the earthly paradise (the prelapsarian, natural state of man), Dante has recovered from the effects of the fall of man; his will is "free, upright and whole," and he receives the crown and miter as both king and priest, symbolizing that he no longer needs the institutional direction of either the empire or the Church. Here he must leave behind Vergil, who has represented earthly reason as a guide and cannot follow into the realms of revelation. At first his tears flow for Vergil, but then for his own faithlessness and sin. Beatrice, his lost love whom he follows first because of earthly love but will later envision as spiritual love, bids him to continue his journey until he can stand to gaze into her eyes. He has already drunk from Lethe, the stream that washes away all memory of sin; now he drinks from Eunoë, the stream that restores all memory of good, and moves on into the heavens.

In the opening canto of the *Paradiso,* Dante reflects on the nature of God as the *Primum Mobile,* or All-Mover of the universe, and how it is natural for all men to seek their place of rest in him, but that some men, as some sparks, fly downward and not upward. Beatrice explains to him the marvelous gift of free will, shared only by angels and men. It is only in the light of free will that the nature of the vow may be understood, as the act by which the free will sacrifices itself. Dante learns too the significance of redemption, wherein God united in his incarnate Self both the unfallen and fallen states of human nature, suffering supremest outrage on the cross. Man was thereby lifted up again and enabled to pursue the moral course (purgatory) that leads to perfect bliss.

In paradise Dante meets various figures of the medieval church, including Albertus Magnus, Thomas Aquinas, Francis of Assisi, Dominic, Bonaventura, Hugh of St. Victor, Joachim of Floris, and Benedict of Nursia. He hears the heavenly choirs sing of the three persons in the one nature of God and of the two natures in the one person of Christ. His sight strengthened by the vision of Christ, he is able to look upon the smile of Beatrice. His faith, hope, and love are tested, respectively, by Peter, James, and John. At last, the intensity of the supernal realm mounting over his consciousness, he is able to behold the full beauty of Beatrice, whose description has passed the limit of his skill. He sees the redeemed rising tier upon tier like the petals of an all-encompassing rose, with all centering upon the triune God. Bernard of Clairvaux, the type of the mystic visionary gifted with immediate contemplation, appears at Beatrice's request to direct Dante to the final vision of divine things in their true form. Bernard beseeches Mary, queen of heaven, to aid Dante in seeing the naked heart of truth. Dante looks into the deep light and beholds things as they are. Here we must permit him to speak for himself:

> Thence forward was my vision mightier than our discourse, which faileth at such sight, and faileth memory at so great outrage.
> As is he who dreaming seeth, and when the dream is gone the passion stamped remaineth, and nought else cometh to the mind again;
> even such am I; for almost wholly faileth me my vision, yet doth the sweetness that was born of it still drop within my heart.[13]

Yet he asks that God may "give my tongue such power that it may leave only a single sparkle of thy glory unto the folk to come" and continues to sketch for us mortals what he saw in that eternal light, until at last his power fails and he puts down the pen.

Little wonder that the *Comedy*'s readers through the centuries have attached to it the epithet "divine"! I have never met the man who would dispute the judgment of T. S. Eliot that "the majority of poems one outgrows and outlives, as one outgrows and outlives the majority of human passions: Dante's is one of those which one can only just hope to grow up to at the end of life." [14]

Exactly what is it about this poem that so overwhelms the reader's senses, so fixes him with "some direct shock of poetic intensity"? To be sure, part of it is in the language itself, which does not in translation suffer entirely the loss of its infinity. But one suspects that much more of it is in the breathtaking magnitude, the sheer totality, of the project. Politics, ethics, history, the arts, cosmology, philosophy—the whole of medieval learning—are caught up in the artist's brush and splayed

[13] *Paradiso,* XXXIII, 19-21.
[14] "Dante," in *Selected Essays,* p. 212.

against an enormous canvas according to the cosmic structure of the queen of knowledge, theology. Somehow one feels that culture, for Dante's time, at least, has come to a perfect head in this poem. Nowhere else is it presented so—the phrase is Shelley's—so "intensely and comprehensively."

Under our present pursuit we are naturally most interested in the specifically theological backgrounds of the poem. Such a subject is doubtless more commensurate to a multivolume treatise than to the brief mention we may accord it here. Dorothy Sayers wisely begins her *Introductory Papers on Dante* with a quotation from Étienne Gilson: "As for the vast literature on Dante, I cannot think of it without experiencing a kind of dizziness. One cannot open an Italian review without saying to one's self: 'Another book, another article that I ought to have read before expressing my opinion on this question!' "[15] And studies of Dante's use of medieval theology are certainly as plentiful as those on any other aspect of his work. Let it suffice, then, inasmuch as this writer is merely an amateur who admires the *Commedia* and as more critical material is so readily available to the interested reader, to sketch here only a few of the more obvious theological relationships of the poem.

First, there is the simple structure of Dante's journey: hell, purgatory, heaven. In a sense, it comprises the total geography of medieval theology. There was in the Middle Ages, of course, a much greater consciousness of hell than there is in the twentieth century. One has only to examine the paintings and drawings of the time, or the stories of Chaucer, to see the preoccupation with death, the devil, and punishment in the afterlife. As for purgatory, the doctrine of its existence had passed into the official theology of the Roman church as early as the days of Gregory the Great. The possibility of such a period of purgation after death had appeared not unlikely to Hermas of Rome, to Cyprian, and to Augustine. Gregory taught in his *Dialogues* that it is a matter essential to the faith. Although the doctrine has always remained rather vague in the Eastern church, it was carefully formulated and annotated in the theology of the Western church and was almost universally accepted by Western Christians in Dante's day.

[15] (New York: Harper & Brothers, 1954).

Actually it was heaven, which today is uppermost in the thinking of most Christians, that was probably furthest from the popular consciousness in the fourteenth century. Dante appropriately associated this part of his journey with thoughts of the Virgin and the great mystics. What is chiefly important about the way in which Dante used the three parts of the journey is the manner in which he was able to telescope the natural into the supernatural, so that the reader never really feels the absence of the earth from any of the three spheres. By remaining in the flesh himself, so that the spectral beings along the way at times took special notice of him, and by depicting along the various stages of his journey notable historical persons, many of whom had either recently died or were yet living, he managed to convey the sense of a "radical continuity" between this life and each of the three stages of the afterlife.

Second, the treatment of many of the characters in the *Commedia* reveals the poet's supreme ecclesiastical awareness. He was no ordinary layman with only a passive interest in the government—or misgovernment—of the Church. There was probably no astuter critic of the imperial-ecclesiastical struggle that had been mounting for centuries and had come to a head in the caricature papacy of Boniface VIII. Dante shows himself to have been a percipient student of church history, especially in Canto XXXII of the *Purgatorio,* where he reviews church-state relations from the time of Constantine to the era of the so-called Babylonian Captivity of the Church. In the *Commedia,* as in his *De Monarchia,* he criticizes papal claims to temporal power, holding that God has ordained the Church to care for spiritual matters and the state for temporal. There was no more relevant or crucial question facing the Church in that day, and it is characteristic of the author of the *Commedia* that he was so vitally involved in the disputation.

Third, the *Commedia* represents another, and perhaps opposite, aspect of the medieval church—devotionalism. Bernard, the mystic reformer of Cluny and Clairvaux and author of *Steps to Humility,* is accorded the place of greatest honor for a historical church figure in the *Paradiso:* it is he who makes the long prayer to the Virgin in the final canto and prepares the moment for Dante's immediate perception of the Deity. Moreover, the adoration of the Virgin (which Henry

Adams considered the high-water mark of devotion in the Middle Ages) is breathed throughout both the *Purgatorio* and the *Paradiso.* It will be recalled that in the *Purgatorio* it is an example from the life of Mary that on each plateau reveals the Christian virtue opposite the deadly sin there punished. And in the *Paradiso* it is she, and she alone, who stands as the final veil between Dante and the Fullness of Mystery and who at last enables the poet to look upon that divine center of all things. Purgatory was essentially ethical in nature, and the Virgin was important there; paradise is essentially devotional and mystical, and here she is supremely important.

Finally, we must mention Dante's general dependence upon medieval theology as a whole. Probably more credit than is necessary is given to Thomas Aquinas for Dante's theology and not enough to such figures as Augustine, Boethius, and Albertus Magnus; but certainly much of the *Commedia* appears to be a literary paraphrase of parts of the *Summa Theologica* of the great Dominican. For instance, the very idea of having Vergil as a guide through the *Inferno* and much of the *Purgatorio* is obviously based on Thomas' assertion that reason, or natural theology, may give an approximate knowledge of God, but that it is finally inadequate and must be augmented by revelation. Vergil is therefore a suitable guide for the lower half of the journey, but surrenders his charge to Beatrice in the latter half. From Thomas, likewise, comes the pervasive Aristotelian flavor of the *Commedia:* the concept throughout of the *Primum Mobile* that motivates all things to movement by love; the refutation of the Platonic doctrine of the plurality of souls (*Purgatorio,* IV) ; and the idea of the entelechy of souls (*Purgatorio,* XXV) . The formulation of the doctrine of the seven deadly sins was of course much older than Thomas, but was given due place in the *Summa.* The idea that pride was the basic sin could be traced back to Augustine, who may himself have owed no little debt to the Greeks and the *hybris* concept on that score; but it persisted in the medieval church and was endorsed by Thomas. The important discussions of the dual nature of Christ in Canticles II and XIII of the *Paradiso,* and of the Trinity in Canticles X and XXIV of that book (which emphasize the *filioque* aspect particularly), follow quite carefully the treatments of those subjects by Aquinas, who in turn essentially held the position of Augustine and the Chalcedonian formula. The important discussion of the doctrine of the Atonement in Canto VII of the *Paradiso* represents Christ's sacrifice as both satisfying God's justice and inspiring man's meritorious response, respectively the atonement positions of Anselm and Abelard which Thomas attempted to fuse. There is evident allusion to the seven sacraments (as enumerated in Peter Lombard's *Sentences* and endorsed in the *Summa*) in Canto XXIX of the *Purgatorio,* as well as a treatment of baptism in Canto IX of that book, and a reference to "substance" and "accident," the theological language of sacramental thought, in Canto XXXIII of the *Paradiso,* in the section previously quoted. The pregnant discussions of free will in Canticles XVI, XVIII, and XXI of the *Purgatorio* and Canto XVII of the *Paradiso* are essentially out of Thomas, who was primarily a determinist, teaching, as Dante does, that freedom of the will can actually be had only by the man of a regenerate nature whose freedom has, for all practical purposes, been voluntarily surrendered to God.

The similarities between Dante's and Thomas' theology might be extended and elaborated until the *Commedia* seemed almost to lie upon the *Summa* part for part, but enough have been mentioned, I think, to suggest the almost total transparency of Dante's writing to medieval theology. Were it not for the other aspects which enter into the *Commedia,* it might almost be said that Dante simply wrote a literary analogue on the *Summa,* so completely did he provide a popular vehicle for the more esoteric doctrines of scholastic theology.

Not that we agree with the premises and conclusions of medieval scholasticism—that is not the point. T. S. Eliot has reminded us that in order to read Dante we must enter the mind of a thirteenth-century Roman Catholic, suspending not only our disbelief, as Coleridge has enjoined us, but our *belief* as well. The point is that Dante, in what still is probably the finest literary creation of all time, gave total and coherent expression to medieval theology. And that is no mean achievement. I cannot forbear repeating the sentiment—and the words—of a student who had just read the *Commedia* for the first time and was still under its mighty spell: "How damned *complete* it is!"

What is true of the *Divine Comedy* is true also, though perhaps to a smaller extent, of such classics as *The Faerie Queene* and *Pilgrim's Progress* [16] and *Paradise Lost*. Although they do not enjoy, as Dante's poem does, a close relationship to medieval European culture, they too are notable fusions of the literary and theological, as well as of the political, social, and economic backgrounds of their times. In fact, it may probably be argued from point of coincidence that the greatest literature the West has known and loved has emerged, in one form or another, from the Christian faith, which until our day at least has been the governing ideological factor in the structuring of Western civilization.

But what has happened to literature since Dante, since Spenser, since Milton and Bunyan? Why do we not continue to have literature of the first magnitude that is total and coherent in its witness to the Christian faith? To be sure, we have had in the last hundred years Hawthorne, Melville, Dostoevski, Tolstoi, Eliot, Faulkner, and a dozen or so other major writers, who have been demonstrably committed to the faith in one way or another. But only in the naming of them one senses how fragmentary on the whole has been their presentation of contemporary trends in theology when compared with that of Dante and the English giants. They have given us scattered and indefinite christological symbols, occasional moments of mysticism—not always of the Christian variety—and a number of isolated and unsystematic theological references; but they have provided us with little poetry or fiction that has seemed to grow organically and immediately out of the world of Christian belief.

One reason may be that the age of the *summa*s is past. Or at least it is assumed to be past. I am not so sure that it really is. Barth seems to be doing very well at providing us with a new one for our time. I like very much George Hendry's description of him, as if he were a character in the first paragraphs of a Hardy novel: "He proceeds on his way like a solitary rider crossing a vast plain, turning aside from time to time to survey the encampments of previous travelers, but always returning to his course, and slowly and steadily advancing to-

[16] Evelyn Underhill has called *Pilgrim's Progress* "the Divine Comedy of Free Church Christianity" (*Worship* [New York: Harper & Row, 1937], pp. 300-301).

wards the distant horizon."[17] It is generally taken for granted today, however, that no one really has time for a *summa*—either to write it or to read it. It has been estimated that there are perhaps ten other theologians in the world who have read all of Barth's massive *Church Dogmatics,* which has thus far run to something over nine thousand pages. Most theologians tend to specialize in some limited area of the theological enterprise and to become identified as authorities within that area. It is not inconsistent with this tendency for literary artists, when they do become especially serious about the Christian faith, to become noted for emphasizing one or two aspects of the faith, as Eliot is for introspection and repentance, Greene for sanctification, and Faulkner for predestination.

Another answer, often given, is in terms of the failure of myth. Our age no longer lives under the unification of the great mythological structure which Dante and Spenser and Milton and Bunyan inherited. Only a great overarching myth is able to provide the ethos in which communication between writer and audience takes place. And our myth has disintegrated. Eliot has taken the disintegration itself as a theme. His broken syntax, pastiche of languages, and complex of mythological references have made his poetry speak to a generation apparently half aware that brokenness itself has become our myth.

Or if our ideological framework has survived it is perhaps today in an inverted condition. In Dante's world nearly everyone participated in the "myth" of God's existence and in all the myths derivative from that one. If we may be said to have a near-common myth in our time, it may be the opposite of Dante's—the Myth of the *Absence* of God. The numinous still appears in our literature—some places are freighted with it—but usually where God *isn't,* not where he is! It is in the southern nights, redolent of magnolia and honeysuckle, in Faulkner; in the "horrorous" darkness and the death-facing of Hemingway; in the rotting, stinking jungles of Conrad and Greene; in the nausea of Sartre and the absurdity of Camus. The numinous is there, but the Christian construct is missing. It is a demonic world, without any sense of the Resurrection's having ever taken place. All there is

[17] "The Dogmatic Form of Barth's Theology," *Theology Today,* XIII (October, 1956), 301.

is a sense of crucifixion—a feeling that perhaps the whole drama of contemporary life is occurring during the dark hours of the Cross, with the graves of our collective unconscious gaping to emit the shadows of our basest inclinations, producing the literature of sex, crime, bestiality, violence—all the photogenic models of naturalism.

There is much talk of creating a new mythological structure for our time—it is, for instance, what Yeats attempted to do and what Freud and Kafka came much closer to doing—or, failing that, of reinvesting the old myth with new relevance. But the moment one approaches myth as something that may be dealt with objectively, it becomes brittle and artificial. True systems of myth evolve slowly and unconsciously, and at their best are as transparent as fine glass, enhancing what they show without calling attention to themselves. To be a mythmaker is to be like a glassmaker—it is to become so conscious of the glass that one loses the world beyond it.

Therefore, the combined mythopoeic activities of our time have been able to produce only abortive and freakish structures, only broken pieces of myth. Scott has noted in *Modern Literature and the Religious Frontier* the configuration of four modern myth-attempts, the Myth of the Isolato, the Myth of Hell (Sartreian, not Dantesque), the Myth of Voyage, and the Myth of Sanctity. But none of these is more than a partial myth, expressing more than a fragmentary area of life or a brief glimpse of the cosmos. And none is really new. The myths of the Isolato and the Sartreian Hell are really inverted cosmological attitudes; they simply internalize the external universe, reducing and compressing it to what may be got within a single human mind; and they are really only contemporary footnotes to the classic image of Narcissus. The modern version of the Voyage is likewise as old as Odysseus, only now it is internalized to become the psychological saga of Leopold Bloom in Joyce's novel; and it is a truncated voyage, beginning and ending with no episodes capable of imbuing the travel itself with meaning. And the Myth of Sanctity is no more than the suspicion of the numinous, with the emphasis we have already noted upon the twisted manner of its visitations. No, if this may be called mythmaking, we have not done very well.

There is perhaps one real myth that is of our time—the Myth of the "Brave New World." The fact that no one has called it a myth only further qualifies it to be one. Made explicit in novels by Aldous Huxley, George Orwell, and Taylor Caldwell, and implicit in much poetry as well as fiction, this myth is, it seems to me, much more total and coherent than the four myths named by Scott. It provides a structure, not just for a few individuals, but for the whole world. It delineates a system of life not only expansive but detailed. This is what strikes me as so terrifying about such futuristic tales that have their origins in the present. They are at once so complete and so finely worked out—and so plausible—that they seem to be almost inescapable. In myths that are partial, one simply shrugs his shoulders and moves elsewhere; but in this one there is nowhere else to go.

Is it possible that we are moving out of the disintegration of one mythological system and into another, frightful in the prospect that it is antithetical to the one from which we have come? That we are entering an age that is godless, technological, and totalitarian? Does the Myth of Voyage really have some sinister hidden meaning, that we are on the way between two worlds, or between two views of what is actually the same world?

Whether we are indeed heading into a collisionless entry into a world view that is totally new and different, and whether it will assimilate old ideologies in such a way as to leave no trace of them, is certainly yet to be seen. Meanwhile, however, we shall continue to ask whence came this disunification of the modern consciousness that has apparently, in many areas of culture at least, led to the atrophy of the Christian mythological structure. Is there a point in history between, say, Dante and modern times where one can lay a finger and say, "Here, just here, the dissolution of the Christian ideal had its beginning"? Basil Willey, in *The Seventeenth Century Background,* suggests that it began with Descartes and the reduction of all ideology to the vanishing point of the *dubito.* Scott agrees with John Crowe Ransom that it was Thomas Hobbes, author of the *Leviathan,* who was really responsible for "the chill" that passed through both poetry and religion in the century following him. Alfred North Whitehead, in *Science and the Modern World,* and Crane Brinton, in *The Shaping of the Modern Mind,* lay the charge upon the first great modern astronomers—Kepler and Galileo and Copernicus. Considering the ubiquity of the motif of decay and mutability in seventeenth-century literature—a motif usually associated with the idea that our solar system is dying—I am more inclined to accept the last view. But it is difficult to say precisely where the change set in. There are so many other names on which the eras might have been hinged. Transition periods are never so susceptible of simplified analyses as we generally suppose from our vantage point of centuries. It is much more accurate to speak of a nexus of persons and events responsible and not simply of an individual or a single idea or discovery.

One thing is clear. The "dissociation of sensibility," as Eliot has called it, did set in sometime before the end of the seventeenth century, because the eighteenth century was of a wholly new character. In literature rationalism led to an undue emphasis on form and, in many cases, an almost utter disregard for content. It was an age of brilliance in technique, but technique by itself offers only a sham splendor. Certainly the satiric writings of men like Molière in France and Pope in England were not without their qualities; but nowhere in the entire century was sounded a diapason note to compare with that of Shakespeare or Milton in the previous century. Dean Swift is, in my opinion, the one man who might have done the Christian epic of the age, but the times were out of joint and turned his ink to vitriol, so that we got a Gulliver instead of a Pilgrim, Brobdingnagians instead of Miltonic Satans, with Laputa for an Eden and Yahoos for sinners. It is almost as if Swift had cleared his throat to sing and had spat instead.

In America a paradigm of the changing times could be seen in the contrast between the careers of Jonathan Edwards and Benjamin Franklin, who were born just three years apart near the first of the century. In outlook they were ages apart. Randall Stewart, in his book *American Literature and Christian Doctrine,* has noted the difference between them:

> Franklin, the greatest of the rationalists, and Edwards, the greatest of the theologians; Franklin, the greatest of the utilitarians, and Edwards, the greatest of the experts in the psychology of religion; Franklin, the greatest of the diplomats, and Edwards, the most intransigent of men—these two giants divided between them the American eighteenth century, and they have divided America and the American mind between them ever since.[18]

[18] P. 34.

Perhaps Stewart is correct in saying that "it is possible that Edwards will yet emerge, is already emerging, as the more useful, the more truly helpful of the two, in man's present distress." I hope so, but I am afraid that the cut of our mind is much more Franklinish than Edwardian.

Consider, for example, this portion of a characteristically amiable letter which Franklin wrote to Ezra Stiles, the president of Yale University, in answer to the latter's inquiry about his religious beliefs:

> Here is my creed. I believe in one God, Creator of the universe. That He governs it by His Providence. That He ought to be worshipped. That the most acceptable service we render Him is doing good to His other children. That the soul of man is immortal, and will be treated with justice in another life respecting its conduct in this. . . .
>
> As to Jesus of Nazareth, my opinion of whom you particularly desire, I think the system of morals and his religion, as he left them to us, the best the world ever saw or is likely to see; but I apprehend it has received various corrupt changes, and I have, with most of the present Dissenters in England, some doubts as to his divinity; though it is a question I do not dogmatize upon, having never studied it, and think it needless to busy myself with it now, when I expect soon an opportunity of knowing the truth with less trouble.[19]

This creed could probably be adopted without dissenting vote by the most amorphous church of suburbia—even those so well described by Martin Marty in *The New Shape of American Religion*. It is boneless and lumpless and highly palatable to the so-called open-minded and unopinionated among us. If Edwards is on the way back, he still has a great deal to do in driving out Franklin from his hegemony over the American mind.

The first complete polarization of the world view expressed in Dante's *Commedia* occurred with the publication, after his death, of Nietzsche's *Thus Spake Zarathustra*. It was incontrovertible evidence of the divorce between literature and the Christian faith. Dostoevski and other authors had given voice to some of *Zarathustra*'s contentions earlier, but not in such chaste form. Here was a radical analogue on the Christian gospel—an antichrist come to save men from the gospel.

[19] Quoted by Stewart, *ibid.*, pp. 32-33.

In numerous ways, Zarathustra is reminiscent of Christ. He is thirty when he leaves home. He is misunderstood, even hated, by most men. He teaches his disciples in parables, and they, like the "straw men" of the Gospels, appear stupid, so that he may make the point of the story clear. He is warned not to enter the city of "The Pied Cow," as Christ was warned not to go to Jerusalem. He moves in and out among the many cripples and beggars who come to him for help. He has not come, however, to save the world from sin, but from saviors. His primary announcement, his *kerygma,* so to speak, is the death of all gods and the birth of the superman. His challenge to those who would be his disciples is not "Deny yourself" but "Overcome!" "Woe to us! Hail to us!" proclaim his followers. "The thawing wind bloweth!"

The thawing wind. Indeed, Nietzsche considered the Christian era an ice age, freezing up the stronger spirits of man, shutting in locked channels his natural impulses, and congealing in his veins the hot blood of human vitality. Christianity, he said, had turned men into herd-seekers, submissive as cattle. And Christianity meant the priests. It was they, dressed always in their dark robes, who had turned the world black and cold. But Zarathustra has come to announce the death of the gods and the overthrow of the priesthood and the coming of the superman. For ten years he has meditated upon his message in a cave high in the mountains; now, out of the overflow of that period, he has come to preach to the world.

A few random passages will remind us of the mood and the lyrical flavor of his pronouncements:

> He whom they call Saviour put them in fetters:—
> In fetters of false values and fatuous words! Oh, that some one would save them from their Saviour!
>
> Do I advise you to neighbor-love? Rather do I advise you to neighbour-flight and to furthest love!
>
> Verily, I have often laughed at the weaklings, who think themselves good because they have crippled paws!
>
> Yea, something invulnerable, unburiable is with me, something that would rend rocks asunder: it is called *my Will.*

> "Thou shalt not rob! Thou shalt not slay!"—such precepts were once called holy; before them did one bow the knee and the head, and take off one's shoes.
>
> But I ask you: Where have there ever been better robbers and slayers in the world than such holy precepts?
>
> This new table, O my brethren, put I up over you: *Become hard!*
>
> Before God!—Now however this God hath died! Ye higher men, this God was your greatest danger! [20]

Zarathustra finally gathers to his cave a little band of Higher Men and gives them a kind of Sermon on the Mount. He retires from the cave for a while, and when he returns he is alarmed to smell incense burning and hear strange noises within. Have the Higher Men reverted to their old faith? Entering, he is highly pleased with the sight: they are all on their knees before an ass, speaking to the beast "a pious, strange litany," and the ass brays "Ye-a" at every interval in the service. When Zarathustra tells them that they must all be as little children to enter into *that* kingdom (pointing aloft with his hands), they reply, "But we do not at all want to enter into the kingdom of heaven: we have become men,—*so we want the kingdom of earth.*"

How far from the universe of Dante! "We want the kingdom of earth." In a sense, this is the evangel of freedom from the old split image, from the hellish schizophrenia of a world torn between the Christian and the secular, and it is the motto of 90 per cent of contemporary writers. It may represent the wheel's coming full circle; that is, it may be a return to the unity of head and heart, of imagination and credo, but this time secular and not religious. It is a post-Christian use of pagan literary standards.

Such a condition as generally prevails in the culture of our time cannot but produce a deleterious effect even upon the work of those writers who are nominally Christian. It is highly questionable whether a Dante or a Milton, writing in the twentieth century, could achieve a fair reading without making certain accommodations to the temper

[20] Tr. Thomas Common (New York: Random House, Modern Library, n.d.), pp. 63, 97, 122, 128, 225, 240, 320. Used by permission of George Allen & Unwin Ltd., publishers.

of the times, or whether the accommodations, if acceded to, might not make him less than a Dante or a Milton. The audience, though often a neglected factor in criticism, is nevertheless a very determinative one in the activity of literary creation. What would be the general attitude toward Faulkner, for example, had he produced a novel of *unmistakably* Christian orientation?[21] Charles Williams, the English novelist, has written some extremely sensitive fiction, but his works are known to comparatively few people, mostly professors and critics. Why? He is too difficult, say some. But nothing he has written is so difficult as Faulkner's *The Sound and the Fury*. What is the difference? Part of it is that Williams has presumed too much on a saturation of culture by Christian doctrine, and his motifs are unintelligible to most of the people who can read and be satisfied with Faulkner.

Perhaps, as Tillich suggests, it is worse than useless to desire a Dante *redivivus* for our time. He says, in *Theology of Culture:*

> An artistic style is honest only if it expresses the real situation of the artist and the cultural period to which he belongs. We can participate in the artistic styles of the past in so far as they were honestly expressing the encounter which they had with God, man, and world. But we cannot honestly imitate them and produce for the cult of the Church works which are not the result of a creating ecstasy, but which are learned reproductions of creative ecstasies of the past.[22]

Agreed. Auden's *The Age of Anxiety* is certainly better Christian art for the twentieth century than a revised *Divine Comedy* would be. But Tillich goes on to say, in an essay on "Protestantism and Artistic Style," that Picasso's "Guernica" is "a great Protestant painting" because of its obvious "negative-Protestant character"; that is, because it suggests "the question of man in a world of guilt, anxiety and despair."[23]

I appreciate Tillich's careful distinction between Protestantism and Christianity. The two are not to be equated. But from the standpoint of the Christian faith, I can see no valid reason for attaching importance to a piece of art for its "negative-Protestant character." By such a standard, the emperor Nero might have been praised for his obvious "negative-Christian character." The perceptive critic may

[21] *A Fable* was not generally recognized by readers as a religious novel.
[22] Ed. Robert C. Kimball (New York: Oxford University Press, 1959), p. 48.
[23] *Ibid.*, pp. 68-69.

doubtless find theological implications in the "Guernica"; but it can hardly be said that there is theology in it.

And this, it seems to me, is pretty much the situation for modern literature as well. There are many implications for theology—indeed, they may be said to abound. And one could not deny that there is a certain *preparatio evangelica* in many works. But there is not very much of what we could call genuine theology. One could hardly fail to be impressed by the extreme fragmentedness of Protestant doctrine when and where it does appear. In short, this is what I mean by "the failure of theology in modern literature." It is not to say that there is no value in literature that is not immediately doctrinal, or that does not spring full grown from the Scriptures, like Minerva from the head of Jove. Certainly God mediates himself to us in nonrational ways as well as rational—a fact of which Catholic authors seem much more aware than most Protestants—and a too-narrow sacramentalism is probably one of the greatest of modern faults. But it is to say that theology *qua* theology has not made a very definite impact on contemporary literature—certainly nothing like that it registered in the times of Dante and Milton.

About the so-called implications for theology there shall doubtless continue to appear many articles, books, and lectures; for precisely what the implications are, and what they mean, is always liable to debate. Literature has a way of becoming public property once it has been printed, so that even the author is no longer the final arbiter of its interpretation. Dorothy Sayers, for example, tells about a priest who commended her for a novel in which she symbolized "the right and proper resolution of a relationship between the soul and God." She had "no such ambitious idea in mind," she confesses, but the priest was finally able to convince her that what he said was true.[24] And Ernest Hemingway once answered an interviewer who was pressing him about symbolism in his writing, "Read anything I write for the pleasure of reading it. Whatever else you find will be the measure of what you brought to the reading." [25]

But theology is another matter. There is a certain *datum*, a given-

[24] *Introductory Papers on Dante*, p. 19.

[25] "The Art of Fiction XXI: Ernest Hemingway," *The Paris Review*, XVIII (Spring, 1958), 76.

ness, about it, by which its presence or absence in works of art may be determined and by which its general shape, when it is present, may be discerned. That *datum* is the historical content of the Christian faith. Although it has a certain fixedness, admittedly it is in many instances still in tension with the living situation; so that it is impossible to pinpoint the relationship of a piece of literature to an *absolute* theology, or a theology to end all theology. But proximate judgments are not thereby ruled out altogether. It is still possible to criticize literature from a particular theological position, albeit one that is acknowledged to be relative. There is a defensible legitimacy, it seems to me, about a Reformed criticism of the arts, or an Evangelical criticism of the arts, or a Roman Catholic criticism, or an Orthodox criticism—or even, perhaps, an ecumenical criticism.

This book does not pretend to be the end-all of such criticism. Its orientation, while it is generally Protestant, is not consistently toward a particular area of Protestantism. I have simply tried, in the following chapters, to examine in a most elemental fashion certain areas of contemporary literature as they are related to several recurrent themes in the theology of the Christian faith. Another writer might have chosen other themes. The ones I have selected are rather basic, I believe, to any theological system. They are, respectively, the Doctrine of God, the Doctrine of Man, the Doctrine of the Church, the Doctrine of the Sacraments, the Doctrine of the Ministry, the Doctrine of Last Things, and the Doctrine of Atonement. The last doctrine might appropriately be dealt with as part of the doctrine of God, but I have singled it out for a chapter of its own because it has been the major emphasis, both liturgically and theologically, of Western Christianity through the centuries.

The final chapter, which I have entitled "The 'Christian' Artist," raises the question of whether, in the last analysis, Christian art is really possible. I only mention it now in order that it may not seem a totally new and preposterous question when we come to it. And, to provide the reader with something to chew on until he reaches that stage of the book, I append here a statement by Geddes MacGregor:

> The purpose of Christian art must include the stimulation of aesthetic experience; but it also includes the initiation of a trend of experience leading

Christians towards union with Christ. So it is that a Christian as such, though he values El Greco, does not really value him so very much more than he does work of a similar kind but of much less artistic merit. For the Christian as such is looking not for aesthetic experience *simpliciter,* but for God, the *terminus ad quem* of that movement of which the aesthetic "moment" is the *terminus a quo.*[26]

[26] "Christian Discrimination in the Realm of Aesthetic Judgment," *The Christian Scholar,* XL (December, 1957), 271.

2

The Absence of God

" 'THE FOOL HATH SAID IN HIS HEART, THERE IS NO GOD.' IT MAY BE SO. Most things said or written have been the work of fools. This thing is certain—he is a fool who says, 'No man hath said in his heart, There is no God.' "[1]

These words, written in 1883, were amazingly prophetic. We are just beginning to realize how prophetic. On every hand now, we are confronted by the fact that we live in an age *"post mortem Dei,"* as Paul Ramsey has called it—an age "after the death of God." Though it dawns on us very slowly, we are at last coming to see that Nietzsche's announcement of the death of God and the transvaluation of all values was not really something that Nietzsche dreamed up on his own, but that he simply saw our times better than we have seen them ourselves. And the same may be said for Dostoevski, whose Ivan Karamazov spoke of a coming age, analogous to a geological period, when all men would deny God and assert themselves in a new titanism. These troubled spirits of the nineteenth century had both the blessing and the curse of Cassandra—they saw what was coming and no one

[1] Olive Schreiner, *The Story of an African Farm* (Boston: Little, Brown & Co., 1905), p. 168.

believed them. Now it is here. Now we are all addressing ourselves to the problems of living in a post-Christian age.

What may we say is the effect of the times upon the literary artists of the present century? How is the matter of living in an era that is *post mortem Dei* reflected in contemporary poetry, drama, and fiction? Edmund Fuller, writing about fiction, had this to say:

> Our present generations now practicing the art of fiction are the first generations in which there have been large, influential, and admired groups of novelists working, in many instances quite unconsciously, on the tacit or declared premise that there is no God, basing the patterns of their work on the implications, again often unconscious, that arise out of that premise.[2]

This is a serious accusation, for if it is true it endorses what is being said about a post-Christian age and posits a climate for modern artistic creation that is the complete opposite of the one in which Dante wrote. God was the glorious center of Dante's universe, "the profound and shining being" toward which all things tended by the movement of love. There is no canto in the *Commedia,* no verse, no line, that is not supremely overridden by consciousness of the Divine; it is this, in fact, that makes the work a "comedy," a sequence of actions through which the protagonist arrives at a happy ending. Has the situation really changed so drastically for writers in our day? Is God, as Fuller suggests, no longer at the center of things, perhaps not even in the picture at all?

Of course there is no simple answer. One cannot say merely that God is or is not there for contemporary authors. There are some for whom he appears to matter more than for others. One would have to say that he is very much in evidence, for example, in the novels of Charles Williams, or in the poetry and drama of T. S. Eliot, W. H. Auden, and Christopher Fry—though even here, especially among the poets, there is a tendency to exploit the critical function, so that what we have is not poetry about God but poetry about a society that has forgotten God. If we may compare Auden's *The Age of Anxiety,* for instance, with Dante's *Commedia,* what we have in the former is a monolithic elegy on the text,

[2] From *Man in Modern Fiction,* by Edmund Fuller © Copyright 1958 by Edmund Fuller. Reprinted by permission of Random House, Inc. P. 8.

Mourn for him now,
Our lost dad,
Our colossal father.[3]

The poem ends with a note of grace and redemption, to be sure—but only after a disproportionately long glimpse of human life in purgatory.

Perhaps the key to the attitude of most modern writers toward God is struck in Aldous Huxley's famous futuristic novel, *Brave New World,* in the scene where the Savage and the World Controller are looking at copies of the Bible, *The Imitation of Christ,* and William James's *The Varieties of Religious Experience.* The Savage inquires whether the World Controller believes there is no God. "No," answers the Controller, "I think there quite probably is one. . . . But he manifests himself in different ways to different men. In premodern times he manifested himself as the being that's described in these books."

"How does he manifest himself now?" asks the Savage.

"Well," says the Controller, "he manifests himself as an absence; as though he weren't there at all." [4]

The Paradox of the Manifest Absence—isn't this what we have discovered in so much of modern literature, especially fiction? It isn't so much that God is dead, as Nietzsche said, but that he just doesn't seem to matter any more. As Richard E. Sherrell has demonstrated in an article about current French drama,[5] the case against God is made by default, not by explicit reference. What we so frequently hear called the atheism of the Gallic theater is not atheism at all. It is simply a view of man disengaged from faith—of man with God absent. I am not sure that even Sartre and Camus should be classified as thoroughgoing atheists; they are only so dedicated to humanism that they would consider it a betrayal of their first cause even to deal seriously with the question of God. It is a matter of priorities. What Sartre calls acting in poor faith (*la mauvaise foi*) is merely the shirking of what he considers to be man's first responsibility—to his own self-

[3] From *The Age of Anxiety,* by W. H. Auden. Copyright 1946, 1947 by W. H. Auden. Reprinted by permission of Random House, Inc., and Faber & Faber Ltd.

[4] (New York: Harper & Row, 1932), p. 281.

[5] "The Case Against God in Contemporary French Drama," *Religion in Life,* XXXI (Autumn, 1962), 610-25.

identity. When Daniel, in *Les Chemins de la liberté,* becomes "religious," his conversion is treated as an atavism, as a desertion of the primary cause of humanism.

But we do not have to go to the French to find significant literature in which God's absence plays an important role.

Consider the novels and short stories of Ernest Hemingway, for example. Elsewhere I have tried to document the similarities between Hemingway's world view and that of the French existentialists.[6] Like the existentialists, Hemingway came to his view through the experience of war. The wound he received as an ambulance driver on the Italian front in the First World War marked every major character he was later to write about—psychically as well as physically, says Philip Young. From there on out, the Hemingway hero was to be a wounded man. And the idea of God hardly seemed to him compatible with the kind of world where a man, if he is any good at all, gets hurt. As he made old Anselmo say in *For Whom the Bell Tolls,* "We do not have God here anymore, neither His Son nor the Holy Ghost."

Faint blushes of the old religious feelings still rise in the Hemingway protagonist from time to time, but mostly when he is tiredest or the night is darkest. As a general thing, if he is strong and the light is bright, he is able to keep them at bay.

"Are you *croyant?*" asks Count Greffi of Lieutenant Henry in *A Farewell to Arms.*

"At night," replies Henry.

"Perhaps I have outlived my religious feeling," says the count a little later.

"My own comes only at night," says Henry.

Henry's wounding occurs almost precisely as Hemingway's had—a random shell, a shower of shrapnel, and a spasm of pain. It is all so senseless, so without reason. The presence of God seems almost unbelievable in such a spectrum of horror. It is all right for the world of quiet Main Streets, soda shops, and civic clubs—the world Hemingway always referred to as "complicated." But it just doesn't belong to a world in combustion.

The nighttime or darkness symbolism figures rather prominently

[6] *Hemingway and the Dead Gods* (Lexington: University of Kentucky Press, 1960).

in many early Hemingway stories and sometimes assumes almost a religious meaning, as in "A Clean, Well-Lighted Place." [7] An old man appears nightly at a little bar, and sits and drinks until the bartenders close and send him off into the night. Outside, the darkness seems to wait like some black beast, panting and restless, to devour him. The total effect is raised to a spiritual pitch by the parody of the Hail Mary as "Hail nada, full of nada," and of the Pater Noster as "Our nada, which art in nada, nada be thy name." *Nada,* of course, is the Spanish word for "nothing." Whatever else it may be, the story, now a classic, is a commentary on a time without God.

Perhaps it is true of the Hemingway personae, as Robinson Jeffers says it is true of a hurt hawk, that they know more of "the wild God of the world" than "communal people." But I doubt it. Somerset Maugham is an old man, and wise in many ways of the world, and he says in *The Summing Up* that suffering, contrary to the general view that it ennobles men, merely makes them mean and animalistic.

Another novelist of the "Lost Generation" who employed the symbolism of nighttime and darkness was Scott Fitzgerald, who continues to claim much critical attention. In *Tender Is the Night* the most peaceful and promising relationships of the novel always seem to be formed at night. Nicole and Dick meet in the rain at night while she is a patient in the sanatorium. She brings a basket of flowers and waits for him in the darkness. Somehow the very night itself seems tender, pregnant with care. Nicole remembers it as "full of the presence of a strange and watchful God." When her marriage becomes sun-parched and desperate, she discovers youth and life again while swimming in the grotto under a full moon. Such night scenes, always soft and mellow, offer an obvious contrast to the glaring scenes along the beach in the daytime, filled with their vacuous chatter, flirtations, and jealousies.

In *The Great Gatsby,* the light symbolism might almost be described as Icarian, for it is consistently reminiscent of the myth of Daedalus and his son Icarus, who flew too near the sun. The furniture in the Buchanan home seems to float, and Daisy Buchanan and her friends appear to sit and walk suspended in the air. The dominant colors in

[7] From *Short Stories* (New York: Charles Scribner's Sons, 1954).

the décor are white and gold. Gatsby's great car, the *instrument de dénouement,* is chrome yellow, foreshadowing his violent end for flying too near the sun. And, if one wishes to press such matters to their utmost, the sun may even be Daisy Buchanan, whom Gatsby has always loved, because "daisy" is etymologically derived from the Middle English "day's eye"—the sun.

Intense heat and dryness accompany the light in the novel, especially in those parts set near the great ash heaps that lie between East Egg and West Egg. Even the people there are ash men: the clothes of Wilson, the garageman who lives by the dump, are always covered with "a white ashen dust," and when he emerges by Gatsby's swimming pool to slay Gatsby, he is an "ashen, fantastic figure gliding toward him through the amorphous trees." Presiding over this arid wasteland society is a monstrous pair of faded eyes on a billboard, advertising an optometrist named T. J. Eckleburg—and somehow suggesting that they represent the sightless vigil of God.

God is not quite present in Fitzgerald's world, and this is what is wrong with it. It is the world that chose Franklin over Edwards. Gatsby, in fact, is a modern-day Franklin, who has practiced Poor Richard's rules for getting ahead in the world. After his death, his father displays a book Gatsby had had as a child. On the flyleaf is inscribed this schedule:

Rise from bed	6.00	A.M.
Dumbbell exercise and wall-scaling	6.15-6.30	A.M.
Study electricity, etc.	7.15-8.15	A.M.
Work	8.30-4.30	P.M.
Baseball and sports	4.30-5.00	P.M.
Practice elocution, poise and how to attain it	5.00-6.00	P.M.
Study needed inventions	7.00-9.00	P.M.[8]

Edwards, who himself was no sluggard and no mean student of science, could have told Gatsby what the missing ingredient in the formula was.

Contemporary fiction is full of Gatsbys—men who have inherited a world that was structured along religious and spiritual lines, but who have drifted away from the rationale.

The characters who inhabit the strange, psychotic world of Franz

[8] (New York: Charles Scribner's Sons, 1925), p. 174.

Kafka, for instance, may appear at first sight to be at the other end of the spectrum from Gatsby. But it is really the absence of God, again, that makes that world so nightmarish and nonsensical. Indeed, one of the most fruitful avenues of critical approach to Kafka's work has been by way of his Jewish heritage—particularly in the area of the Law. All experiences in his novels are truncated and frustrated because they are begun under the premise of God's existence but incapable of being completed under the same premise. Kafka's universe therefore becomes one of unlimited ricochet: emotions are never consummated, but bound back and forth endlessly in a sealed world, crisscrossing and returning, returning and crisscrossing, until the characters (and perhaps even the reader) sink into exhaustion and quiet despair. It is little wonder that Joseph K., at the end of *The Trial,* feels that he is dying "like a dog." It would be different if only God were present.

Nathan Scott has spoken somewhere of the "soulscape" of modern novels. Perhaps this is their "Godscape." Few characters actually go so far as Anne Dubreuilh, in Simone de Beauvoir's *The Mandarins,* who says, "I've never felt sorry about losing God." But the *deus in absentia* is such an obvious feature of contemporary life in general that we really should not marvel at finding it so frequently in the literature of the time.

What has happened, both in the world of fiction and in the real life it is supposed to body forth, to convince men of God's absence? Hosts of answers have been given: the Copernican revolution; the Renaissance and the rebirth of humanism; the scientific spirit of Newton and Bacon and Hobbes and Descartes; deism; Darwinism; higher criticism; progressivism; two world wars and the onset of twentieth-century pessimism. Certainly all these have been involved, one way or another, in the debacle of faith. But beyond all of them, or perhaps through them and involved in them, there is a more direct answer—one given from a theological point of view.

What, after all, is the primary mode of relationship between God and the world? Nature has of course always been one mode of relationship. Paul began the argument of Romans there: God's self-revelation in nature has left all men without excuse. But beyond nature is God's ultimate revelation of himself in the Incarnation. That which Tillich calls the "Christ-event" has always, for the Christian faith, been the real ground of interaction between God and man. "God was, in Christ, reconciling the world unto himself."

Here is the reason the world has lost God: it has first lost Christ, and the loss of Christ means the loss of relation.

Not that Christ does not appear in contemporary writing. One does not obliterate him and his effects upon history simply by saying to him, as Dostoevski's Grand Inquisitor did, "Go, and come no more." Jeffers was right when he said,

> His personal anguish and insane solution
> Have stained an age; nearly two thousand years
> are one vast poem drunk with the wine of
> his blood.[9]

There are numerous references to Christ in modern literature—countless symbols, analogues on his ministry and passion, even direct references.

But the majority of the better-known Christ figures are ineffectual ones, like Jeffers' "young Jew writhing on the doomed hill in the earthquake." [10] Alan Paton and Liston Pope, discussing the prevalent ideas of the Christ symbol in an article on "The Novelist and Christ," said that "apparently any fictional character qualifies who is innocent, selfless, and strange, even if he is banal or amoral or utterly humanist." [11] Herman Melville's Billy Budd, according to critic James Baird,[12] is merely the apotheosis of the *puer aeternus*. Steinbeck's Casy, in *Grapes of Wrath,* is a holiness preacher who gets his head smashed by a pick handle during an attempt to organize a fruit pickers' union. George Brush, in Thornton Wilder's *Heaven's My Destination,* is a fundamentalist textbook salesman who is given a

[9] "Dear Judas." Copyright 1929 and renewed 1957 by Robinson Jeffers. Reprinted from *Dear Judas and Other Poems,* by Robinson Jeffers, by permission of Random House, Inc.

[10] "Meditation on Saviors." Copyright 1928 and renewed 1956 by Robinson Jeffers. Reprinted from *The Selected Poetry of Robinson Jeffers,* by permission of Random House, Inc.

[11] In the *Saturday Review,* December 4, 1954, p. 15.

[12] *Ishmael: A Study of the Symbolic Mode of Primitivism* (New York: Harper & Row, 1960), p. 205.

kind of Christ-before-Pilate trial for trying to break a thief from stealing by giving him money. Hemingway's Santiago, in *The Old Man and the Sea,* loses his fish to the galanos and falls wearily under the weight of his ship's mast as he bears it up the hill. Faulkner's Benjy, in *The Sound and the Fury,* is a thirty-three-year-old idiot who has been gelded to keep him from molesting little girls; and Joe Christmas, in *Light in August,* is a half-breed who is murdered and mutilated for killing a spinster woman to whom he has made love.

This is not to say that there have not been some beautiful and inspiring uses of the Christ image. F. W. Dillistone has discussed several of them in *The Novelist and the Passion Story:* Mauriac's *The Lamb* and *A Woman of the Pharisees,* Melville's *Billy Budd,* Kazantzakis' *The Greek Passion,* and Faulkner's *A Fable.* There is absolutely no doubt of Mauriac's intention of making Xavier Dartigelongue, in *The Lamb,* a Christ figure. His life is surrendered in one great passion for other persons; again and again he gives himself that they might have life. Especially poignant is the scene in which he carries a ladder through the dark night to put against the window where the boy Roland is imprisoned. He has put off his shoes in order to make no noise when passing out of the house, and the furze bushes and pine cones are giving him excruciating pain as he half carries, half drags, the ladder along. Mauriac says,

> It was the very flesh of his body now that was being torn and mangled. In the past he had talked endlessly of the Cross, had fed his meditations on the thought of it, but only here, in the loneliness of a cold, dark night, was it born [*sic*] in upon him that he had never understood its full meaning, had never truly merged himself with the experience. The Cross was not, as he had once believed, a love withdrawn, an agonized bending of the spirit, an humiliation, an obstacle; it was, quite simply, a crushing weight of timber, a bruised and tortured shoulder, carried on feet flayed by stones and earth.[18]

In the end, Xavier dies a ridiculous death—he is struck by an automobile while riding a bicycle. But the driver of the vehicle, Jean de Mirbel, is strangely "redeemed" by the death.

Faulkner's *A Fable* is probably the most intricate refashioning of the Passion narrative to appear in the last half century. It is a "big" novel, capturing innumerable facets of life along the wavering battle-

[18] Tr. Gerard Hopkins (New York: Farrar, Straus & Company, 1956), p. 104.

fronts of Europe in the First World War. In my opinion, it is the finest novel Faulkner ever wrote and the nearest thing the English-speaking world has ever had to put against the grandeur of Tolstoi and Dostoevski. The plot centers in upon an act of passive resistance by a regiment of soldiers in the Allied trenches. An old general holds the power of life and death over them. At the center of the resistance is a little band of thirteen men, of whom a certain corporal (*corpus:* incarnation!) is the leader. Ironically, the corporal is discovered to be the illegitimate son of the general. In a private interview, the general offers him a limousine to escape to the coast, but the corporal refuses; he will not desert his men. The old man reminds him that one of them has already deserted him and that the others will probably do likewise when given the chance, but he is obdurate. The order is given and the corporal is executed—on a post between a thief and a murderer. His body is taken away by friends and buried on French farmland. When the bombardment has fallen on the farm again, leaving it pockmarked with craters, the peasants rush to the place where they had entombed him, only to find a crater there, and some fragments of the unpainted wood of the coffin. They search the area and find a few more shards and pieces of the coffin; but the body itself is gone.

The unfortunate ingredient in the novel, from the Christian viewpoint, is Faulkner's known humanism, which he puts eloquently into the words of the old general during his interview with the son he is trying to save. The son tells him not to be afraid. "Afraid?" he says.

> No no, it's not I but you who are afraid of man; not I but you who believe that nothing but a death can save him. I know better. I know that he has that in him which will enable him to outlast even his wars; that in him more durable than all his vices, even that last and most fearsome one; to outlast even this next avatar of his servitude which he now faces: his enslavement to the demonic progeny of his own mechanical curiosity, from which he will emancipate himself by that one ancient tried-and-true method by which slaves have always freed themselves: by inculcating their masters with the slaves' own vices—in this case the vice of war and that other one which is no vice at all but instead is the quality-mark and warrant of man's immortality: his deathless folly.[14]

[14] (New York: Random House, 1954), p. 352.

In words Faulkner himself repeated when he accepted the Nobel Prize for Literature, the old general says that man and his folly "will prevail."

Dillistone is probably correct when he says that any attempt to present Christ again in fiction is sure to involve the artist in heresy of one kind or another, for the *work* of a Christ figure must always fall short of the work of Christ. As Paton and Pope remind us in "The Novelist and Christ," the plot involving a Christ figure is prescribed at the outset, and the writer's failure to bring it off theologically is unavoidable:

> The end is inevitable from the beginning, whatever form the crucifixion may take. Hence he can write only tragedy if he is faithful. He does not have the consolation of the Gospels, which transcend tragedy in the Resurrection. Most often in modern fiction the Christ figure is lost "in the gathering fog" or exiled or executed; we know of no novelist who has undertaken to depict the ultimate triumph. Hence the reader is compelled to behold the agony again without the promise; the Christ figure is reduced to a victim of history, largely without hope other than a vague appeal to the future.[15]

Perhaps the triumph Faulkner reveals in *A Fable* is penultimate; but it can hardly be said to be ultimate. What is impossible for fiction is probably not so impossible for poetry: one thinks of Hopkins' "The Windhover," for example, or Auden's *For the Time Being*. But fiction, as a rule, when it attempts to present the figure of Christ, is limited to the presentation of a kind of spiritually scented humanism in which the most it can say is little more than was said of the Crucified by one of the soldiers in Hemingway's "Today Is Friday": "He was good in there today." It is good humanism, but it is truncated Christianity. It is the earth's-side version as told by the buzzard in Robert Penn Warren's "Pondy Woods": "The Jew-boy died."

Perhaps some authors sincerely believe they are doing Christ a service by rescuing him from the gray supernaturalism that tended to enshroud him in the pietistic literature of earlier generations. But the real result is that they have depicted him as an ineffectual, as a Revelation who does not reveal and a Redeemer who cannot redeem. Consequently the doctrine of God is obscured at a vital point, for

[15] P. 59.

the Christian faith has always placed a premium upon the indivisibility of Father and Son, God and Incarnation. As Gabriel Vahanian has suggested,

> While the literary effects, even the religious ones, can be tremendous, the theological implication is disastrous. The Christ-figure is a result of the process of leveling down. If all is grace, any man can take on the marks of Christ; and Christ, the unique, according to Christian theology, becomes a mere mask, suitable to any man. The Christ-figure is but another devaluation of Christianity. It is expressive of the broad secularization of Christian concepts, whose content has been hollowed out. The humanization of God—or the deification of man which takes place in many ideologies, from communism to some forms of existentialism—indeed goes hand in hand with the secularization of Christ and the assimilation of Christianity with a culture which *ipso facto* is less and less Christian.[16]

Nor has the doctrine of the Holy Spirit fared much better in contemporary writing, unless lack of treatment could itself be called better. Hopkins, Eliot, and Auden allude to the Spirit in several places, but I can remember very few such allusions in the prose of our time. One that I do remember vividly is in Camus' *The Fall.* Clamence is discoursing to his *"cher compatriote"* about the "beautiful negative landscape" of Amsterdam. He observes how horizontal, how colorless and lifeless it is—a soggy kind of hell. His friend apparently observes in return that the sky seems to be alive. "You are right, *cher ami,*" says Clamence.

> It thickens, becomes concave, opens up air shafts and closes cloudy doors. Those are the doves. Haven't you noticed that the sky of Holland is filled with millions of doves, invisible because of their altitude, which flap their wings, rise or fall in unison, filling the heavenly space with dense multitudes of grayish feathers carried hither and thither by the wind? The doves wait up there all year round. They wheel above the earth, look down, and would like to come down. But there is nothing but the sea and the canals, roofs covered with shop signs, and never a head on which to light.[17]

The reference is clearly to the descent of the dove upon Christ at his baptism and to the traditional identification of the dove as the Holy

[16] *The Death of God* (New York: George Braziller, 1961), p. 131.

[17] Albert Camus, *The Fall,* tr. Justin O'Brien (New York: Alfred A. Knopf, 1957), p. 73.

Spirit. But in the flat and colorless modern world there is no head on which the dove may light. Without the Second Person of the Trinity, there can be no Third Person. Without the Third Person, there can be no true community; and therefore man in the contemporary world is condemned to Clamence's existential hell of introspection and monological discourse. It is a dreary prospect.

Admittedly it is a difficult thing to refer directly to the Holy Spirit in a piece of fiction. The New Testament itself does not fully articulate a doctrine of the Spirit. That task was left to the church councils. But if, as most contemporary theologians insist, the doctrine of the Trinity is the Church's reference to her *experience* with God, to the manner in which she has known him, then it seems reasonable to expect the "Christian" writer to do more writing as John of the Apocalypse did, "in the Spirit," or as Milton did in *Paradise Lost,* under an invocation to the Spirit.

How does one recognize a literary composition that has been written "in the Spirit"? I am not sure that there are any suitable criteria. But I think it is something that the reflective Christian can intuit. Charles Williams' *War in Heaven* and *Descent into Hell,* for example, exude a kind of spiritual quality that strongly suggests such composition. On a different level, James Street's *The High Calling* gives me such a feeling. I cannot put my finger precisely on the thing that evokes this feeling. Sometimes I think it is a happy combination of *knowledge* and *love:* a kind of doctrinally informed compassion. It is not precisely what Arnold meant by "sweetness and light," but they are the words, when set in the reverse order, I should like to use. Perhaps it is a case of our spirits bearing witness with his spirit that we are the sons of God.

Even with such a generous criterion as this, though, there seem to be few writers on the contemporary scene bearing such a witness. The doves simply do not light.

George Santayana once wrote, in an essay about Dante: "If any similar adequacy is attained again by any poet, it will not be, presumably, by a poet of the supernatural. Henceforth, for any wide and honest imagination, the supernatural must figure as an idea in the human mind—a part of the natural. To conceive otherwise would be to fall short of the insight of this age, not to express or to complete it."[18] In a similar vein, Charles Glicksberg says that

> No writer of our time who has been exposed to the teachings of Darwin, Freud, Dewey, Russell, Carnap, and Einstein can hope to recapture the medieval intensity of faith in the supernatural. The revival of interest in the work of Kierkegaard serves but to reinforce the impression that doubt in our age is universal. The strenuous attempts of Christian apologists to revive the faith so that it will once more impregnate the body of modern literature have not borne much fruit.[19]

Literary realism devoid of supernaturalism was probably an inevitable corollary of the loss of God. It is worth noting that there was an incipient "realism," a strain of vulgarity,[20] in some of the best literature of the neoclassical period, when the influence of deism was most strongly felt; and that naturalism *per se* was the product of the latter half of the nineteenth century, when the real erosion of faith was under way. One of the main tenets of the naturalism of Zola, Gissing, Hardy, Norris, and Dreiser was the certainty that there is an inexorable mechanism or determinism at work in man. It is this secret and baleful force that accounts in many instances for the degradation of a worthy character or the rewarding of an unworthy one. Considered from the moral aspect, then, naturalism is a literary revolt against the traditional belief that God is a rewarder of those who "do justly and walk uprightly." It preaches with relentless dogmatism the blindness of justice—and the absence of God.

At the *fin de siècle,* the primary aim of naturalism was to provide a kind of photographic realism in writing; it was espoused by writers reacting strongly against the saccharinity of most late-Victorian prose and melodrama. Had the movement remained merely a corrective, we should owe it much. But soon the literary "photographers" were enthusiastically arranging their own scenes. Setting up their cameras in the kitchen or the bathroom, they left the dirty dishes in the sink, even added a few more for good measure, strewed a month's collection of moldy garbage and cigarette butts on the floor, and arranged a couple

[18] *Three Philosophical Poets* (Cambridge: Harvard University Press, 1935), p. 134.

[19] *Literature and Religion,* p. 92.

[20] A vulgarity qualitatively different from the earthiness of Chaucer or of Luther.

of cadavers in a suggestive position somewhere in the sideground with a mangy cat eating on them. The whole effect was as far from real life on one side as sentimentalism had been on the other. But whereas in earlier literature God had stood around like some embarrassed entrepreneur waiting to reward virtue and punish vice, now he was nowhere around. He had simply been written out of the plot.

And although the passionate naturalism of Zola's generation has by and large given way to the more casual sort of naturalism discoverable in the works of such men as John Steinbeck and Erskine Caldwell and Mickey Spillane, it requires but the mention of these names to remind us of how completely a modified naturalism dominates the literary scene in our day. It takes but a glance at the contents of the average newsstand bookrack to see how far we have come from William Dean Howells' "smiling" aspects of life or Henry James's incisive gentility. I cannot help thinking there is a fortuitous—though perhaps unintentional—description of the present literary malaise in the opening lines of Robert Penn Warren's "Pondy Woods":

> The buzzards over Pondy Woods
> Achieve the blue tense altitudes,
> Black figments that the woods release,
> Obscenity in form and grace,
> Drifting high through the pure sunshine
> Till the sun in gold decline.[21]

The buzzards could symbolize the triumph of the predatory spirit in contemporary writing. Woods have long suggested darkness and evil—as witness the first lines of the *Inferno* and the secret meetings of Hester and Arthur in *The Scarlet Letter*. The "black figments that the woods release" might then be the compositions of the naturalists—"obscenity in form and grace." Much of the literature of the naturalists does have form and grace, to be sure; but like the buzzards it is also dark, menacing, and associated with death. And "the sun in gold decline": could this not be Dante's "profound and shining being," the God who has gone from the scene?

But I have spoken of the Paradox of the *Manifest* Absence. It seems to me that we must distinguish between that literature from which

[21] From *Selected Poems 1923-1943* (New York: Harcourt, Brace & Co., 1944). Copyright © 1944 by Robert Penn Warren.

God is *merely* absent and that from which he is plainly, or manifestly, absent. And it may well be the fact that we have always made this distinction, whether consciously or unconsciously, that has caused us to respect some works of realistic literature over others and to apply to them the adjective "serious." Why else would a critic like Hyatt Waggoner write an article about Hemingway's contribution to Christian thinking in our time,[22] when Hemingway was rather obviously something of a nihilist? Or why do we return again and again to Faulkner's Latinate, mesmeric descriptions of the decadent South? Why indeed, unless we find there is something in the way these writers depict the godless world that actually speaks to us of God, that makes plain to us what is missing from the picture?

As I try to discover what it is that makes such writers different from other competent writers, I find myself coming back repeatedly to the feeling I find in them for the demonic. Is it not precisely this—the sense of the demonic—that haunts the pages of a writer for whom God is manifestly absent? Certainly it was very strong in Melville and Hawthorne and Dostoevski, the very figures who had most to say in their time about a coming age of apostasy from the Christian faith. Ivan Karamazov even said that he found it easier to believe in the devil than to believe in God.

Hemingway's world may lack the depth and the height of a good supernaturalism, but where in his world does the supernatural come closest to appearing? Where but in the light-and-dark symbolism of which we have spoken earlier? An acute sensitivity to darkness informs scenes in many of his stories and novels, culminating, probably, in "A Clean, Well-Lighted Place," where the darkness surrounding the neat little bar is almost animated. It is not simply a matter of a childish fear of the dark. With Hemingway it is something much more sinister. The darkness threatens. It menaces. It breathes annihilation—or at least *nada*.

Or take the works of Thomas Wolfe. The demonism there is far less subtle. The starched and decent Presbyterianism of Altamont, in *Look Homeward, Angel,* is too tame and orderly for Eugene Gant's wildish centaur heart, but he does believe in the dark beings of the

[22] "Ernest Hemingway," *The Christian Scholar,* XXXVIII (June, 1955), 114-20.

air. When his brother Ben is dying, he begins suddenly, "under the mastering surge of his wild Celtic superstition," to pray. "He did not believe in God," says Wolfe, "nor in Heaven or Hell, but he was afraid they might be true. He did not believe in angels with soft faces and bright wings, but he believed in the dark spirits that hovered above the heads of lonely men." [23] After Ben's death he continues for a long time to pray at night—

> not from devout belief, but from the superstition of habit and number, muttering a set formula over sixteen times, while he held his breath . . . not to propitiate God, but to fulfil a mysterious harmonic relation with the universe, or to pay worship to the demonic force that brooded over him. He could not sleep of nights until he did this.[24]

But it is Faulkner's world that is most truly demonic—the world of the Compsons and Sartorises and Snopeses. At first this strikes us as being a strangely incongruous fact in light of the strong tinge of Calvinism we find also in his writing. Some inexorable predestination seems to manipulate his characters, lending to his fiction the sense that something far larger than man is just behind the veil of history. But then we remember Hawthorne and Melville and the same strange blend of darkness and doctrine in them. The combination has even prompted Randall Stewart to suggest that the two greatest corpora of American literature have come from the two special loci of Puritanism —Hawthorne and Melville in New England, and Warren and Faulkner in the South.

If it is God who is behind the veil of Faulkner's world—and his repeated use of Christian imagery would argue that it is—then he is evidently the *deus in absentia,* and the absence is what accounts for the radical dementia of that freakish world. God is not far away, to be sure—if he were, some kind of order might be achieved on the human level. But neither is he very near, or he would introduce his own order, the order of his presence. It is the nearness and the farness together that confound Faulkner's South and hurl it into the most profound agitation. The propinquity of the holy, when it fails to be-

[23] (New York: Charles Scribner's Sons, 1929), p. 556.
[24] *Ibid.*, p. 611.

come articulated into explicit terms or relationships, throws life into twistedness and torment.

Consider, for example, the plot of *Sanctuary*,[25] all of which takes place during a four-week period ten years after the violent death of young Bayard Sartoris in the novel *Sartoris*. For ten years Horace Benbow has been living with his wife Belle in Kinston. Every Friday afternoon he has met the train and carried a package of fresh shrimp home for her; he is repulsed to think that for ten years his life has been represented in those faint-smelling blotches of shrimp drippings on the pavement between the depot and his home. Now, at the beginning of *Sanctuary*, he has left Belle and is on his way home to Jefferson. He stops for a drink at a spring somewhere in Yoknapatawpha County, and looks up from the water's edge to see standing before him an undersized man with a colorless face and eyes like "two knobs of soft black rubber." Thus begins a story of almost incredible windings and turnings, with episodes where the strands cross that are even more incredible.

Popeye—that is the name of the man at the spring—is a petty despot in a nest of moonshiners that includes an idiot named Tommy, a truck driver named Van, an ex-convict named Lee Goodwin, and Lee's wife Ruby, who carries about a baby that has never come more than half alive.

One night a man named Gowan Stevens and a co-ed named Temple Drake are driving drunkenly through the country and crash into a tree lying across the road at a point adjacent to Popeye's domain. They are made prisoners of the bootleggers. Stevens manages to sneak off the next day. Temple, apparently pleased with her role as main temptress in the camp, sets man against man until Popeye finally shoots the idiot Tommy. After the murder, he flees to Memphis, taking Temple with him. Lee sends Ruby for the sheriff. When the sheriff arrives, he arrests Lee and takes him to Jefferson, because everyone else has fled.

In Memphis, Popeye establishes Temple in a house run by a fat, asthmatic woman named Reba Rivers. He showers her with expensive clothes and perfumes and makes love to her by proxy—he

[25] (New York: Modern Library, 1931).

brings a man named Red who lies in bed with her while he himself bends over the bed without so much as his cap off, whinnying and making other strange noises. But when Temple and Red try to run off together, he shoots Red and flees to Pensacola, where, of all things, he annually visits his mother.

Red's funeral is held in a speakeasy, where a jazz band plays "Nearer, My God, to Thee" while the crowd gets high on illegal booze. At one point, a drunk lurches at the orchestra and tips over the coffin so that Red's body rolls out and the wax plug in the forehead where the bullet entered is knocked out and lost.

Horace Benbow, who has assumed the job of defending Lee Goodwin against a murder charge, hears that Temple is in Memphis and has her brought to Jefferson as a witness for the defense. Evidently fearful of Popeye's vengeance if she should incriminate him, she testifies that Lee really did murder Tommy. The D.A. holds up a corncob with some muddy brown stains on it, makes some muted references to a gynecologist's having connected the stains with the sacredness of womanhood, and leaves the court assured that Lee has abused Temple's body. The jury is out only eight minutes, and returns the verdict of guilty.

Sick at the outcome, Horace prepares to return to Kinston. He is waiting at the station for his train when he hears the cry of "Fire!" He joins the crowd rushing toward the alley by the jail. Lee Goodwin has been dragged outside by a mob and burned alive in coal oil.

Popeye is picked up by the police in a southern city on the charge of having killed a policeman on the very night when he had actually murdered Red. For some unknown reason, he sullenly declines to combat the accusation, refusing even the entreaties of a sharp Memphis lawyer who has got him off on worse charges several times before. As the minister's voice drones quietly, the sheriff throws the trap of the gallows floor and Popeye swings silently at the end of a rope.

In the Luxembourg Gardens, Temple Drake strolls with her father, Judge Drake. Fall, "the season of rain and death," is in the air.

What an intense spectrum of horror! Faulkner has seemed to ignore deliberately the more genteel aspects of life in favor of the ugly and the perverted and the grotesque. The result is a world of monstrous distortion and terror. Halford Luccock has said that Faulkner revolted "against the predominance of honeysuckle and magnolia in the Southern vegetation" and "planted his own garden with thistles and skunk cabbage." But it is more than that. The very title of *Sanctuary*—a word that once meant a refuge given under religious auspices—implies that there is more than that.

Here is a world that is a kinetoscope of terror because it is a world without God. It is the outcome of Goodman Brown's apostasy in Hawthorne and Ahab's sky-hurled defiance in Melville, and it is terrifying to behold. Its twistedness is so ultimate that even Christ is represented as an idiot in *The Sound and the Fury,* and as a half-Negro murderer in *Light in August.* Nothing is safe from distortion. The truancy of God has thrown everything into convulsion.

It was Luther who first formulated the paradoxical statement that where God is revealed, there he is also hidden, and where he is hidden, there he is also revealed—the *deus revelatus* is always *deus absconditus,* and vice versa. Is there some sense in which this is true also of God in modern literature? Is not his very hiddenness there charged with the tension of his presence? We should like to think that this is so—for the works of some authors, at least. When a writer is as sensitive and serious about life as Faulkner, for instance, it is probably safe to assume that many readers are able to see the God behind his world, revealed *as through torment.* Or, when a poet like Jeffers is so bitter about humanity and so lavish in his praise of jagged rocks and turbulent waters and strong animals, he doubtless inadvertently tells us something about God and his relationship to the created sphere. Or even when a playwright like Beckett confronts us with the nihilism and despair of a *Waiting for Godot,* we think that we can discern the subtle, oh-so-subtle overtones of the *mysterium tremendum* that does not blush to reveal itself even in negativity.

But again, these are only the *implications* for theology from contemporary writing—*they do not necessarily proceed from the Christian faith.* They are not, like Dante's *Commedia,* a direct product of the faith. Some of them are not even by-products. They are not kerygmatic or didactic in their orientation, but incidental, and there is a vast difference in that. Literature that reflects only the loss of God is not Christian literature, any more than a pamphlet on anarchy is pro-government because it happens to use the word government in every other sentence. Its real shortcoming is that it fails to reflect fully, if at all, the mighty facts that are central to the Christian faith—the Incarnation of God and the resurrection of Jesus Christ. In the face of the true gospel, it might almost be said to be blasphemous.

3

The Journey into Self

"OUR WISDOM, IN SO FAR AS IT OUGHT TO BE DEEMED TRUE AND SOLID wisdom, consists almost entirely of two parts: the knowledge of God and of ourselves." Thus began John Calvin's *Institutes of the Christian Religion*. For the great reformer, the doctrine of God and the doctrine of man were from the first inseparably linked. Man is not understandable apart from God. He was created in the image of God, and his nature and condition are discernible only in relation to that image. He is not a law unto himself; he is a dependent creature. There have been two major facts in his history: the Fall, by which the *imago Dei* was marred; and Redemption, by which the image is restored, now in part and later in full.

The greatest literature of the Western world in the last thousand years has consistently reflected this view. Dante, Shakespeare, Milton, Goethe, Hawthorne, Melville, Dostoevski, and Tolstoi all assumed, as part of their basic attitudes toward life, that man is known truly only as he is seen over against the Ultimate Being, only as he reflects in his fragmented way the glory and image of his Creator. It is surely this that Roland Frye has in mind when he speaks of the way literature "both undergirds and increases the greatness of man," [1] for the

[1] *Perspective on Man: Literature and the Christian Tradition* (Philadelphia: The Westminster Press, 1961), p. 57.

best literature always has a way of helping man to see himself as he exists before God.

This point of view has not exactly vanished in our time. There is a strong, though somewhat refracted, example of it in the works of Faulkner. His Calvinism is largely residual, but he is still heavy on the themes of original sin and predestination. The saga of Yoknapatawpha County is really the story of human pride, told over again in local terms. The Sartorises have tried by human means—a name, a dynasty, a culture—to raise a bulwark against time itself; but they have failed, and the novels in which they appear are the epic of that failure. And, because the Fall involves also the loss of free will, the air of foreordination hangs over all Faulkner's people. Of Joe Christmas, for instance, who knew before he did it that he would murder Joanna Burden, it is said that "he believed with calm paradox that he was the volitionless servant of the fatality in which he believed that he did not believe." [2] And young Bayard Sartoris, the last of his clan, is said to live in the isolation of "that doom he could not escape." [3] There is little redemption in Faulkner's world, to be sure; his only *sursum corda* is the word that man "will prevail." But there is some understanding of the nature of man in the light of that which is more than man.

Another novelist of our day who has treated the theme of the *imago Dei* is Graham Greene. All Greene's serious works have dealt in one way or another with the idea of the mingled grandeur and misery of man. Here, for instance, is that wonderful passage from *The Power and the Glory* in which the refugee priest, leading his mule through the jungle with the repulsive Judas slung across the saddle, ponders the ironies of life:

> Sometimes, instructing children in the old days, he had been asked by some black lozenge-eyed Indian child: "What is God like?" and he would answer facilely with references to the father and the mother, or perhaps more ambitiously he would include brother and sister and try to give some idea of all loves and relationships combined in an immense and yet personal passion. . . . But at the center of his own faith there always stood the con-

[2] *Light in August* (New York: Random House, 1950), pp. 244-45.

[3] *Sartoris* (New York: Harcourt, Brace, 1929), p. 380.

vincing mystery—that we were made in God's image—God was the parent, but He was also the policeman, the criminal, the priest, the maniac, and the judge. Something resembling God dangled from the gibbet or went into odd attitudes before the bullets in a prison yard or contorted itself like a camel in the attitude of sex. He would sit in the confessional and hear the complicated dirty ingenuities which God's image had thought out: and God's image shook now, up and down on the mule's back, with the yellow teeth sticking out over the lower lip; and God's image did its despairing act of rebellion with Maria in a hut among the rats.[4]

This is a radical identification of man with the image of God, even man in his most obviously fallen state. It fairly insists that there can be no understanding of him—even as criminal or maniac or traitor—apart from the God in whose likeness he was created.

It is part of our admiration for writers like Faulkner and Greene that they satisfy at least partially the nostalgia we feel today for the great novels about man and God in the nineteenth century. They are still dealing with our essential nature, with our origin in the *imago Dei,* and not merely with our "existential" nature. They provide, often eloquently, a real sense of the combination in man of the lustful and the pure, the timely and the timeless, the effete and the fecund. They speak to us, as few voices outside the Bible itself do, of the contrarieties of our existence.

But, having said this, we must go on to say that such writers are probably the exception in our day, not the rule. Eugene O'Neill, discussing *The Hairy Ape,* said, "The subject here is the same ancient one that always was and always will be the one subject for drama, and that is man and his struggle with his own fate. The struggle used to be with the gods, but is now with himself, his own past, his attempt 'to belong.'"[5] In a sense, this is the story not only of most modern drama, but of poetry and fiction as well—man's struggle is no longer with God, but with himself. Any statement of the general tone of contemporary literature must include a reference to its pervasive humanism. Its study of man—the perennial subject, as O'Neill said—is mainly from the human viewpoint, not the divine. It is largely

[4] (New York: The Viking Press, 1946), p. 136. Used by permission of the publisher and Graham Greene.

[5] In *Playwrights on Playwriting,* ed. Toby Cole (New York: Hill and Wang, 1960), p. 237.

lacking in theological reference of any kind. Its world is a truncated affair where God is manifest only as an absence and mysticism is merely the experience of vacancy.

The notable literary critiques of man in our age seldom berate him for failing to be related to God, or even imply, for that matter, that such a relation is possible; instead they chide him, if at all, for his failure to be true to his own nature (a dubious norm, indeed!) or for his seeming inability to adjust the relative differences between his libido and the world of real experience around him. We get the idea that he, and he alone, is important in the universe.

This completely tosses out the idea of sin and introduces a false kind of compassion for the sinner, who, if there are no such absolutes as good and evil, can never be guilty of more than harmless indiscretions. Edmund Fuller, in his book *Man in Modern Fiction,* says that we began by feeling sorry for the lovable bums of William Saroyan and John Steinbeck and ended by going soft on "the genial rapist, the jolly slasher, the fun-loving dope pusher." Mr. Fuller particularly has in mind James Jones's *From Here to Eternity,* which was hailed by many critics as a "compassionate" novel, though it is full of sentimentalisms on drunkenness, whoring, violence, and defiance of authority. "Imagine *Crime and Punishment* or *The Brothers Karamazov,*" says Fuller, "if Dostoevsky had thought that the good and evil in those books were wholly a relative matter and had had no conviction about them." [6]

The result of this modernization is a ranch-style universe with everybody, saint and sinner alike, living together on one floor.

This does not mean, however, that man in modern literature has found himself, or that he knows exactly who he is and why he is and what he is capable of. Far from it! He is almost always questing—even though he is not often sure what grail he is looking for. If he were not questing, in one way or another, there would be nothing for the author to write about.

But the quest in our day takes a different form. It has been largely internalized, so that it is the distance the character traverses in discovering himself or his own identity that really constitutes the journey.

[6] P. 40.

The paradigm is Joyce's Leopold Bloom, the modern-day Ulysses. As Halford Luccock once said, the old cry of "Westward, Ho!" has given way to a new one—"Inward, Ho!"

Joyce, of course, was not the first writer of psychological novels. Their roots go all the way back to Chaucer's *Troilus and Criseyde* in the fourteenth century, and to Lyly's *Euphues* and Shakespeare's drama in the Renaissance, and to the novels of Defoe and Richardson and Sterne and George Eliot. But it was he who used the stream-of-consciousness method so daringly and so brilliantly that practically every writer since has performed under obligation to him. He has left his mark on literature for all time. Even the drugstore novel, written, as likely as not, by someone with no direct acquaintance with *Ulysses* or *Finnegans Wake,* from time to time slips into the technique of the uncensored flow of talk.

Ulysses will always remain the shining example of the twentieth century's literary voyage into the self, the journey motif turned inward. It represents dramatically the distance we have come from the world of the real Odysseus. Even though the fabulous voyage of that traveler was made in an imaginary world, with its Circe and Cyclops and Lotus Eaters, it was at least in an external, objective world. But Leopold Bloom's journey, in Joyce's novel, is to an internal world, to a world that consists mainly of the reflection, imagination, and thought association of Leopold Bloom. It is mainly a solipsistic world, a realm of private experience and rumination without objective reference, save the Homeric framework and classical allusions, to the world that is common to all men.

This is the hell of isolation for contemporary man, that he is no longer related to a world of common experience. He has lost his polestar. His struggle for self-understanding and self-definition is with himself, and no longer with God or his fellows. And his paradise has become a wasteland littered with the failures of what O'Neill called "the attempt to belong."

A few authors have, of course, made their way through the wasteland to spiritual affirmation. T. S. Eliot, for example, having in "The Hollow Men" verbalized the results of the loss of spiritual direction, followed five years later with "Ash-Wednesday," which Randall

Stewart calls "perhaps the chief Christian poem of our time." [7] It is not hard to see that Dante was a major influence on this pilgrimage. There are long sections in "Ash-Wednesday" that echo the *Commedia* in almost every line, as does this one:

> Lady of silences
> Calm and distressed
> Torn and most whole
> Rose of memory
> Rose of forgetfulness
> Exhausted and life-giving
> Worried reposeful
> The single Rose
> Is now the Garden
> Where all loves end
> Terminate torment
> Of love unsatisfied
> The greater torment
> Of love satisfied
> End of the endless
> Journey to no end
> Conclusion of all that
> Is inconclusible
> Speech without word and
> Word of no speech
> Grace to the Mother
> For the Garden
> Where all love ends.[8]

Here is a turning, a new note sounded because man is seen in relation to that which is more than man, because the wasteland is viewed over against the "Garden where all love ends."

But unfortunately the majority of contemporary writers have not followed Eliot. They are still somewhere out in the wasteland, giving us clinical cases of men who are trying to discover the meaning of life without reference to any fixed point outside themselves. Many of the better-known characters in recent novels and plays are as lost as

[7] *American Literature and Christian Doctrine,* p. 130.

[8] From "Ash-Wednesday" in *Collected Poems of T. S. Eliot,* copyright, 1936, by Harcourt, Brace & World, Inc., and reprinted with their permission, and by permission of Faber & Faber Ltd.

Willy Loman in Arthur Miller's *Death of a Salesman,* so that the word Biff speaks about Willy at the end of that play—"He never knew who he was"—might stand as an epitaph for any of them. Miller has confided that the first image that occurred to him that was to result in *Salesman* was "an enormous face the height of the proscenium arch which would appear and then open up, and we would see the inside of a man's head. In fact, *The Inside of His Head* was the first title. It was conceived half in laughter, for the inside of his head was a mass of contradictions." [9]

Socrates' *gnothi seauton* is good advice, and it is still the business of literature to depict the struggle of man to know himself. Moreover, a writer may be said to be doing us a service if he does no more than hold the mirror up to life, as Miller did in the case of Willy Loman. But the search for the self in modern literature has failed, for the most part, to reveal more than a sub-Christian doctrine of man, because the pattern or image of what the self ought to be is rarely given. We are made to see the frustration of man in his attempt at self-discovery, but we are not presented with the archetype against which it would appear patently clear whence the frustration arises.

This is not to say that we are not given partial archetypes, for we are. Ours is an age seriously in search of a new doctrine of man, and ordinarily we do not give two cents for any so-called "serious" author who is not concerned with this enigma. The most celebrated authors of the last 150 years have, as a rule, been those who enunciated a definite view of man, usually with some distinctive emphasis. Consider the names that would appear on any list of major writers of the times—Goethe, Wordsworth, Coleridge, Carlyle, Nietzsche, Melville, Whitman, Dostoevski, Tolstoi, Zola, James, Eliot, Proust, Gide, Faulkner, to name a few. Not one of them lacked his own private doctrine of man or failed to contribute to the shape of the composite view of man in the modern age.

But the point is that in an age so characterized as ours is by the processes of disintegration the view of any particular author tends to be unique—as unique as he can make it, for ideational exaggeration is one of the secrets of style in most contemporary writing. It is his

[9] In Cole, *Playwrights on Playwriting,* p. 261.

particular hobbyhorse, so to speak. The harder he rides it, the more it contributes to his own identity as an author. I admire the kind of faith in the total literary enterprise that this presupposes—the belief that the whole will always act as a corrective on the part. Talk about the communion of saints! Here is a communion of artists, new in our time. But the practical effect, from the theological viewpoint, is that few writers adequately present what would be adjudged an orthodox doctrine of man. Many of them deal with facets, or aspects, of such a doctrine; but they do it in such an isolated fashion that partial truths often become, from a Christian perspective, less than true.

For the sake of illustration, let us consider at some length three of the most prominent emphases in contemporary fiction: the mystiques of sex, heroism, and revolt. They are by no means new. As a matter of fact, the works in which they appear in their purest forms are quite commonly referred to as classical or neoclassical. And there is certainly a place for each of them in the Christian view of man. But behold what has happened to them as isolated motifs.

If there is one writer who is more than any other to be identified with the sex mystique, it is surely D. H. Lawrence. Regarded by the more prudish as a *bête noire* and by the more liberal as a prophet, Lawrence's true stature is still difficult to assess. One critic says that he "was a religious artist, and that all his work was governed by religious ends." [10] In one sense, the Dionysian sense, this is true. Lawrence deplored the lack of vitality in modern life, the lack of imagination, the lack of creativity, the lack of sexual robustness. Therefore he preached a new "organicism" for our time: a reuniting of mental and physical vigor capable of restoring to man in this age the wholeness and harmony he enjoyed in earlier ages. As Spilka says, Lawrence "found the very goal of life in the achievement of organic being, and the only major sin—its degradation or denial." [11]

Forget that he is concerned with sexuality in its broadest sense (as Freud used it) as the answer to technology and materialism and

[10] Mark Spilka, *The Love Ethic of D. H. Lawrence* (Bloomington: Indiana University Press, 1955), p. 3.

[11] *Ibid.*, p. 9.

the lack of personal vigor in the twentieth century, and you must conclude that he is what the Mrs. Grundys have insisted that he is—a gross immoralist distilling into literature the lascivious crudity of the human posture in the sexual act, putting into books, as Mark Twain would have said, what little boys write on back fences. But read him against the real passion of his life—to cause the "primitive indefinite" to assert itself against Victorian prudery and industrial capitalism—and you have more nearly seen the real Lawrence.

Even *Lady Chatterley's Lover,* the novel that stirred up such a hornet's nest in this country as a borderline "pornographic" work, contains impassioned protests against the industrialism that controls nations and despoils countrysides. The miners of Tevershall have become hopeless drudges in black overalls—shapeless and thoughtless creatures speaking ineffectually of socialism and bolshevism and various other "isms." The gamekeeper Mellors, in whom some considerate force has kept alive the ruddiness of old paganism, is a passionate man who seizes the great physical pleasures of life, who pursues the formula of Carlyle and Thoreau that reduced spending equals fewer monetary demands and more genuine independence, and who preaches that if all miners would only wear red tights, bright red tights, they would begin to think better of themselves as men and their women would begin to be real women and their whole world would come right again.

The dialectic between vitality and sterility is symbolized by the difference between Mellors and Clifford Chatterley, the crippled industrialist. Clifford is described by Lawrence as "almost a *creature,* with a hard efficient shell of an exterior and a pulpy interior, one of the amazing crabs and lobsters of the modern, industrial and financial world, invertebrates of the crustacean order, with shells of steel, like machines, and inner bodies of soft pulp." [12] His impotence, according to Spilka, is the result of a failure that is really *sensual,* and not merely sexual. He lacks the larger human sympathies.

Machines have taken the energy, the willfulness, the spunk out of the common people. Mellors says:

> Motor cars and cinemas and aeroplanes suck that last bit out of them. I tell you, every generation breeds a more rabbity generation, with india

[12] (New York: Grove Press, 1959), p. 156.

rubber tubing for guts and tin legs and tin faces. Tin people! It's all a steady sort of bolshevism just killing off the human thing, and worshipping the mechanical thing. Money, money, money! All the modern lot get their real kick out of killing the old human feeling out of men, making mincemeat of the old Adam and the old Eve. They're all alike. The world is all alike: kill off the human reality. Pay money, money, money to them that will take spunk out of mankind, and leave 'em all little twiddling machines.[13]

Merrie olde Englande is producing a new kind of man, "over-conscious in the money and social and political side, on the spontaneous, intuitive side dead,—but dead!" [14]

The only hope seems to lie in the vitality of sex—in the energy of the egg. Frost, in his poem "The Egg and the Machine," threw a turtle egg, a primitive blob of protoplasm, against an onrushing train, symbol of the juggernautish machine age. Lawrence too turns to the symbolism of the egg, as Connie Chatterley goes down on her knees in ecstasy beside a cage of gamebirds on a lovely sunny day in the copse. One tiny chicken prances around in front of the coop, and the mother hen clucks in terror.

The slim little chick was greyish-brown with dark markings, and it was the most alive little spark of a creature in seven kingdoms at that moment. Connie crouched to watch in a sort of ecstasy. Life, life! Pure, sparky, fearless new life! New Life! So tiny and so utterly without fear! Even when it scampered a little, scrambling into the coop again, and disappeared under the hen's feathers in answer to the mother hen's wild alarm-cries, it was not really frightened; it took it as a game, the game of living. For in a moment a tiny sharp head was poking through the gold-brown feathers of the hen, and eyeing the Cosmos.[15]

It is sex that awakens new life in Mellors. "Now I've begun again," he says to Connie.

"Begun what?"

"Life."

Connie begins to feel it too, and one day she argues with Clifford, who tends to find solace for his own sterility in the idea that the universe is gradually burning out and the religious impulse battening.

[13] *Ibid.*, p. 278.
[14] *Ibid.*, p. 205.
[15] *Ibid.*, pp. 160-61.

"I think there is something in the idea that the universe is physically wasting and spiritually ascending," he says. "Do you?" replies Connie. "Then let it ascend, so long as it leaves me safely and solidly physically here below."

"The life of the body," says Clifford, "is just the life of the animals."

"And that's better than the life of professional corpses," answers Connie. "But it's not true! The human body is only just coming to real life. With the Greeks it gave a lovely flicker, then Plato and Aristotle killed it, and Jesus finished it off. But now the body is coming really to life, it is really rising from the tomb. And it will be a lovely, lovely life in the lovely universe, the life of the human body." [16]

So there are converse trends in the universe. One, implemented by mechanization, is toward the extinction of the human. The other, implemented by the disintegration of the religious ideal, is toward the reassertion of the human, and of the *physical* as the essential nature of the human. The criticism of contemporary religion is that it no longer represents life but instead a renunciation of man's natural modes of expression, represented most crucially in the sexual act. Long centuries of asceticism and the monastic ideal have sucked the blood from a religious faith which, as any good student of early Christianity knows, was once more full of hardy life than any paganism.

Perhaps this is a valid criticism; perhaps modern Christendom no longer addresses man's vital nature in terms that are relevant to the needs and impulses of his deeper, organic self; perhaps we have permitted the idiom of our religion to become archaic, so that the symbol of the Cross is no longer made to speak effectually to men riding subways or operating elevators or watching television.

But whether it is valid as an indictment of contemporary Christianity as it is preached and practiced by the majority of Christians is not entirely within our elected jurisdiction here. What is important to our study of theology in modern literature is the view of man which Lawrence propounds—the attitude that man in his primitive nature, uncorrupted by science and anemic religions, is basically good.

[16] *Ibid.*, pp. 297-98.

This new Rousseauism, emboldened by the new freedom to discuss sex frankly before mixed audiences, characterizes one large and significant segment of the literature being written today. It has especially flourished since the Second World War. War, in addition to tearing up countrysides, tears up mores as well, resulting in unusual directness in dealing with certain topics; and, at the same time, it has a way of causing men to reflect more upon primitive values than they ordinarily would. Hence the open depiction of the purely sexual—apart from the sanctions of love and marriage—in a host of postwar stories and novels.

In a chapter in *Man in Modern Fiction* entitled "The Female Zombies," Edmund Fuller explores the thesis that what the new sexual freedom really means is that the male characters are able to use the female characters as objects or receptacles and not as persons, making love where and when they want without consequent responsibility, all as part of the great modern "non-fertility rite." Examining novels by James Jones and Norman Mailer, both of whom appear in their writing to "requite love at the drop of a halter," and by John Steinbeck, William Faulkner, A. B. Guthrie, Madison Cooper, and Philip Wylie, all of whom have contributed notably to "the great whorehouse mystique," Fuller concludes that the more recent writers have considerably out-Lawrenced Lawrence.

The result is not only that literature is the poorer—"too many brothels spoil the book"—but that the view of man is immeasurably distorted, so that it is really impossible to see what his true virtues and vices are. There is no longer any such thing as sin—there are only mistakes and errors in judgment.

I am not certain that the implication is present in *most* of the new literature that bashfulness and sexual purity are bad and to be identified at least in part with the taboos of the Christian religion, and that the recrudescence of pagan amoralism is both good and healthy, but I know that it is present in much of it. And the inevitable consequence of such an implication, deprived as it is of the vertical reference in Calvin's formula for human self-understanding, is further confusion in a doctrine of man that is already somewhat less than crystal clear.

As Fuller has put it rather well,

There are two great facets of sex in the life of man. It is both unitive and procreative—and it is these things above and beyond anything else that can be made of it. The radical disorders of the sexual life to which all of us are variously liable, and to which it is true that errors of the religious and moral sense often contribute, can at their extreme make of sex something divisive and fruitless—the complete thwarting of its two supreme functions. But we are confronted with writers who do not know these functions, or do not believe in them, or who reject them. They show us the symptoms or last states of disordered sexuality and say that this is indeed the nature of the sexuality of man. My quarrel, again, is not against portraying the disorder—it is against failing to recognize the disorder for what it is and failing to have some vision or concept of a proper state for man's sexuality.[17]

This, in my opinion, was the failure of Lawrence's view. I do not think he was a mere trafficker in "the symptoms or last states of disordered sexuality"; but I do think he lacked a proper vision of the total setting for human sexuality. He tended to survey only the possible ends to be achieved by the release of the sexual urge at all its levels, and not the origin of sex itself. He tried to get back to the first Adam without going by way of the second Adam. And he produced a rash of imitators whose failure, because the quality of their vision is even less lustrous than his, is more patent than ever.

Just as the name of Lawrence is associated with the revival of sex in literature, the name of Hemingway is readily identified with the cult of the heroic. It is perhaps remarkable that there should even be a noticeable emphasis on heroism in an age when most characters, as Malcolm Cowley complains in *The Literary Situation,* are victims instead of heroes. One thinks, for example, of the early plays of Ionesco and the novels of Kafka, where wholesale victimization is part of the internal structure of the human situation. But, while it is true that Hemingway's personae feel that they are being victimized by the age in which they live—by war and violence and suffering and stupidity and bureaucracy and whatever else happens to be bothering them at the moment—it is also true, in turn, that they become heroes by behaving with courage before these things. It is almost impossible, after nearly forty years of Hemingway fame, to discuss his male characters without using the stock epithet of the critics, "the Hemingway

[17] *Man in Modern Fiction,* p. 117.

hero." Heroism—courage—"grace under pressure"—is his doctrine of man.

The hero, for Hemingway, is the man who earns integrity and form for his life by making proper choices—so that his total life assumes an aesthetic flavor, even in the selecting of sausages, in the killing of kudu, or in making love—and by having courage in the face of death or great pain. The choices must be made without external reference —"We do not have God here anymore," says Anselmo—and only in accordance with rigorous personal criteria. What matters most in every situation is to behave properly—not to be "messy"—and he who behaves well is worthy of all reverence.

It is difficult, without seeing the total pattern of the novels, to imagine the premium Hemingway put upon relentless, unmerciful self-judgment. Colonel Cantwell holds himself accountable for the wartime deaths of his troops, even though they were caused by "stupid orders from higher-up." Robert Jordan, after killing a Fascist cavalry officer who has ridden into camp during his love feast with Maria, checks out his own actions and finally says, "You behaved O.K." Harry Morgan lies in a rocking boat after being fatally shot in the stomach and quietly "takes it." The old man of the sea, Santiago, when the line to his great fish is cutting his hand, holds out stoically against the pain, whispering, "I will show them what a man can do and what a man endures." And in *Green Hills of Africa* the author himself says, "Every damned thing is your own fault if you're any good."

In a world without God, right behavior is extolled as the single dignity that is left to man.

Perhaps the essence of Hemingway's philosophy of the hero and the good life was captured in the novel that was both his worst and most autobiographical book, *Across the River and into the Trees.* The title is from Stonewall Jackson's dying words, "Let us cross over the river and rest under the shade of the trees." The main character, Colonel Cantwell, is transparently Hemingway himself. He is fifty years old (Hemingway's age at the time the book was written) and knows he is going to die soon of a heart condition. He motors to Venice, where he plans to spend the short time remaining in a moderate orgy of sensibility. On the way, he makes his peace with old memories by stopping at the exact spot where he was wounded thirty years earlier, relieving himself there, and burying with the excrement some money to pay for the medals he received for being wounded.

In Venice he hunts ducks in the bay, savors the foods in the marketplace and fine restaurants of the city, repeats "fraternal" secrets with the Gran Maestro of the hotel, reflects on the decisions that have made him the man he is, and makes love to Renata, a beautiful young Italian countess whom he calls Daughter. Love is one of the grand sacraments of life for him, "the only mystery that he believed in except the occasional bravery of man." He would like to marry Renata and have enough sons to send to all the corners of the world, but, knowing that death is imminent, he will not put upon her the burden of marriage.

After a sequence of charades in the city of Venice, summarizing the Hemingway attitude toward life and death and love, Cantwell directs his orderly to drive him out into the country, and death comes in the back of the limousine.

The whole story has unfolded under the shadow of death. A man's life has reared itself briefly but defiantly against the threat of impending annihilation and has gone out bravely. The Spanish have a word for it—*pundonor*. Hemingway described it once, in that minor classic on bullfighting, *Death in the Afternoon,* as "honor, probity, courage, self-respect and pride in one word." A good man sets his own high standard of excellence and then, with his own conscience as his only tribunal, does his utmost to perform at that level, simply for the personal honor that is involved.

"Man's chief end is to glorify God and to enjoy him forever," says the catechism. But in a world without God man's chief end becomes the glorification of man himself—there is no other end conceivable. And Hemingway attempts this. He attempts it through the transmutation of ordinary man, with violence or imminent death or extreme pain for a catalyst, into the highest kind of man he knows: the hero.

Hyatt Waggoner has done us a service, I think, by identifying Hemingway's world view as sub-Christian instead of anti-Christian. "The implication of Western middle-class prudential morality from the novelists Defoe and Richardson to Honesty-is-the-best-policy Franklin to How-to-win-friends Dale Carnegie," he writes, "is that goodness is worth while *because* it pays off, very tangibly, in the world's goods," while "the implication of the cross is that goodness must be ready if necessary to face crucifixion." "Needless to say," he continues,

> Hemingway's work is in direct conflict with any such interpretation of the ways of the world or of Providence. The good, as Frederick Henry realizes, die young, are broken by the world early. Only in some transcendent moral sense, with no cash value, are we ever among the "undefeated." Richardson has his Pamela remain shrewdly chaste until her "virtue" pays off in the form of a rich husband, but Hemingway's old fisherman must endure the sight of the sharks destroying his great fish.[18]

This is a modern kind of sainthood, and it may well have been part of what one critic had in mind when he said that "the theologian can well put himself to school to the modern artist to free himself from hang-overs of old fashions in transcendence."[19] But I cannot help agreeing with Waggoner that, while it is not anti-Christian, it is certainly sub-Christian. Admirable as it is—it has elicited the whole genre of "hard-boiled" novels and movies—its vision is very, very low.

There is a sense in which the mystique of revolt in contemporary writing is part of the mystique of heroism. That this is so is evident in what I have said about Hemingway: the code for the hero definitely involves a kind of defiance. But when I proposed to examine the subject of revolt, I had in mind, more than Hemingway, that group of writers generally classified as existentialists, especially Sartre and Camus and their followers. And, as Lawrence and Hemingway stand *pars pro toto* for the literatures of sex and heroism, existentialism represents the whole literature of revolt, philosophical and nonphilosophical, extending even to the works of the beatniks and the "angry young men."

For two decades now, existentialism has probably been the most influential current of thought in western Europe. Its mood of austerity seemed particularly well-suited to the days of the occupation and to

[18] "Ernest Hemingway," p. 119.

[19] Amos N. Wilder, "Art and Theological Meaning," *Union Seminary Quarterly Review,* XVIII (November, 1962), 39. Used by permission of the copyright holder, the *Quarterly Review.*

the task of reconstruction after the war. It said, "Well, here we are, naked and hungry, thrown out into a scarred and ugly world. We have nothing but our selves, nothing but our own wills. Let us work from that."

Most of the twentieth-century existentialists, as opposed to Kierkegaard, conceive of value only in human terms. This is particularly true of Martin Heidegger, the author of *Sein und Zeit,* and of his most famous disciple, Jean-Paul Sartre. Without God in the world man is thrown back upon himself, not only for the maintenance of the self, but for its very creation as well. Traditional philosophy and theology usually emphasized the *essence* of man—his given nature. But a favorite saying of the existentialists insists that for man "existence precedes essence." That is, man alone, of all creatures, can decide his existential relationship to life, and thereby his essence. A unicorn may have essence and still not exist; but man must choose existence before his essence is determined: in a sense, he chooses his essence when he chooses his existence.

This is not to say that there is no norm for the self in existentialism. On the contrary, there is a very demanding norm. It is the freedom of the self from all alien powers—from the tyranny of society, of culture, of religion, even of God. The devotedness of the religious man is regarded as a retreat from the responsibility for forging the self without the benefit of external patterns and criteria. It is at this point that the nontheists among the existentialists disown the theists, claiming that they do not carry the revolt far enough, but, having rejected the domination of all natural tyrannies, end by surrendering to a supernatural one.

Mathieu Delarue in Sartre's *Les Chemins de la liberté,* for example, repudiates his friend Daniel because the latter disclaims the responsibility of human freedom by becoming a *religieux.* Daniel writes a long letter to Mathieu, describing his conversion as a result of his becoming aware that God sees him and thereby constitutes his existence:

> I used to long to become invisible, to go and leave no trace, on earth or in men's hearts. What anguish to discover that look as a universal medium from which I can't escape! But what a relief as well! I know at last that I am. I adopt for my own use, and to your disgust, your prophet's foolish

wicked words: "I think, therefore I am," which used to trouble me so sorely, for the more I thought, the less I seemed to be; and I say, "I am seen, therefore I am." I need no longer bear the responsibility of my turbid and disintegrating self: he who sees me causes me to be; I am as he sees me.[20]

In disgust, Mathieu crushes the letter and hurls it away.

To those of us who are of the Christian persuasion, Daniel may seem in this excerpt to come off better than Mathieu; but for Sartre, under the perspective of the total narrative, he is only another instance of man's having acted in *la mauvaise foi,* shuffling off onto the idea of a Berkeleian God the responsibility for his own existence.

Similarly, Albert Camus repudiated Kierkegaard for taking what the Danish theologian called a "leap of faith"—that last, desperate leap after God when one has come to the end of logic's tether. Real freedom for the self, said Camus, lies in remaining at the end of that tether, in choosing to live in what he called the "absurd."

The absurd is really the dialectic between the being of man and the objective world around him; it arises whenever man tries to exist as a subject in a world of objects; then he becomes aware of the insane character of daily living and of the fact that he is really an alien in the world. Authentic existence, for Camus, is for man both to accept and to rebel against this absurdity—to accept it in that he is aware of it and does not retreat from the facts, but to rebel against it in that he loves existence and clings to life in spite of the facts. Therefore Camus defined the true rebel as "a man who says no: but whose refusal does not imply a renunciation." [21] Kierkegaard, he claimed, tries to make meaning of the absurd by relating man's existence to God's; but actually he destroys the meaning of human existence by subsuming it under divine existence.

To abolish conscious revolt [wrote Camus] is to elude the problem. . . . Living is keeping the absurd alive. Keeping it alive is, above all, contemplating it. Unlike Eurydice, the absurd dies only when we turn away from it. One of the only coherent philosophical positions is thus revolt. It is a constant con-

[20] Jean-Paul Sartre, *The Reprieve,* tr. Eric Sutton (New York: Alfred A. Knopf, 1947), p. 407.

[21] *The Rebel,* tr. Anthony Bower (New York: Alfred A. Knopf, 1954), p. 19.

frontation between man and his own obscurity. . . . It challenges the world anew every second.[22]

It is not difficult to sense the blatant humanism here. The mythical Sisyphus, whose name is part of the title of the book from which I have just quoted, is a symbol of the man who is in revolt against the order of things, including the divine order. He was accused of levity against the gods and as punishment was in the underworld put to rolling an immense stone up a long hill, whence it invariably plummeted back to the bottom again. But even in the dullness and drudgery of this enslavement to an objective task—the absurd—he continued always to cherish his life as a human being and remained defiant of the gods. The revolt of which Sisyphus is thus a symbol, wrote Camus, "gives life its value. Spread out over the whole length of a life, it restores its majesty to that life. To a man devoid of blinkers, there is no finer sight than that of the intelligence at grips with a reality that transcends it. The sight of human pride is unequaled." [23]

Nor is it too difficult to see in these words part of the reason for the strong appeal of existential philosophy in postwar Europe. It is so much more challenging than the cold nihilism that has gripped the hearts of so many young people there. John Wild, in his book *The Challenge of Existentialism,* has noted some reasons for its special appeal at this time:

Its point of view is starkly realistic. It suppresses no uncomfortable facts. Many of its leading exponents have lived through revolutions, terrors, and occupations. They have fought alone in the Resistance against hopeless odds. They express the unvarnished thought of men caught in the mass confusion and conflict of the modern age—weak and fragile men, weighed down by physical bodies, goaded by physical needs and desires, suffering from lethargy and sickness, lacking strength, and lacking knowledge. It is from such men and from such struggles that this ideal has emerged—solitary men struggling against might forces, alone in ignorance and in the dark. It is amazingly timely and relevant. It has been movingly expressed in poetry, drama, and novel; clearly analyzed and justified in philosophical prose. It embodies freedom and the dignity of the individual person, two of the great ideals of

[22] *The Myth of Sisyphus,* tr. Justin O'Brien (New York: Alfred A. Knopf, 1955), p. 40.

[23] *Ibid.,* pp. 40-41.

Western civilization. Hence it has deeply stirred the minds and hearts of multitudes of our contemporaries.[24]

The key issue for us, in our study of theology and literature, is the insistence of Camus, and most of the existentialists who write novels and plays and short stories, that man's true dignity is possible only if all theological reference is removed from the world. This is the very antithesis of the Christian viewpoint. It is as thoroughgoing a humanism as it is possible to find at any moment in the history of the world.

And, as I have taken Nietzsche's *Thus Spake Zarathustra* to be the classic statement of the humanistic viewpoint in the last century, so I take Camus' little novel *The Fall* to be its classic statement in this one. Its exceptionally rank humanism is only intensified by the fact that it is an analogue on the Christian doctrine of the fall of man and that, in its own way, it too deals with the questions of penance and redemption.

Jean-Baptiste Clamence, the narrator of the story, has been a very respectable lawyer. Professionally, he accepted the cases of the poor and the defenseless; privately, he was known to be kind to the aged and liberal with beggars. But in the absence of a God such respectability lacked a transcendent basis and had no intrinsic worth. He was merely cultivating a legend about his own goodness. Actually he performed no good work without an ulterior motive; the surface of all his virtues "had a less imposing reverse side." As he now puts it himself, he was "playing a role," and was absent at the moment when he seemed to take up the most space.

"To be sure," he says,

I occasionally pretended to take life seriously. But very soon the frivolity of seriousness struck me and I merely went on playing my role as well as I could. I played at being efficient, intelligent, virtuous, civic-minded, shocked, indulgent, fellow-spirited, edifying. . . . In short, there's no need of going on, you have already grasped that I was like my Dutchmen who are here without being here: I was absent at the moment when I took up the most space. I have never been really sincere and enthusiastic except when I used to indulge in sports, and in the army, when I used to act in plays we put on for

[24] (Bloomington: Indiana University Press, 1955), pp. 55-56.

> our own amusement. In both cases there was a rule of the game, which was not serious but which we enjoyed taking as if it were. Even now, the Sunday matches in an overflowing stadium, and the theater, which I love with the greatest passion, are the only places in the world where I feel innocent.[25]

The fall of man, the loss of innocence, for Clamence, involves the loss of honesty. His life became a cheat, a lie, a pretense.

Two experiences occur to challenge the lack of seriousness in his life. The first is on the Pont Royal. Clamence is crossing the bridge late at night, and passes a young woman leaning against the rail and looking down into the murky waters. The impressionism of the moment attracts him, and he is stirred by the sight of the nape of the woman's neck, cool and damp between her black coat and dark hair. He has gone only fifty yards or so past her when he hears a falling object strike the river. Intuitively he knows it is the woman. He stops short, but does not turn around. He hears a cry, repeated several times, moving downstream. Then it ceases. He still does not move, but begins to tremble. He knows he must be quick, but feels flooded by an irresistible weakness. Then it is too late, and he goes on in the rain.

The second experience likewise occurs on a bridge, this time on the Pont des Arts one evening shortly after dark. But let Clamence tell it in his own words:

> I had gone up on the Pont des Arts, deserted at that hour, to look at the river that could hardly be made out now night had come. Facing the statue of the Vert-Galant, I dominated the island. I felt rising within me a vast feeling of power and—I don't know how to express it—of completion, which cheered my heart. I straightened up and was about to light a cigarette, the cigarette of satisfaction, when, at that very moment, a laugh burst out behind me. Taken by surprise, I suddenly wheeled around: there was no one there. I stepped to the railing; no barge or boat.[26]

Nor does he ever discover the source of the laughter, even though he hears it again on another occasion. I shall not pretend to know why this strange teasing noise is able to do so—though I suspect it has something to do with what George Meredith in his fine essay called the Comic Spirit, that is the real judge of values and value-relationships in the world—but it cracks the glass house of Clamence's role

[25] Camus, *The Fall*, pp. 87-88.
[26] *Ibid.*, pp. 38-39.

and pursues him down the labyrinthine corridors of his complexity, mocking his "respectability" at every turn.

The combination of these unnerving experiences works a hole into the fabric of his mask. He begins to care about honesty. Almost passionately he goes about correcting the opinions that people have formed of him, rectifying them in many cases by behavior diametrically opposite that which had earned him the reputation of respectability. He is discourteous to the elderly; he spits into the faces of blind men on the street; in short, he becomes almost the antithesis of what he has been. The major difference is that now he obeys his natural impulses instead of his synthetic ones.

The whole narrative of his reduction from what he was to what he now is is presently being related as a kind of confession to an auditor Clamence has buttonholed in an Amsterdam bar called the *Mexico City*. Thus he is a kind of Ancient Mariner figure with, it seems to me, a much more credible listener than that stopped by Coleridge's seaman. The purpose is the same as the Mariner's: the listener will recognize his own sin in the confession, and will go his way "a sadder and a wiser man."

When he begins his confession—in the *Mexico City*—Clamence's sophistication and complexity of intellect contrast vividly with the stark simplicity of the bartender. The silence of that simian character, who only manages to grunt from time to time, Clamence describes to his newfound confessor as "deafening"—"It's the silence of the primeval forest, heavy with threats." "One of the rare sentences I have ever heard from his mouth," says Clamence, "proclaimed that you could take it or leave it. What did one have to take or leave? Doubtless our friend himself. I confess I am drawn by such creatures who are all of a piece. Anyone who has considerably meditated on man, by profession or vocation, is led to feel nostalgia for the primates. They at least don't have any ulterior motives." [27] A bit later, Clamence says, "If that be foolish . . . ," and stops. "Ah," he says, "I see you smile at that use of the subjunctive. I confess my weakness for that mood and for fine speech in general." [28] The grunt and the subjunctive are obviously at antipodes, are the symbols of the dialectic between the primate and

[27] *Ibid.*, p. 4.
[28] *Ibid.*, p. 5.

contemporary man. The inarticulate bartender is the apotheosis of the Noble Savage, and the subtle barrister is the product of an age of *raffinement.*

The Fall in this novel, then, is a second-level fall—not from Adam to the Savage, but from the Savage to the Sophisticate. It is a fall determined not in the light of the *imago Dei,* as with Calvin, but of the *imago hominis,* represented by the bartender. Clamence calls the bartender a "Cro-Magnon man lodged in the Tower of Babel"—he is the symbol of unity, integrity, and honesty, and Clamence is the symbol of fragmentation, duplicity, loss of innocence.

Camus is vitally concerned in this story with the subject of freedom —basic freedom, the freedom simply to be what one is. The only way to achieve it completely is to be alone; Clamence guesses that the price of it is the depopulation of the world. But there is one way to achieve partial freedom, and that is the way Clamence takes: to divest oneself of all pretensions, to live openly before the world the way one wishes to live, to live by what Paul Lehmann calls the "unredemptive indicative," as opposed to the ethical imperative. After all, it is the harlots and publicans of the world who are free, not the Pharisees.

Therefore, he who has been a legalist, a Pharisee, becomes a penitent, perpetuating freedom by living in honest confession and involving the listener too in the confession by causing him to see mirrored there his own hypocrisy. "A ridiculous fear pursued me, in fact," says Clamence, that "one could not die without having confessed all one's lies." Salvation, which he defines as "the right to disappear definitively," involves getting rid of one's lies before he dies. And so he conceives of his mission as a judge-penitent.

The critics have constantly noticed a certain obvious similarity between *The Fall* and Dante's *Commedia.* Clamence himself draws attention to the fact that Amsterdam's concentric canals resemble the circles of hell—"The middle-class hell, of course, peopled with bad dreams. When one comes from the outside, as one gradually goes through those circles, life—and hence its crimes—becomes denser, darker. Here, we are in the last circle." [29] But it is no comedy of which Camus writes, for it ends a long way from paradise. It is true that

[29] *Ibid.,* p. 14.

there is something of purgatory in *The Fall*—Clamence is trying to cleanse himself by confessing. But there is certainly no beatific vision at the end of it. The height of Clamence's ambition is "to disappear definitively"—and he must be purged even for that.

And what a flat universe his is, when compared with Dante's. Amsterdam, the international city at the crossroads of the modern world, is as level as a table—a "beautiful negative landscape," with ashes and gray dikes and livid beaches and "the sea the color of a weak lye-solution with the vast sky reflecting the colorless waters." "Is it not universal obliteration, everlasting nothingness made visible?" asks Clamence. Once, when he and his friend are riding in a boat on the Zuider Zee, shrouded in fog, he says, "You are wrong, *cher,* the boat is going at top speed. But the Zuider Zee is a dead sea, or almost. With its flat shores, lost in the fog, there's no saying where it begins or ends. So we are steaming along without any landmark; we can't gauge our speed. We are making progress and yet nothing is changing. It's not navigation but dreaming." [30] Clamence's own description is most fitting: "A soggy hell, indeed!"

But it is the colorless hell of man without God, thrown back upon himself to determine on his own the degree of integrity by which he shall live. The only purgation he knows is of a limited nature, a catharsis in which he tries to get rid of his dishonesty by confessing it to someone else whom he addresses as *mon cher compatriote* because that one too has been dishonest. And as for heaven, that is an impossible bliss beyond man's greatest dreaming, approximated only by the feeling that comes when one has extirpated all his lies.

We have come full circle, then, on the doctrine of man—from Dante and Calvin to Lawrence and Hemingway and Camus, Camus returning us, in a sense, to Dante. But there is something definitely impoverished about the world of the latter-day prophets—as if God had somehow withdrawn and man were left alone on the wide expanse of a morally neutral universe, eating his viscera, as Stephen Crane has pictured him in "The Heart," and finding them bitter. It is a world of bleakness and fog, a world where Dante's supernal sun never breaks

[30] *Ibid.*, p. 97.

through to illumine the journey. It is a world where the measure of all things is anthropological and not theological, because it is the world of man without God. "Glory to Man in the highest, for Man is the master of things!"

Sex, courage, rebellion: they only spell out again the old story of human pride and the loss of Eden. Literature, to be sure, performs a real service by giving form and shape to the human condition, so that we see ourselves there in our need. No truer word may be spoken than Amos Wilder's, that the Christian faith, recurrently threatened by docetism and irrelevance, is perpetually in need of "baptism in the secular, in the human, to renew itself. It has to be continually re-immersed in the vitalities of nature to be saved from a spurious and phantom Christ. Art mediates this order of creation to us." [31] But there is a great difference between man as fallen and man as redeemed, and recent literature has not, for the most part, taken cognizance of the second order. It is the task of theology, in any coming dialogue between the Church and the arts, to insist upon the relevance of the higher order. The circle of man's self-understanding must become an ellipse again, including God; for as the three wise men in W. H. Auden's Christmas oratorio say,

> To discover how to be human now
> Is the reason we follow this star.[32]

[31] Wilder, "Art and Theological Meaning," p. 39.

[32] *For the Time Being.* Copywright 1944 by W. H. Auden. Reprinted from *The Collected Poetry of W. H. Auden,* by permission of Random House, Inc., and Faber & Faber Ltd.

4

The Unredeemed Community

"EXTRA ECCLESIAM NULLA SALUS," SAID CYPRIAN—"THERE IS NO SALVATION outside the Church." *That* from the third century.

"It seems to me that the will of God is that I should not enter the Church at present," wrote Simone Weil to a friend. "I cannot help still wondering whether in these days when so large a proportion of humanity is submerged in materialism, God does not want there to be some men and women who have given themselves to him and to Christ and who yet remain outside the Church." [1] *That* from the twentieth century.

These two statements represent something of the polarization between the orthodox Christian view of the Church and the secularist Christian view, the latter being a way of thinking with which we have become much more familiar of late.

Dante certainly agreed with Cyprian that there is no salvation outside the Church. He agreed in spite of the fact that he condemned papal abuses so strongly as to endanger his life. In the *Commedia* he wrote of emerging from hell to stand at the shore with other souls looking across to the sunrise in purgatory: through the mist, they descry a strange, red glow coming swiftly toward them over the water, growing

[1] *Waiting for God,* tr. Emma Craufurd (New York: G. P. Putnam's, 1951), pp. 47-48.

larger as it comes: suddenly white wings appear out of the glow, and Vergil cries to Dante to fall on his knees before the messenger of God —it is the angelic counterpart of Charon, come to ferry the souls of the redeemed to the other side. "Wherefore I," wrote Dante, "who now was turned to the seashore where Tiber's wave grows salt, kindly by him was garnered in." [2] The Tiber, of course, is the river at whose mouth Rome is situated—Rome, the heart of medieval Christendom.

The Reformers, too, agreed with Cyprian. We have but to reflect on such phrases as "the Church within the Church" or "the Church hidden and the Church visible" to refresh our memories about how seriously they rethought and refurbished the concept expressed by Cyprian. They still regarded the Church, both visible and invisible, as the only community of saints on earth. The really new note in their doctrine was an emphasis on the Word of God as that which is deposited in the Church and which judges the Church at all times. The Church that was born at the Reformation was a Church both strangely humbled and strangely exalted.

It is true that the doctrine of the Church fell on evil days during the age of rationalism, and that the devastation done to it by deism and the *Aufklärung* was all the more severe because of their pretension to be Christian and to represent the finest flowering of the theological endeavor. But Pietism, Evangelicalism, and the Oxford Movement each contributed in its own way to the beginning of the slow and arduous recovery of what had been eroded by the Enlightenment; and Albrecht Ritschl, an influential theologian of the latter half of the nineteenth century, helped to stake down the gains of these movements by insisting that human salvation is possible only through contact with the redemptive work of Christ, and that this contact comes solely through the mediation of the Church as the community of believers, the living fellowship in which Christ is present and the gospel is preached.

And strangely enough it is in our own century, in the time of Simone Weil and other secular Christians, that the doctrine *extra ecclesiam nulla salus* has most fully come into its own again. This "renewal," as it is frequently called, is reflected in several areas of the Church's life. It is seen, for example, in the work of the theologians themselves, and

[2] *Purgatorio,* II, 34.

perhaps nowhere more clearly than in the title of the most important single theological treatise of our time, Karl Barth's mammoth *Church Dogmatics*. Originally Barth intended to call this project *Christian Dogmatics,* and the first volume was actually published under that title. But he was disappointed with this beginning and so began again, reorienting himself and calling the new work *Church Dogmatics*. So influential has Barth been that he has re-created, almost single-handedly, a theology of the Word for our time, with the Church resuming its role as the place where the Word of God is heard and proclaimed, proclaimed and heard, where God's self-revelation takes place in the fellowship of the saints.

What is "mere" theology, moreover, is constantly passing into life and actuality in several ways. For one thing, there are the ecumenical conversations so much in the air these days, expressing the desire of many Christians for a reunified household of faith, or at least a diversified household where the various churches can participate in what W. A. Visser 't Hooft describes as "the dialogical situation." There is a growing feeling today that, as P. T. Forsyth put it, "each Church has the right to live only in virtue of the contribution it makes to the great Church." [3] There are, of course, many obstacles to reunification, some liturgical, some doctrinal, some political, some just plain human. But there are very few Christians who are not encouraged by the new reverence that is being felt for the concept of the universal Church of Jesus Christ, which transcends all barriers, ideological as well as physical, and reasserts to us the more sensitive meaning of the third-century dictum of Cyprian.

For another thing, renewal is also being expressed in the life of the laity of the Church. Not since Luther's insistence on the priesthood of every believer has that idea been taken so seriously; perhaps not even since the days of the early church itself has it been practiced so extensively. In Britain and Japan it is reflected in the great "house church" movement, with laymen gathering in neighborhood homes for worship and Bible study. All over the world it is mirrored in new lay interest in promoting theological study, witnessing to the gospel, and revitalizing

[3] *The Church and the Sacraments* (London: Independent Press Ltd., 1955), p. 8. Distributed in U.S.A. by Allenson's, Naperville, Illinois.

the Church. Hendrik Kraemer, writing in *The Theology of the Laity,* says that the vigorous new appraisal of the place and responsibility of the laity in both the Roman and non-Roman worlds "is a justification for speaking of 'signs of the time.'" And the important thing about it, as he sees it, is that it is more akin to the great lay movement of the fourteenth century, which stressed personal responsibility, than to that of the nineteenth century, which was largely organizational in character: the present movement is getting to the roots of what it means to be a Christian in modern society.[4]

Still another indication of renewed interest in the Church is the widespread renascence of worship, a revival of liturgical uses that has stirred nearly as much excitement in the free churches as in the established ones. The conviction expressed by Donald Macleod in his book *Word and Sacrament,* that "there is a holiness of beauty as well as a beauty of holiness," seems to have been quickened even in churches of normally Puritan leanings. Perhaps one thing it spells out rather clearly is that something does—or should—go on in the worship service of the Church that cannot be duplicated by any rite or ritual outside it, something transcendent, metarational, and, apropos of our own time, metatechnological. If it does carry overtones of Romanism, that is not necessarily a matter for deprecation, for that, after all, is the clay from which we are digged. And if both ecumenism and the revival of worship signalize something like rapport between high Protestantism and low Catholicism, that is not exactly unsalutary; it represents the fact that there are spiritual currents passing in the air from pole to pole, and we should be glad to be alive in a time when the currents have been turned on again.[5]

The short text of the matter is that these are exciting days for the theology of the Church, both as reflected in the literature of the

[4] (Philadelphia: The Westminster Press, 1958), pp. 46-47.

[5] James H. Nichols, among others, has noted the irony in the fact that while some Protestant groups are moving the communion table against the wall (making an altar of it), employing more and more solos, anthems, and choral responses (proportionately withholding the participation of the laity), and generally heading in the direction of more formal worship, there are a number of Roman Catholic churches moving the altar out (making a table of it), honoring more and more congregational participation (including the use of a vernacular mass), and seeking spiritual power in a freer type of service.

Church and as enacted in the parliaments of the Church. We are indeed a long way from Antioch, or Rheims, or even Geneva; but we have had preserved to us a root, and it has begun to turn green again. Nor for centuries has there been such a high and sensitive doctrine of the Church.

It is time, then, to put the question. How do we explain the fact that, in the light of all the developments in recent years issuing in the renewal of the Church, such a person as Simone Weil, highly admirable as she was, should choose to remain an outsider? Of course, we could resort to casuistry, juggling the Reformed concepts of the Church visible and the Church invisible, and argue that she was certainly a part of the latter whether she thought so or not. But that is surely to evade the real issue. There is something more important involved here. She herself gave numerous reasons for not entering the Church, including the suspicion that if she did enter she could not continue to love those on the outside merely for themselves, as she did then, and the fear that she would feel oppressed and constricted as part of an institution that must assume, for necessary reasons, a social structure. But there must be something even behind these reasons, something that accounts, at a more basic level, for their existence: perhaps a mood, or an atmosphere, or an assumption, that has grown tacitly but surely into the modern mind with regard to the Church: something that affects the ecclesiastical attitudes, though ever so slightly, even of those inside the Church.

I believe that the answer is partly reflected in the literature of the time and that an examination of the doctrine of the Church as found in contemporary fiction will tell us as perhaps nothing else could what it is that disturbs all the Simone Weils about the Church in our age. Therefore, I re-put the question thus: How has the evident renewal in the theology and life of the Church today been mirrored in modern literature? Has the picture of the Church drawn by contemporary writers really shown what we feel is the success of the Church, or has it depicted something less encouraging, even discouraging? Has it revealed a Church carrying on a strong existential dialogue with itself and hearing always the word of divine judgment upon it, or a Church hardened to any voices except those of wealth, prestige, and power? Has it revealed a Church gathered by the hand of God and set against the forces of selfishness and materialism in the world, or a Church formed merely by human incentive and bound together only by ulterior motives? The answer must be two-pronged.

First, the positive. There has always been, and probably will continue to be, a small corpus of sentimental literature that is distinctively ecclesiological in its orientation—novels like Charles Sheldon's famous *In His Steps,* Agnes Sligh Turnbull's *The Bishop's Mantle* and *The Gown of Glory,* and James Street's *The Gauntlet* and *The High Calling.* There is definitely a commercial element in such writing, a kind of *Reader's-Digest* tone of voice that tends to garble the more sensitive meaning of the Church in a lot of platitudes and moralisms. But despite its false notes it generally attempts a better tune than the kind of anti-ecclesiastical literature we are so familiar with.

More important as literature than all these saccharine accounts is William Faulkner's description of the Negro church in Dilsey's section of *The Sound and the Fury.* Here is an example of real writing "in depth" about the Church.

In *The Sound and the Fury* Faulkner was treating his favorite theme of the decay of the generations and the dissipation of the energy that is expended on obsolete cultural forms. This time it is the story of the Compsons, one of the families that originally settled and controlled the town of Jefferson, Mississippi. From its illustrious progenitor, Jason Lycurgus Compson, who owned a square mile of property right in the center of what was later to be Jefferson, the line has descended to Jason, Jr., a grandson who is employed in a local hardware store, and nervously and parsimoniously plays the cotton market; Caddy, who has an illegitimate child and leaves home, eventually becoming the mistress of a German army officer; Quentin, Caddy's brother, who loves her so possessively that he contemplates incest in order to damn them both by a classic sin, and who finally commits suicide at Harvard; Benjy, a thirty-three-year-old idiot who has been gelded to protect the little girls in the neighborhood; and young Quentin, Caddy's illegitimate daughter, who runs off at last with a man in a traveling show. The single force holding all these disparate and degenerate elements of a worn-out family together is the old Negress Dilsey, the matriarch of the family servants. Contrasted with the sickness and evanescence of the white clan, she is both therapeutic and durable. Her character—large, brown, primitive—is of the earth, and the earth endures beyond the changes upon its surface. Quentin, at Harvard, pierces his finger on the hands of an heirloom watch and submits to the whelming flood of time, desiring the peace of death and no-time. In contrast, Dilsey and the Negroes seem to rise granitic, rocklike, indestructible, in the stream. "They endure," says Faulkner.

The Negro church service bears the same sense of the primitive, the elemental, the durable. Staged in the most austere setting imaginable, it develops into something that not only defies but actually seems to transform its physical and temporal environment. This is the way Faulkner describes the route to the church:

> A street turned off at right angles, descending, and became a dirt road. On either hand the land dropped more sharply; a broad flat dotted with small cabins whose weathered roofs were on a level with the crown of the road. They were set in small grassless plots littered with broken things, bricks, planks, crockery, things of a once utilitarian value. What growth there was consisted of rank weeds and the trees were mulberries and locusts and sycamores—trees that partook also of the foul desiccation which surrounded the houses; trees whose very burgeoning seemed to be the sad and stubborn remnant of September, as if even spring had passed them by, leaving them to feed upon the rich and unmistakable smell of Negroes in which they grew.[6]

Further on, the road appeared to stop short between the red clay banks, and beside it "a weathered church lifted its crazy steeple like a painted church, and the whole scene was as flat and without perspective as a painted cardboard set upon the ultimate edge of the flat earth, against the windy sunlight of space and April and a midmorning filled with bells." [7]

The Negroes, despite their colorful clothes and bright bonnets, do not seem to contrast at all vividly with the landscape. They throng toward the church with "slow sabbath deliberation." The men stand outside and talk until the bell ceases to ring. Inside, the church has been decorated with sparse flowers from kitchen gardens and with

[6] From *The Sound and the Fury,* by William Faulkner. Copyright 1929 and renewed 1956 by William Faulkner. Reprinted by permission of Random House, Inc. Pp. 306-7.

[7] *Ibid.,* p. 308.

streamers of colored crepe paper. Over the pulpit, which is empty, hangs a battered Christmas bell of the accordion sort.

Somewhere a real bell sounds, and the congregation hushes with expectancy. It sounds again, and the choir begins to sing. Six small children proceed up the aisle, followed by the pastor of the church and the visiting preacher from St. Louis. A sigh of disappointment goes up from the congregation when they see the insignificant-looking visitor, who contrasts so unfavorably with the magisterial figure of their own minister. He is undersized, has a little black face like a small, aged monkey, and is dressed in a shabby alpaca coat. The rich, unctuous tones of the pastor's voice seem even to increase his countriness and insignificance.

"En dey brung dat all de way fum Saint Looey," whispers one of the congregation, incredulously.

When the visitor rises to speak, he sounds like a white man. His voice is big and cold and inflectionless. The Negroes listen, as if they were hearing a little black monkey talking like a white man. They even forget his insignificant appearance. Suddenly a strange voice from within him says "Brethren." And here we must turn to Faulkner's description:

> The preacher had not moved. His arm lay yet across the desk, and he still held that pose while the voice died in sonorous echoes between the walls. It was as different as day and dark from his former tone, with a sad, timbrous quality like an alto horn, sinking into their hearts and speaking there again when it had ceased in fading and cumulate echoes.
>
> "Brethren and sisteren," it said again. The preacher removed his arm and he began to walk back and forth before the desk, his hands clasped behind him, a meagre figure, hunched over upon itself like that of one long immured in striving with the implacable earth, "I got the recollection and the blood of the Lamb!" He tramped steadily back and forth beneath the twisted paper and the Christmas bell, hunched, his hands clasped behind him. He was like a worn, small rock whelmed by the successive waves of his voice. With his body he seemed to feed the voice that, succubus like, had fleshed its teeth in him. And the congregation seemed to watch with its own eyes while the voice consumed him, until he was nothing and they were nothing and there was not even a voice, but instead their hearts were speaking to one another in chanting measures beyond the need for words, so that when he came to rest against the reading desk, his monkey face lifted and his whole attitude that of a serene, tortured crucifix that transcended its shabbiness and insignificance

and made it of no moment, a long, moaning expulsion of breath rose from them, and a woman's single soprano: "Yes, Jesus!" [8]

Subtly, almost imperceptibly, the preacher's intonation, his pronunciation, become negroid. At what moment, the congregation cannot say. They just sway a little in their seats as the voice repeating "I got de ricklickshun en de blood of de Lamb!" seems to take them into itself, and they moan, "Yes, Jesus!" Outside, a car passes along the road, its wheels laboring in the sand; but they are rapt in the words of the messenger:

"O blind sinner! Breddren, I tells you; sistuhn, I says to you, when de Lawd did turn His mighty face, say, Ain't gwine overload heaven! I can see de widowed God shet His do'; I sees de whelmin' flood roll between, I sees de darkness en de death everlastin' upon de generations. Den, lo! Breddren! Yes, breddren! Whut I see? Whut I see, O sinner? I sees de resurrection en de light; sees de meek Jesus sayin' Dey kilt Me dat ye shall live again; I died dat dem whut sees en believes shall never die, Breddren, O breddren! I sees de doom crack en hears de golden horns shoutin' down de glory, en de arisen dead whut got de blood en de ricklickshun of de Lamb!" [9]

When the service has ended and the congregation has dispersed along the road, Dilsey still weeps softly on the way home. "Whyn't you quit dat, mammy?" says Frony. "Wid all dese people lookin'. We be passin' white folks soon."

"I've seed de first en de last," says Dilsey. "Never you mind me."

"First en last whut?"

"Never you mind," answers Dilsey. "I seed de beginnin', en now I sees de endin'."

Her reference, as Amos Wilder has observed, is dual—to the cycle of the Compson generations, now played out in the *non compos mentis* Benjy, and to the Alpha and Omega, who has been present in the little Negro church.

"The one true Church," says P. T. Forsyth in *The Church and the Sacraments,*

is where the Gospel heartily is, where it is taken seriously as man's chief end; where that Gospel is lived for and worked for; where it is the source

[8] *Ibid.*, p. 310.
[9] *Ibid.*, pp. 312-13.

> of our supreme action, namely, worship, common worship; where it takes its own native form in the existence of a Church speaking by Word and Sacrament; where it is the inspiration of all the energy and kindness that flow out toward men when we have really been dealing with God; and where it makes the Church the prophet of righteousness to nations and their States, bearding kings, sobering soldiers, and moralising finance.[10]

Surely, if the one true Church has been anywhere, it has been in this little Negro church.

In a way, *The Sound and the Fury* is one long footnote to the first line of Eliot's *The Waste Land,* "April is the cruellest month," with its paradox of death and rebirth. Faulkner's story, too, is set in April. The old white families reek with the odor of death and decay. Benjy plays with a Jimsonweed, which feeds on rubbish and destruction. He is a gelding as well as an idiot. Quentin commits suicide. The very setting of the Negro church is reminiscent of a wasteland. But the rebirth that takes place in the saga occurs in that church, in the basic primitiveness and timelessness, in the rapture and transposure from self that occurs to the Negro congregation in the act of hearing, in their ageless dialect, the Word of God.

Study that Negro sermon. Besides being among the choicest bits of Negro dialect in our language, it is also, from the Protestant point of view, theologically unimpeachable. I am sure that Faulkner was well aware of the connection between the statement he made in this book about the Negroes—"They endure"—and the optimistic prediction he made years later in his Nobel Prize acceptance speech, that man "will prevail." Some critics, at the latter occasion, attacked the word "prevail" as vague, colorless, and barren of content. But Randall Stewart, I believe, has the last word on that: "I would suggest," he says, "that it might be helpful to look up the word in Cruden's *Concordance* to the Bible, and then read the passages (there are sixty-five) in which it occurs. In general, *prevail* occurs in contexts where a victory is won with God's help. *Prevail,* as Faulkner uses it, has nothing to do with modern technology. It is a Biblical word, and has a religious connotation."[11] And, we may add, the heart of such prevailing

[10] P. 49.

[11] *American Literature and Christian Doctrine,* p. 141.

is seen nowhere more nakedly than in this inspired passage about the Negro church in *The Sound and the Fury.*

Seldom, however, do we find a picture of the Church at once so compelling and winsome as this one. This is the negative side of the situation. Not even Faulkner has produced anything else comparable to it. When he describes white churches, as he does, for example, in *Light in August* and *Sanctuary,* he depicts them merely as organizations drawn along social lines, with no true sense of the transcendent that might purify and redeem them. There is real irony in *Light in August* at the point where the men return to town with the dogs during the search for Joe Christmas: "When they crossed the square the church bells were ringing, slow and peaceful, and along the streets the decorous people moved sedately beneath parasols, carrying Bibles and prayerbooks." [12]

The very title *Sanctuary* is a sharp indictment of the institution that once stood for social refuge as well as spiritual. Lee Goodwin, an ex-convict falsely charged with murder, is awaiting trial in the county jail, and his wife Ruby seeks temporary asylum in a local hotel. On Sunday morning, the pastor of the Baptist church takes Lee as the text, subject, and argument of his sermon; says he is not only a murderer and an adulterer, but a polluter of the free Democratic-Protestant way of life in Yoknapatawpha County as well; and strongly recommends that both he and "that woman" be burned at the stake as a moral lesson to the senseless little baby she carries in her arms. The Baptists descend *en masse* on the hotel manager and force him to turn the mother and child out of the establishment—it is a modern instance of "no room in the inn." And when Lee Goodwin is finally dragged from the jail and burned to death in an alley by a mob, one need not strain his imaginative powers to conjecture that there were some Baptist deacons and laymen in the crowd. Faulkner's condemnation of the contemporary religious cultus, in its distance from the transcendent experience of the Negro church in *The Sound and the Fury,* is not difficult to discern. The modern church has degenerated from a vital ideological structure into a staid form of moral-

[12] P. 260.

ism now in the hands of a group of separatists devoid either of basic Christian charity or of the complete devotion to their religion which was, in some ways at least, the saving grace of New England Puritanism. From a large, expansive, spiritual religion, Christianity has dwindled into something mean and strict and utilitarian. No truly religious person can ignore the pungency in the words of Horace Benbow as he turns away from the hotel clerk who has been "reached" by the local Baptists: "Christians! Christians!"

Criticism of the visible Church is not new. It was not new in the time of Dante and Chaucer. But it has been generally much more good-natured than this. The gentler chidings of authors such as Trollope and Henry James—mere chitchat about cathedrals—have passed into the stringent, almost caustic attacks of more recent years. Indeed, the ugliness of the human side of the Church seems lately to have become such an obsession with some authors that they find it impossible to see another side. Chaucer's tone and manner assure us that, beyond the fun he has with what H. O. Taylor has called "the spotted actuality" of the medieval church, he bore great and sincere respect for its ideality, at least partially realized in the church of his age. But we do not sense such respect in the attitude of a writer like, say, Sinclair Lewis, when he is dealing with the church of our age; nor, for that matter, do we sense that he is really having any fun, for there is a little too much bitterness and disgust in most of his portraits of church members to call what he is doing fun.

We shall have occasion later to look into *Elmer Gantry,* Lewis's scathing report on the insincerity that blights so much of evangelical fundamentalism; but here it is much to the point to look into another of his novels, which, though it lacks the concentrated power of *Elmer Gantry,* has entered its title into our language. That is *Main Street.*

This particular Main Street—in Gopher Prairie, Minnesota, which has a population of "over three thousand"—is really an extension of Main Street in every small town in the United States. It is the symbol of the bourgeois, materialistic, and Philistine character of the broadest section of the American populace. Lewis's novel is a tirade, a Philippic against all provincialism and lack of sensibility—including narrowness and callosity in matters religious.

Gopher Prairie's Main Street is seen through the eyes of Carol Milford, a librarian from St. Paul who marries Dr. Will Kennicott and gets her first glimpse of the little town as a bride. She is young and fresh, and has a yearning to be creative; and the entire narrative is spun out of her conflict with the conservatism and inertia she encounters there. She tries to enrich the cultural program of the local Thanatopsis Club, but is overruled. She approaches the wives of important citizens about building a new town hall and school but finds them too absorbed in their own affairs to welcome large changes in the town. She sponsors a play which is a theatrical flop because the players are not at all interested in serious drama.

She finds only a few compatriots for her dreams. One is Guy Pollock, a lawyer with a fine soul but with too much timidity to be very effectual. Another is Fern Mullins, a wholesome young teacher who is dismissed from her position because of the false accusation of Widow Bogart that she has tried to seduce her teen-age son. Another is Erik Valborg, a tailor's apprentice with Keatsian sensitivity, who leaves town because he and Carol fall in love and he does not wish her to be hurt. And another is Miles Bjornstam, town handyman and town atheist, who marries Bea, Carol's maid.

Throughout the book, one of the main targets of Lewis's flaying satire is the denominationalized, "respectable" religion of the small town—a religion grossly insensitive to the real currents of damnation and grace in the world. The theology of Main Street Lewis characterizes as a "sanguinary and alien theology"—sanguinary because of its preoccupation with the blood of Christ to the exclusion of all the other aspects of the Incarnation, and alien because it never really penetrates through the crustaceous hearts of the people. Doc Kennicott's attitude is typical: he thinks religion is a "fine influence" to keep the lower classes in order, and guesses that theology is "O.K." because a "lot of wise old coots figured it all out, and they knew more about it than we do." [13] Widow Bogart is the strongest supporter of the local Baptist church—and the town's most slanderous busybody. And the Reverend Mr. Edmund Zitterel's ministry in that church is summed up in the onomatopoeic effect of his name: he is narrow, shallow, and generally

[13] Sinclair Lewis, *Main Street* (New York: Harcourt, Brace, 1920), p. 328.

irrelevant, with no trace of the real vitality of the true Hebraic-Christian tradition. He has been completely homogenized to his culture, which, in this case, is a very mean little culture. When he preaches on the subject "America, Face Your Problems!" he defines the American problems as being summed up in two monstrous evils—Mormonism and Prohibition. He denounces socialism and cries up the good old democratic ideals, and thinks the legislature ought to step in on the Seventh Day Adventists for insisting that Saturday is the Sabbath. And when Fern Mullins is wrongly accused of immoral deportment, he stands with the Pharisees in condemning her.

Carol is hardly so crass. When Fern says that God may be punishing Mrs. Bogart through her son, Carol says, "My dear, Mrs. Bogart's god may be—Main Street's god. But all the courageous intelligent people are fighting him . . . though he slay us." [14] The twisted quotation from the lips of Job is a poignant one. Carol is determined to resist Main Street and its god, even unto death. Once, when her husband suggests that they have their son Hugh christened by the Reverend Mr. Zitterel, she explodes, "I refuse to insult my baby and myself by asking an ignorant young man in a frock coat to sanction him, to permit me to have him! I refuse to subject him to any devil-chasing rites! If I didn't give my baby—*my baby*—enough sanctification in those nine hours of hell, then he can't get any more out of the Reverend Mr. Zitterel!" [15] Perhaps there is a certain lack of understanding of the nature of the ministry here, a failure to see the minister as one small link in the historical continuity of a great spiritual Church, blessing, performing the rites, declaring the Word from its bosom. But there is no failure to recognize the inadequacy of the present minister and the local church as they are judged by that continuing ministry and that great Church, no failure to see this church as a mere confluence of heterogeneous social forces gathered under the sanctioning name of a spiritual body, as a mere unredeemed community posing as the redeemed one. Carol sees that there is more true spirituality in a man like Erik Valborg, whose Keatsian sensuousness has for most people

[14] *Ibid.*, p. 384.
[15] *Ibid.*, p. 241.

in the small town stamped him as a "fleshly" man. "I tell you," she says to her husband, "he thinks about God, the God that Mrs. Bogart covers up with greasy gingham wrappers!" [16]

Lewis was not simply being unkind to the type of religion found in small towns. He had the clinical eye, and it roved everywhere. In another of his major novels, *Babbitt,* he exposed the pretensions and frailties of the plush "oaken and velvety" Chatham Road Presbyterian Church of Zenith, a mythical midwestern industrial city.

George F. Babbitt, a Zenith real-estate broker, is as typical of the occasional churchgoer as he is of the American entrepreneur, the family man, the club member, and the dallier in extramarital affairs. A simple man, who thinks in broad terms like patriotism, honesty, and neighborliness, he likes his religion simple too. Wrote Lewis:

> Actually, the content of his theology was that there was a supreme being who had tried to make us perfect, but presumably had failed; that if one was a Good Man he would go to a place called Heaven (Babbitt unconsciously pictured it as rather like an excellent hotel with a private garden), but if one was a Bad Man, that is, if he murdered or committed burglary or used cocaine or had mistresses or sold non-existent real estate, he would be punished. Babbitt was uncertain, however, about what he called "this business of Hell." He explained to Ted, "Of course I'm pretty liberal; I don't exactly believe in a fire-and-brimstone Hell. Stands to reason, though, that a fellow can't get away with all sorts of Vice and not get nicked for it, see how I mean?"
>
> Upon this theology he rarely pondered. The kernel of his practical religion was that it was respectable, and beneficial to one's business, to be seen going to services; that the church kept the Worst Elements from being still worse; and that the pastor's sermons, however dull they might seem at the time of taking, yet had a voodooistic power which "did a fellow good—kept him in touch with Higher Things." [17]

Only twice in his adult life does Babbitt become more than casually interested in the church which he spasmodically attends. The first time is when he is appointed as one of the leaders in a special Sunday-school drive to make Chatham Road the biggest Sunday school in town. His scheme for accomplishing this goal is to divide the Sunday

[16] *Ibid.*, p. 397.

[17] Sinclair Lewis, *Babbitt* (New York: Harcourt, Brace, 1922), pp. 207-8.

school into four armies, depending on age, and to give everyone a military rank according to how many new members he introduces to the organization. He also suggests hiring a real press agent for the Sunday school to keep all the information about it before the public: "Not only the big, salient, vital facts, about how fast the Sunday School—and the collection—is growing, but a lot of humorous gossip and kidding: about how some blowhard fell down on his pledge to get new members, or the good time the Sacred Trinity class of girls had at their wieniewurst party." [18] And on the side, thought Babbitt, the press agent might even tout the lessons, advertising them with trick titles, such as, should the lesson be about Jacob, "Jake Fools the Old Man; Makes Getaway with Girl and Bankroll." Babbitt's special reason for his enthusiastic service on this committee is the association it affords him with another member of the committee, prominent banker William W. Eathorne. When he has just concluded a profitable financial arrangement with Eathorne, involving a rather shady public real-estate deal, he announces to his son Ted, "I tell you, boy, there's no stronger bulwark of sound conservatism than the evangelical church, and no better place to make friends who'll help you to gain your rightful place in the community than in your own church-home!" [19]

The second occasion on which Babbitt becomes more than tangentially interested in the church follows an extramarital relationship that has been terminated by his wife's appendectomy and his fearful return to morality and "religion." He is not quite sure there is a heaven or a hell, but he wants to be on the safe side. One day he drops by the office of his pastor, Dr. John Jennison Drew, and tries casually to confess that he has been guilty of backsliding. Drew seems to take a pernicious kind of delight in probing into his sins. " 'Don't hesitate to tell me, brother! That's what I'm here for. Been going on joy-rides? Squeezing girls in cars?' The reverend eyes glistened." [20] Drew says he has two meetings pressing him, one with the Don't-Make-Prohibition-a-Joke Association and the other with the Anti-Birth-Control Union, but that he will take five minutes to pray with Babbitt,

[18] *Ibid.*, p. 216.
[19] *Ibid.*, p. 223.
[20] *Ibid.*, p. 394.

and, fish-like, flops down beside his chair and begins to pray. Midway through one of the most unctuous prayers in literature, Babbitt squints up between his fingers and beholds the pastor glancing at his watch as he concludes with a swelling, "And let him never be afraid to come to Us for counsel and tender care, and let him know that the church can lead him as a little lamb." [21] Sheldon Smeeth, the Y.M.C.A. director who has come in during the prayer and has moaned "Yes, Lord! Help our brother, Lord!" throughout, as if to authorize what Drew has prayed, offers to remain and pray further with him, but Babbitt bounds for the door, muttering something about not having the time. "Thereafter," concludes Lewis, "he was often seen at the Chatham Road Presbyterian Church, but it is recorded that he avoided shaking hands with the pastor at the door." [22]

Babbitt has failed his church, it is true. But the church has also failed Babbitt. It can hardly be said to be a redemptive community—unless keeping the Worst Elements from getting worse is a redemptive function. It plainly lacks a real sense of the ecclesiastical function, of the message, the mission, the *raison d'être* of the Church. Oh, it is a real community center, all right. As Lewis says, it has "everything but a bar." It has a nursery, a gymnasium, a Thursday evening supper "with a short bright missionary lecture afterward," regular movies, and a library of technical books for workmen—though, as Lewis points out, no workman ever enters the church except to wash the windows or repair the furnace. But all these "attractions" serve only to point up the vacuum that exists where the real drawing power of the Church ought to be: in its ministry of the Word that challenges and converts men from their disparate and failing existences into the united and prevailing body of Christ. Chatham Road is a church embarrassedly naked because it is adorned only by the accoutrements of modern religion—which might as easily go with any other religion—and not in the signal garb of the redemptive community of Jesus Christ.

But perhaps we shall be accused of loading the dice we are playing with. Lewis was unquestionably set against organized American religion, and could be trusted to lash out at it at every opportunity.

[21] *Ibid.*
[22] *Ibid.*, p. 395.

What about authors who are less vitriolic? Surely no other writer of more recent years has painted such a picture of the church.

But then we pick up a book like Peter de Vries' *The Mackerel Plaza* and find a comparable criticism in a different vein. If Lewis dealt with the more traditional Protestant denominations, inclining usually to a panning of hidebound fundamentalism, then de Vries goes to the other extreme. The church he depicts in *The Mackerel Plaza* is a silky, spineless thing in a commuter's haven near New York City—its members, explains Mr. Mackerel, the pastor, live in "a kind of hand-to-mouth luxury, never knowing where their next quarterly instalment of taxes or the payment on a third car is coming from"—and it is called People's Liberal. Chameleon-like, the church is colored almost entirely by the special nature of the community, where cleaning women have washing compulsions, where lawn benefits are held for folk singers who have escaped from jail, and where Max Kaminsky, Messy Williams, and other noted trumpeteers come up from New York to play for Easter services.

Mackerel, in the introductory part of the novel, delivers a brief explanation about the church:

> Our church is, I believe, the first split-level church in America. It has five rooms and two baths downstairs—dining area, kitchen and three parlors for committee and group meetings—with a crawl space behind the furnace ending in the hillside into which the structure is built. Upstairs is one huge all-purpose interior, divisible into different-sized components by means of sliding walls and convertible into an auditorium for putting on plays, a gymnasium for athletics, and a ballroom for dances.[23]

Then, almost parenthetically, he adds, "There is a small worship area at one end." This he describes as having

> a platform cantilevered on both sides, with a free-form pulpit designed by Noguchi. It consists of a slab of marble set on four legs of four delicately differing fruitwoods, to symbolize the four Gospels, and their failure to harmonize. Behind it dangles a large multicolored mobile, its interdenominational parts swaying, as one might fancy, in perpetual reminder of the Pauline stricture against those "blown by every wind of doctrine." Its proximity to

[23] From *The Mackerel Plaza* © 1958 by Peter de Vries, by permission of Little, Brown & Company, publishers. P. 10.

the pulpit inspires a steady flow of more familiar congregational whim, at which we shall not long demur, going on with our tour to say that in back of this building is a newly erected clinic, with medical and neuropsychiatric wings, both indefinitely expandable. Thus People's Liberal is a church designed to meet the needs of today, and to serve the whole man. This includes the worship of a God free of outmoded theological definitions and palatable to a mind come of age in the era of Relativity.[24]

Liberal indeed is the theology espoused by such a church. Mackerel preaches sermons based on texts from Havelock Ellis. When nearby areas have been inundated by a flood, he prays from the pulpit, "Let us hope that a kind Providence will put a speedy end to the acts of God under which we have been laboring." [25] And, again, "We know thou hast a difficulty for every solution." [26] One of his favorite remarks, always well received by the congregation because of its apparent religious flavor, is that "it is the final proof of God's omnipotence that he need not exist in order to save us." [27]

Such criticism as is implicit in these passages is of course not unfounded. Mackerel's semantical hocus-pocus strongly reminds us of the emasculated version of the Apostles' Creed Martin Marty quotes in *The New Shape of American Religion* as the credal statement of a typical community church:

I believe in God, the Father, all-loving;
Maker of all that is;
And in Jesus Christ,
loveliest of His many sons, our friend;
who was born of the Mother, Mary;
moved by the Spirit of God;
suffered under the systems of men;
was crucified,
and died for the sake of truth and right.
Yet he lives again in the lives made
beautiful by His truth,
ascending into the hearts of men,
and working at the right hand of
God, the Father who works all that is good.

[24] *Ibid.*
[25] *Ibid.*, p. 24.
[26] *Ibid.*
[27] *Ibid.*, p. 10.

I believe in the Holy Spirit of truth,
beauty, and goodness;
the ministering Christian Church;
the communion and cooperation of
good men with God and with each other;
the destruction of sin by righteousness;
the worth and beauty of human personality;
and the everlastingness of the life that
is in God. Amen.[28]

If, as George Buttrick has said, a creed is "that by which we dare ourselves against the universe," then the dare has been removed. We are in the world that is the making of Benjamin Franklin and the pleasant benevolence of deism, not in the world of Jonathan Edwards and the sterner theology of another day.

Edwards was dismissed in 1750 from his pastorate in Northampton, Massachusetts, for his rigorous insistence that Communion in the church should be offered only to believers and not to nonbelievers. The end result of the laxism that triumphed there is seen in the very architecture of Peoples' Liberal: a large hall convertible as a gathering place for various kinds of social entertainment, with a diminutive worship area at one end. The world has so swamped the church that the church is no longer sure of her purpose and, no longer sure of her purpose, is no longer certain about her message. What a world of difference there is between the descriptions of People's Liberal, with its free-form pulpit and interdenominational mobile and psychiatric clinic, and the spare little Negro church in Faulkner's *The Sound and the Fury,* with its crazy white spire and battered Christmas bell and handmade pews!

Perhaps there *is* a doctrine of the Church among modern authors, and they are using it to point up the shallowness, inefficacy, and offense of contemporary churches. Or, more likely, they are merely more sensitive to the general illnesses of the society in which we live, and, in their constant probing, now and then hit the raw nerves of pain and disease in our makeup.

One recent novel about the Church is professedly by a minister

[28] From *The New Shape of American Religion* by Martin E. Marty. Copyright 1959 by Martin E. Marty. Reprinted by permission of Harper & Row, Publishers.

writing under the pseudonym of Gregory Wilson. It is called *The Stained Glass Jungle*. As the title implies, it is basically a job of formula writing. But in certain instances it is powerful and telling in its judgments—especially those against organizationalism and ecclesiastical politics.

Even modern technology has entered the field for organizationalism. One scene in the novel is a candid view of a meeting of Methodist ministers, called to enable the chairman of a new pledge campaign to distribute bundlesome mimeographed material for the campaign. The instructions to each minister include a precise timetable that he must follow in the campaign, a specified order of service for the Sunday worship of his church, and even a canned sermon which he must "preach" lest he fail to give proper emphasis to the pledge system. Perhaps the most horrifying item of all is the Electronic Kingdom Commitment Card, which the campaign director explains thus:

> Let us now turn to the Electronic Kingdom Commitment Card. Note that I am rubbing the electrographic pencil so as to black in the square directly to the left of the words, "I commit myself to the practice of daily prayer". . . . The first three code letters designate the district, conference, and jurisdiction; the first numeral indicates the pastoral charge; the last five digits designate the individual prospect. Use of code numbers instead of proper names for prospects enormously simplifies the computation of results. Thus, when prospect has recorded his commitments in this fashion, pledging himself to pray, to read his Bible, to attend church, etc., the card is forwarded to campaign headquarters and within a matter of hours we are in position to flash the word to the most distant charge in the conference as to its precise standing, the district's comparative status, and various items of interest to the pastor, such as the median number in attendance at midweek services, etc.[29]

Talk about depersonalization—this is I.B.M. religion at an ultimate!

But the real "message" of the novel is about the rank and frank politics of the Methodist church's ministry. Fred "Beloved" Worthington, a little butterball of a man who is one of the slickest district superintendents a Methodist ever met, says to Jack Lee, a young minister on the idealistic side,

[29] From *The Stained Glass Jungle* by Gregory Wilson. Copyright © 1962 by Doubleday & Company, Inc. Reprinted by permission of the publisher. P. 236.

Possibly the first Christians *were* as selfless and unworldly as is generally assumed; certainly they were few in number, their organizational structure was quite modest, and they anticipated the end of history at an early date. But time went on, the church grew, its shadow lengthened, and the motives which had empowered a band of lay preachers in a temporary world soon proved insufficient for the full-time professionals of an on-going organization. So title and rank and salary and seniority had to be wedged in among love and sacrifice and faith.[30]

Later, Jack says, "Then you actually can't put the Kingdom of God first, and the Holy Spirit has no place in a cabinet meeting."

"Of course it has a place!" says Worthington. "I've seen problems unraveled which could only have found solution through a wisdom more than human. I've seen the whole cabinet stop dead for prayer. I've seen superintendents in such agony in their desire to be fair to every man, not to penalize or hurt any man, that they broke down and cried."

"But if a big church—"

"Oh, come, come, beloved! Everyone knows that the Holy Spirit has nothing to do with the big church appointments—those are all settled by wealthy laymen. But the Spirit certainly does exercise an influence in the medium and lower brackets." [31]

Jack is engaged to Worthington's daughter Patricia. But he rebels against Worthington and the machine, loses Patricia, and is sent to the one church in the conference where he had wished never to go. He realizes that Patricia, as the daughter of the D.S., has never recognized ministers as being any more than religious career men. "The stained glass jungle was her native habitat, and she no more expected ministers to be like Christ than she expected her Greek grocer to quote Euripides."

This is the report on the Church in modern literature. We could look further, at works such as Thornton Wilder's *Our Town,* with its representative, though sentimentalized, small-town church, or Wolfe's *Look Homeward, Angel,* with its protagonist too passionate and sensitive to be satisfied with the Altamont churches that have

[30] *Ibid.,* p. 175.
[31] *Ibid.,* pp. 175-76.

more than half forgotten the mythological vitality of their heritage, or Joyce's *Ulysses,* with its devastatingly satirical passage about a worship service in a Catholic church. But everywhere the story is the same. It is the story of a church that has become either so esoteric and cabalistic as to be completely out of the main stream of life or so adapted and acculturated to its surroundings as to have ceased to judge them, with the result that in either case it has lost, unforgivably, its redemptive efficacy, and, what is more, is unaware that it has lost it.

The following items, it seems to me, are most generally associated with the Church as it is delineated in contemporary writing:

(1) A new kind of exclusivism of membership—not the kind that separated the Christians from the non-Christians in the early church, but the kind that results from splinterish sectarianism or that makes radical moral distinctions between the socially acceptable church member and the unimportant church member or nonchurchgoer;

(2) A narrow moralism, the emptiest kind of Phariseeism, substituted for the more sweeping demands of biblical religion, such as those stated by Micah, to do justly, to love mercy, and to walk humbly with God, or that inculcated by Paul, that we be crucified with Christ;

(3) A modernization of organizational structure, to bring the Church into line with the insights of contemporary business, politics, and advertising;

(4) No experience of the numinous, without which it is impossible to perceive the vertical relationship of the true Church;

(5) Hence, no amalgamating, forging spiritual experience to bind the membership into the realized body of Christ on earth, so that they remain disparate and unrelated elements in a fellowship that is always at least a little bit alien to them;

(6) No real maturation of the members, such as the early Christian fellowship seems to have provided; and, finally, climactically, most important of all,

(7) No experience of redemption.

Three remarks are in order.

First, there are many instances in which the Church deserves such criticism. There are whole areas of modern life in which the Church has failed stupendously and overwhelmingly. For this reason, churches should pay far more attention than they do to the censures of contemporary artists.

Second, the Church is not wholly unaware of its deficiencies. Its own intelligence system provides for self-criticism. For example, a recent study prepared by the General Assembly of the United Presbyterian Church and edited by Robert Clyde Johnson as *The Church and Its Changing Ministry* states, and then takes up in detail, three major accusations against the Church:

> (1) The Church does not understand itself; it is confused about its real nature and about its intended mission as the Body of Christ in the world. (2) The Church is virtually paralyzed by a crippling self-preoccupation. (3) The Church is increasingly inflicted with what can be called "organizational sclerosis," that is to say, a hardening of its institutional arteries that prevents it from swimming in the main currents of twentieth-century life.

This is what Paul Tillich calls "the Protestant principle"—the principle of self-examination—at work.

Third, there is really no doctrine of the Church in modern literature. Instead, there is a statement of extremely negative character about what the churches generally are in practice. It is not theology but sociology. The emphasis is upon what the Church has failed to be, not upon what it aspires to be. Authors seem all too frequently to write about the Church from outside it, instead of inside it, where they might be more sympathetic. As P. T. Forsyth has said,

> Religion is confused and pathless chiefly to those who treat the greatest concerns with most levity. And it is clear and great not from without the Church, but from within. To look at a building like the Albert Hall, or even St. Paul's, from the outside, you would have no such impression of its vastness or grandeur as you receive from its interior. And so with Christian truth. It is really and mightily true only from within.[32]

But, having made this assertion about the absence of a real doctrine of the Church in contemporary writing, let us grant to the *littérateurs* what they appear to insist upon: that in many cases the Church is an

[32] *Positive Preaching and the Modern Mind* (London: Independent Press, 1957), p. 90.

irrelevance in the modern world. Let us see to the end what the ramifications of this insistence are.

Because the Church in its local manifestations is so often an unredeemed and unredemptive community, it becomes an offense in a world that is full of community attempts. It is viewed as a shell, a form-survival that has lost the creative myth that formerly charged it with power. Consequently, men looking for redemption look elsewhere. They renounce the community, the *koinonia,* and seek their maturity and fulfillment in isolation.

The failure of the Church to provide the incandescent redemptive experience for our time is, it seems to me, one of the signal reasons for the contemporary apostasy from community and flight into individualism. Father Zossima, in Dostoevski's *The Brothers Karamazov,* saw a great spirit of isolation coming upon men. When asked what he meant by isolation, he spelled it out more carefully:

> Why, the isolation that prevails everywhere, above all in our age—it has not fully developed, it has not reached its limit yet. For every one strives to keep his individuality as apart as possible, wishes to secure the greatest possible fullness of life for himself; but meantime all his efforts result not in attaining fullness of life but self-destruction, for instead of self-realization he ends by arriving at complete solitude. All mankind in our age have split up into units, they all keep apart, each in his own groove; each one holds aloof, hides himself and hides what he has, from the rest, and he ends by being repelled by others and repelling them.[33]

Every student of religion, of philosophical movements, or of literature knows what he meant. From Melville's Ahab through Camus' Meursault—there has never in history been such a period bent upon the individualization of man, never such a current to the extrication of the single human soul from the whole of human society. Isolationism and the isolato are such a frequently repeated motif in the literature of the last hundred years that Nathan Scott, in *Modern Literature and the Religious Frontier,* speaks of it as one of the outstanding literary myths of our time.

Never have we been made more sensitive to heterogeneity. There

[33] Tr. Constance Garnett (New York: Modern Library, 1950), p. 363.

almost seems to be something in the air forbidding communi
feeling of Simone Weil is not uncommon: said she,

There is a Catholic circle ready to give an eager welcome to whoever enters it. Well, I do not want to be adopted into a circle, to live among people who say "we" and to be part of an "us," to find I am "at home" in any human *milieu* whatever it may be. In saying I do not want this, I am expressing myself badly, for I should like it very much; I should find it all delightful. But I feel that it is not permissible for me. I feel that it is necessary and ordained that I should be alone, a stranger and an exile in relation to every human circle without exception.[34]

A spirit of isolation haunts even those who are in the Church—even they tend to be suspicious, distrustful of the motives of others, perhaps because they do not, in an age of moral scholasticism and sophistication, trust even themselves. Where men have not committed themselves fully enough to the binding fire and the fusing light, they live in perpetual fear of other people, of the community itself, so that no true and complete community is really possible for them. They end "by being repelled by others and repelling them."

It is perhaps fitting for Franz Kafka to be called by critics the Dante or the Goethe of our time, as being largely representative of the spirit of the age. His famous short story "Metamorphosis" is the classic parable of isolationism. Gregor Samsa, who has been a traveling salesman, wakes up one morning to find himself in an unbelievably grotesque predicament—his introverted nature and his generally unspecific detestation of other people have become concretized in a physical condition. But here, in Kafka's disarmingly simple style, is the first paragraph of the story:

As Gregor Samsa awoke one morning from uneasy dreams he found himself transformed in his bed into a gigantic insect. He was lying on his hard, as it were armor-plated, back and when he lifted his head a little he could see his dome-like brown belly divided into stiff arched segments on top of which the bed quilt could hardly keep in position and was about to slide off completely. His numerous legs, which were pitifully thin compared to the rest of his bulk, waved helplessly before his eyes.[35]

[34] *Waiting for God,* p. 54.
[35] Tr. Willa and Edwin Muir (New York: Modern Library, 1952).

Thus begins one of the most frightening sagas in the annals of literature. Samsa discovers, successively, that he is unable to communicate with his family, his maid, his employer, his sister's beau—with anyone at all; that he is singularly abhorrent to all who see him; that he cannot perform the simplest human functions; in short, that he is summarily cut off from the whole realm of human community. Kafka has managed, in a single story, to show us the entire situation of contemporary man in isolation from his fellows, whether by choice or happenstance, by temperament and inclination, or by the mood of the times—or even by what Iris Murdock has called "the sickness of the language." More than most of us realize, we awake daily into Samsa's predicament, where we too are crustaceous, armor-plated, "cut off."

It is almost impossible to speak of Kafka's world without calling it the world of the nightmare. Indeed, another of the chief critical approaches to his work (we have already mentioned that through Judaism) has been through Freudian dream analysis—both Gregor Samsa and Joseph K. (in *The Trial*) *awake* into their predicaments, so that each might wonder if he is in the waking world or still in the dream world. And one of the characteristics of most nightmares is the extreme isolation and loneliness of the dreamer: he is in a distorted world that howls centrifugally around him, so that he is made to wonder whether it is he or the world around him that is warped and crazy; it no longer submits to logic, to the mind order he has been taught by the community; and he therefore faces it in a radically peculiar experience, one that cannot be shared with the human community at large.

The same seems true to a large extent for Meursault in Camus' *The Stranger*. Meursault appears to be caught in the destroying intersection of two worlds, the world of the human community, where he necessarily has some roots, and the world of private experience, which in his case has taken priority over the other world. Much of what Camus in his essays calls "absurdity" arises from the contiguity of the two worlds and from the impossibility of the human to satisfy the demands of both. Because the world of private experience has loomed larger in the consciousness of Meursault than the world of community, he seems to live with a recklessness for the traditions and mores of the community, so that in the end the community must destroy him for its own preservation. Significantly, the only time Meursault becomes angry, truly angry, in the whole business of his extermination by the community, is when the priest urges him to confess and be forgiven. The forgiveness he seeks is not from the community *per se* or the community as represented by the Church. These, for him, are not redemptive communities. The redemption he seeks, if he may be said to seek such, he must search for in isolation.

Kafka and Camus are of course both grouped with the existentialist writers of our century. And the glorification of the isolato is one of the major undertakings of all existentialism from Kierkegaard on. Kierkegaard, in whose thought Lutheranism played a much more formative role than most of his critics have allowed, tried, by assailing the idea of the collective experience of grace, to correct a situation Luther had unwittingly left in the institution of a state-church. The individual—that is the basic integer of all spiritual experience, he declared. He set himself like the soldier at Thermopylae to encounter every man at the moment of dread when he must enter the pass singly and alone. No man can be saved, he declared, without first knowing himself as a sinner; and one can know himself as a sinner only by being alone before God. Perhaps Kierkegaard is not to be blamed for his strong strain of anti-ecclesiasticism; he knowingly overstated himself on many points in order to exert the corrective influence that he felt necessary. But, if the truth be spoken, he as much as Nietzsche is responsible for the flight from the community that is mythologized in so much of modern literature.

This strong emphasis upon individualism is by no means confined to the literature of existentialism alone, though. It is to be found in much of the finest writing of the last thirty or forty years. For instance, it is the hallmark of the works of Ernest Hemingway, who, although he was at last buried by the Church, throughout his adult life wrote about men who discovered what he called "the separate peace." This kind of peace he conceived of as being won only through the clear, tough honesty of radical self-identification and the complete repudiation of the easier world of intrigue and mass culture. The extreme violence which characterizes his writings—wars, fistfights, gun battles, bullfights—is not merely incidental to his storytelling; it is part of the method by which he makes his characters aware of their unique selves. They experience what Martin Heidegger has named *das Sein zum Tode* (being towards death)—that is, as they face the possibility of their own imminent annihilation, of their own ceasing to be, all cultural complications drop away, and they realize what their naked, unadorned souls are. And once a good man has seen his soul thus, he can never again retreat with full comfort into life in the collective form, whether the collectivism be of politics, social structure, or religion. The Hemingway hero, as he has been dubbed by the critics, has passed beyond the Church and the Christian era. I suspect that here Hemingway has been much influenced by Nietzsche; perhaps not, but his characters frequently speak of the superannuation of religion in terms reminiscent of Zarathustra. At least, like Nietzsche, he views the Church as a development of the herd and must abjure it along with all the other aspects of life in community.

How intense, how devoted, how almost mystical are these writers in dealing with the theme of isolation! Their *spiritus sanctus* seems to be one not of unification but of dissolution and separation. How clairvoyant Dostoevski's Zossima was!

What has been the Church's attitude toward the separatist, the individualist, in our day? Has it encouraged uniqueness of personality and expression, depending on the gravity of its redemptive message and mission to offset all centrifugal activity and hold things together at the center, or has it tended to manufacture an artificial center by repressing idiosyncrasies and binding the *élan* of the individual?

Remarkably, it is the Roman church that has taken the larger view in the last century. Protestantism, with its numerous vying sectarians, and often with no clear vision of its principle of authority, has established numerous small authorities and orthodoxies, with the result that the really popular view of the Protestant church is that of an army divided, with every corps in it admitting precious little deviation on the parts of its adherents. Whereas the Roman church not only shelters but generally sanctions the work of François Mauriac and Graham Greene, and even made overtures of acceptance to Camus in his latter days, most Protestant denominations have been embarrassed to own the most talented critics who have arisen within their ranks, stumbling at minor points of moral and doctrinal divergence. Protestantism, in other words, because of its careful attention to the formulation of doctrine, has been far more cautious than Catholicism about including in its fold those writers who display not orthodoxy but heterodoxy. I do not say that Protestantism is culpable at this point. Catholicism has a Gargantuan digestive system for assimilating strong individualism without ever changing its total form; Protestantism, much more sensitive, much more fluid, is ever subject to alterations in its total form when it admits changes within its parts. The natures of the two are simply different. But the result is that Protestantism often seems more resistant to change and individualism than Romanism, and this may be one reason for the tendency notable in major authors like Eliot and Tate to move in the direction of the older church.

This is not to say that Protestantism has entirely discouraged the spirit of creativity among its artists; certainly not—the branch of the World Council of Churches devoted to the arts is said by some persons to be one of the most distinguished and liberal arms of the Council. But it has often, especially at the grassroots level, appeared to discourage real art. The failure of the average layman to appreciate and be receptive to the more creative efforts being made by artists interested in religion has tended to mark all Protestantism as grudging and recalcitrant to change. And, for better or worse, the genius of Protestantism, unlike that of Romanism, lies with the laity.

It is difficult to say whether it is the Church or the individualist who is more to blame for the estranged relationship. Probably the fault lies with both. Pär Lagerkvist, in his novel *Barabbas,* however, puts the onus of guilt upon the Church, and he is worth listening to. The exclusivistic ethics of the Church, which began to crop out in the injunction in I John to "love the brethren," is echoed in *Barabbas* by the repetitive, "Love one another." Ironically, it seems the Christians do not love Barabbas, or, for that matter, anyone beyond the fold of the elect. The unspeakable *agape* that has embraced them they have not learned to direct toward others. It is almost as if they alone had the power of redemption over Barabbas, as if only their society could cure the restlessness, the longing, the sickness of his soul. And yet they retreat from him in what amounts almost to a frenzy of loathing and hatred.

What strikes the reader so forcibly is that Barabbas is far more distinctive as a person than the Christians are. He actually seems more worthy than any of them. To be sure, he is "Barabbas the acquitted"—Christ has died in his stead. But might not as much be said for any of them? Never was a man more steadfast a seeker after some redemptive relationship to Christ. And yet he never seems to find salvation and peace because the Christian community refuses to receive him and guide him in his search. The reader's sympathies are definitely with Barabbas and against the Christian fellowship, which appears selfish, fearful, small, and meanly restrictive.

Lagerkvist was writing from within the biblical reference. It is easy to see how the artist who deals with a more contemporary setting can exalt the individual at the expense of the community, which tends almost invariably to have a lower mean intelligence, humor, and spirit than the individual and which tends therefore to crucify the individual out of an unreasonable fear for its own preservation. Thus the Church, in the Protestant communion at least, is so often denigrated as a provincial, narrow, and haughty-spirited institution bent upon preserving the *status quo* by crushing every appearance of novelty and uniqueness.

This, then, is the report from modern literature: that the individual, the isolato, the man in revolt—he is called by many names—is the real myth of our time, and not the redeemed community, which was the myth of Dante's day. Because there is no longer any real redemption in the community, but only stultification, shallowness, and ennui—"My parish is bored stiff," says Bernanos' country priest—the vital man searches for redemption alone, and the only true creative fellowship in the world is a kind of understanding among those who have been rebels and have achieved some kind of salvation in isolation. The only peace for our time is "the separate peace," a kind of tenuous half-peace that is won by the lonely gladiator.

One can hardly forbear noting the contrast between Dante's figure of the boatload of the redeemed at "the seashore where Tiber's wave grows salt" and Kierkegaard's modern picture of faith: a single man in a leaky boat, headed, oddly enough, not for harbor but for open water.

Perhaps this helps us to understand the Simone Weils a little better. When the Church ceases to live on the frontier between the world and the great Mystery, it becomes an irrelevance to the keenest intellectual and "spiritual" souls of its day; they may indeed feel that God has called them to remain outside the Church. The *true* Church, the Church that is experiencing renewal in our age, surely cannot fail to consider the report from contemporary literature a clear call to repentance and a challenge to a more sensitive understanding of its role of redemption in the world.

5

Sacraments and Sacramentalism

HAVING DEALT WITH THE DOCTRINE OF THE CHURCH, WE MUST NOW TURN to the subject of the sacraments. But because the sacraments are the sacraments *of the Church,* what was said in the last chapter will inevitably pertain to what must be said here. If it be true, as was observed there, that loyalty to the Church has in our time given way before an allegiance to individualism, then it naturally follows that a new attitude toward baptism and the Lord's Supper has obtained, and that it too will be mirrored in the poetry and drama and fiction of the age.

First we must be clear about what we mean by the word "sacrament." The classic definition is that it is "an outward and visible sign of an inward and spiritual grace." There are two aspects of this. First, the sacrament is a sign or a symbol, a visible reproduction of an inward drama. Baptism is a picture of Christ's death, burial, and resurrection —and not of his only, but of those of the baptisan and the entire congregation. The Lord's Supper, in the fraction and eating of the bread and the drinking of the wine, re-presents the suffering of Christ on the cross and the believer's appropriation of that act in his own behalf. Second, the sacrament is more than a sign, even more than a symbol. As theologians are wont to say, it is a "means of grace," or a "channel of grace." It is a gift to the Church wherein God continues to act upon the wills of men. Therefore it is not a magical thing, as the Roman church has been accused of implying, with an automatic effect regardless of the faith of the participant; nor is it, as unimaginative, right-wing Protestantism insists, merely a memorial. Something does happen to the votary in the sacrament, though not apart from his moral will.

It was the special work of the Reformation to achieve a better balance between the objective and subjective factors in the sacraments. Luther said in *A Treatise concerning the Blessed Sacrament of the Holy and True Body of Christ* that "the sacrament must be external and visible, and have some material form; the significance must be internal and spiritual, within the spirit of man; faith must apply and use both of these." The emphasis is upon faith, and faith depends upon hearing the gospel. The sacraments are objectively valid when they are recognized by the participant as presentations of the gospel in nonverbalized form. The objective and subjective aspects are not *in*dependent, but *inter*dependent.

The phrase that has therefore become almost indispensable to any discussion of the Reformed view of the sacraments is "Word and sacrament." Remove the Word, and the sacrament becomes a mere magical rite. The Word, which is both the Scripture and more than the Scripture, must be made known to the people in order for the sacraments to be rationally comprehensible and meaningful. Christ's words of institution must be read at the moment of the sacrament to take it out of the realm of mere thaumaturgy and put it where it belongs, in the province of faith and appropriation. The liturgical rites of the Roman church were all in Latin. Luther considered this to be part of "the Babylonian captivity of the Church" and said it bereft the people of the real meaning of the sacraments. Protestantism took one step toward the restoration of the meaning by restoring the words of institution in the vernacular.

But the balance between objectivity and subjectivity is a difficult one to maintain; and the pendulum, having swung away from the magical view, moved, in the generations following the Reformation, to the other extreme. The Reformed churches put so much emphasis on rationality and subjectivity that they began gradually to abandon all belief in the intrinsically sacramental qualities of the elements themselves. The lustrative power of water in baptism and the mystical process of nutrition in the Lord's Supper were largely forgotten; the contributions of archetypes to the symbolism of the Christian rites were greatly underestimated or purposely overlooked. In short, the rational aspect was so celebrated as to make the verbal word itself the complete bearer of the sacramental grace, leaving the sacraments themselves as little more than pictorial aids to reflection upon the Word. As Hugh T. Kerr has suggested in a monograph entitled *Mystery and Meaning in the Christian Faith,* Protestantism has so exalted the *meaning* of the faith—resulting in numerous biblical translations, commentaries, creeds, catechisms, confessions, and elaborate educational systems, all having to do with meaning and interpretation—that it has done little justice to the abiding mystery of the faith.

The result of such an imbalance is obvious. There has been a deplorable depreciation of the sacraments among nearly all the churches of contemporary Protestantism. Not that we have discarded the celebration of the sacraments. The so-called "renascence of worship" has at least temporarily reintrenched them in some denominations; and, besides, we are slow to kick over old ways of doing things. But we have developed a strain of Protestantism that is sacramentally obtuse and insensitive. Probably more persons today than ever before can *explain* the symbolism of the sacraments; but these same persons have difficulty in feeling the sacramental magnitude involved in actually receiving the sacraments. The dramatic effect of the sacramental act—an effect that could almost be described as traumatic among the early Christians—has been lost in the process of intellectualization. We *know* all about the sacraments; but we have lost the power to *experience* them.

I suspect that part of this is due to the fact that the means of enacting the sacramental dramas of Christianity are not exactly indigenous to our culture. We have no ready reference in common experience, as the early Christians had, for the forms of the sacraments. There is, of course, some discernible relationship between submerging oneself in a steaming tub of hot water in the privacy of one's bathroom and being baptized in the River Jordan; and between eating a meal or attending a cocktail party with friends and sharing bread and wine in the communion meal. But the relationship is immediately diminished when baptism is administered as a few drops of water sprinkled titillatingly on one's pate by a grandfatherly clergyman, or when communion is celebrated with neat little crackers and diminutive cups of grape juice. Everything is subjective. We are asked to make believe, not once, if you please, but twice. To make believe once is not difficult, and it was the original intention of the sacraments that we should do so. Plunged beneath the waters of a river, one can imaginatively claim the experience of being born from the womb again spiritually, of passing through the Red Sea and the Jordan, of dying with Christ and being raised with him; eating a fistful of bread torn from the loaf by the host, or quaffing a cup of wine passed around, mouth by mouth, from the host, one can realize with vividness the occasion when Christ ate thus with his disciples. But to make believe twice—to make believe that being sprinkled with a few drops of water is equivalent to being immersed in a river, before one can make believe that he is being baptized into Christ's death, and to make believe that a crumb of bread and a sip of juice are a hunk of bread and a chalice of wine, before one can make believe that they are the body and blood of the Lord—overtaxes the imagination. What I am trying to say, and am saying badly, is that the very forms of the sacraments have been so abused in contemporary urban civilization as to forbid the mystery for us. The rationale is all. The sacraments speak to the mind but not to the whole man. They become part of the fragmentedness of modern life. Consequently we are witnessing, to use Tillich's phrase, "the death of the sacraments."[1]

Let us turn now to the literature of our period and see how the objective and subjective emphases are worked out there. First we must note the generally high regard in which the sacraments—especially the Eucharist—are held by Catholic authors. There is of course that "obscene Eucharist" in Joyce's *Ulysses,* but there are also the beautiful stories of sacrifice and compassion in Ignazio Silone's *Bread and Wine* and Graham Greene's *The Heart of the Matter* and *The Power and the Glory.* Silone's novel, which is about the corrupt conditions in Italy during the thirties, implies in its title the need for some Christ-like sacrifice to purify the country. Near the end of the story, the aged

[1] *The Protestant Era* (Chicago: University of Chicago Press, 1948), p. 94.

priest Don Benedetto, who has sympathized with the revolutionaries, dies while celebrating the Mass. Both of Greene's stories likewise feature protagonists who sacrifice themselves in behalf of others. In *The Power and the Glory* it is the renegade priest, who turns back from safety to give communion to a man who has betrayed him, and is caught and executed. In *The Heart of the Matter* it is Henry Scobie, who commits suicide in order not to hurt his wife and a friend.

The Heart of the Matter dramatically illustrates the Catholic reverence for the objective nature of the Eucharist. In fact, I know of no other novel in which a sacrament is so inextricably involved in the plot.

Scobie is the Deputy Commissioner of Police in a West African district during the Second World War. He is fiftyish, careful, guileless, and meticulously honest, in a position and location not particularly noted for the latter characteristics. His wife Louise is fond of poetry, bored with the town full of black people and rats and heat, and distressed by the fact that all her friends have left to go to South Africa, where a semblance of British order is still maintained. She wishes she could go ahead to South Africa too, where Scobie could join her when his leave is due. Scobie manages to borrow the necessary money, and sends her on ahead.

After Louise's departure, Scobie is summoned to Pende to take charge of a small group of survivors from a boat sunk by the Germans. They have been afloat for forty days and are in wretched condition. Scobie's heart goes out to two victims especially, a little girl who has lost her parents and who reminds him of his own daughter, who died as a child, and a young married woman who has lost her husband and is still clutching a stamp album that belonged to him. The child dies, but the young woman, whose name is Helen Rolt, mends and eventually comes to live in Scobie's community. An involvement with her ensues.

Then Scobie receives word that Louise has felt guilty about leaving him alone in the awful community and is coming back to endure it with him until his leave. He is faced by a major dilemma: he pities both women, Louise and Helen, and doesn't want to do anything to hurt either of them. His immediate problem is that Louise will suspect something if he does not accompany her to Mass. But to receive communion without having confessed his sin and sworn to forego it forevermore is to eat damnation for his soul. He is firmly convinced of this. In the end, it is his "terrible automatic pity" that decides the issue—he takes the Eucharist and damns himself.

Protestants who have made light of Catholic seriousness about the Mass cannot fail to be impressed by the high drama of Scobie's approach to the altar. As he kneels, he tries to excuse his disobedience to the Church by his compassion for the two women. He says to Christ, speaking to the crucifix, "You can look after yourself. You survive the Cross every day. You can only suffer. You can never be lost. Admit that you must come second to these others." He watches the priest pour the wine and water into the chalice. "And myself," he thinks, "I must come last: I am the Deputy Commissioner of Police: a hundred men serve under me: I am the responsible man. It is my job to look after the others. I am conditioned to serve." The bread is given. He makes one last attempt at prayer: "O God, I offer up my damnation to you. Take it. Use it for them." And then, says Greene, he senses "the pale papery taste of his eternal sentence on the tongue." [2]

All that is left is to will physical death. It soon becomes apparent to Scobie that he must go all the way if he is not to hurt Louise or Helen—or God—any longer. He has dreamed several times of suicide. As affairs become more and more complicated, it seems the only out. Still, it is his pity for the others that rules him: he must make his death appear natural. He studies the symptoms of angina and simulates them so convincingly that even a doctor believes he is suffering from the disease. The doctor gives him evipan to help him sleep. He caches ten doses, writing each time in his diary that the dose has helped him to sleep. Then, with all in order, he takes twelve doses at once, and dies.

How completely the communion motif is involved even in the death is indicated by Scobie's final visit to the church, shortly before he takes the evipan. He clutches the narcotic in his pocket and sits at the back of the church, "as far as he could get from Golgotha." He says:

[2] Graham Greene, *The Heart of the Matter* (New York: The Viking Press, 1948), pp. 248-50. Used by permission of the publisher and Graham Greene.

O God, I am the only guilty one because I've known the answers all the time. I've preferred to give you pain rather than give pain to Helen or my wife because I can't observe your suffering. I can only imagine it. But there are limits to what I can do to you—or them. I can't desert either of them while I'm alive, but I can die and remove myself from their bloodstream. They are ill with me and I can cure them. And you too, God—you are ill with me. I can't go on, month after month, insulting you. I can't face coming up to the altar at Christmas—your birthday feast—and taking your body and blood for the sake of a lie. I can't do that. . . . I'm not pleading for mercy. I am going to damn myself, whatever that means. I've longed for peace and I'm never going to know peace again.[3]

This writing has what Matthew Arnold called "high seriousness." It is the objective view—but even to a Protestant it is deeply moving. The theology of the sacrament and the plotting of the story are so inextricably intertwined and interfused that each gives reality and meaning and depth to the other. For my money, this is *the* novel about a sacrament.

What has Protestantism, for all its insistence that its concept of the sacraments is higher than that of the Roman church, to match against *The Heart of the Matter?* Very little, to my knowledge. We are indicted by the fact that the most famous communion scene in non-Catholic literature is Aldous Huxley's vicious parody of the Lord's Supper in *Brave New World.* Twelve men and women sit around making the sign of the "T"—a truncated cross, for Ford, who is the deity of the New Age—and getting drunk on strawberry soma and soma wafers while they wait for the theophany of the great Ford. They sing their "solidarity hymns"—

Orgy-porgy, Ford and fun,
Kiss the girls and make them One.
Boys at one with girls at peace;
Orgy-porgy gives release[4]

—and presently they reach a state of delirium, and they dance and shout that they hear their divinity coming. Even Bernard Marx, one of the few reflective characters in the book, jumps and shouts with the rest of them, "I hear him; He's coming!" "But it wasn't true," says

[3] *Ibid.,* p. 289.
[4] P. 100.

Huxley. "He heard nothing and, for him, nobody was coming. Nobody —in spite of the music, in spite of the mounting excitement. But he waved his arms, he shouted with the best of them; and when the others began to jig and stamp and shuffle, he also jigged and shuffled." [5]

For seriousness and sensitivity, this is poles apart from Greene's treatment. It is negative where he is positive. It satirizes; he depicts sympathetically. It speaks from without, from the context of criticism; he writes from within, from the community of faith.

But this seems to be the situation for Protestantism. There has passed away a grandeur from the sacraments. In our attempt to state the meaning of them, to rationalize them, we have lost the sense of their mystery. It is with baptism as with the Lord's Supper. We recall Carol Kennicott's vituperative tone when speaking about "devil-chasing rites" in Sinclair Lewis' *Main Street.* We have become largely antisacramental. We ask with straight faces the question posed merely for rhetorical purposes by Donald Baillie in his book *The Theology of the Sacraments:*

> Why should not intelligent and educated Christians be content with the more reasonable and rational elements in public worship, preaching and praying and the reading of Scripture and the expression of praise in musical form? Why should they perpetuate such non-rational practices as the sprinkling of water on the head of an unconscious child or the consuming of tiny quantities of bread and wine to the accompaniment of solemn words? [6]

We have no capable Protestant writer working today who has been fundamentally and seriously impressed by either the mystery *or* the meaning of the Christian sacraments—at least, not seriously enough to cause him to make them the unifying motif of a major work of art, as Greene has done.

The word communion itself is instructive. It signifies identification with something beyond the self—with God, or with one's fellow men. Or even with nature. Basically, it is something that all men seek. And the means by which they seek it is always some kind of sacramentalism, whether Christian or not. If the Church has failed to

[5] *Ibid.*, p. 99.

[6] (New York: Charles Scribner's Sons, 1957), pp. 41-42.

make its sacraments seem relevant and meaningful, then men will seek other avenues to the fulfillment of the self. For example, we cannot help witnessing the reverence, spoken or unspoken, that some men have in our day for the kind of mass life that is the product of modern technology. With a few it amounts almost to a mysticism between the individual and the new society. The individual endures the painful periods of preparation—adolescence, college, job placement—until the moment when he can suddenly break through to the nirvana of life in lower-middle-class suburbia, with a split-level house on a standard-sized lot, a station wagon with an average-sized complement of children, membership in the country club, the P.T.A., and a community church, and a budget large enough to cover all the gadgetry, repairs, drugs, and psychiatric treatment required by such an existence. Then he belongs. Then his wife feels that she belongs. Then the children feel that they belong. They feel a kind of vague "togetherness" with the whole anonymous society of which they are a part. It is a form of communion, *à la moderne,* in which the invitation to swim in the neighbor's pool replaces baptism and the cocktail party does a stand-in for the Lord's Supper.

There has also been a resurgence of real primitive sacramentalism in our time. Because the sacraments of the Christian faith have appeared too limited and too contrived—perhaps too rationalized—there has been a tendency to go behind them in favor of their own archetypes. Not just the Church's baptism, but any water becomes purgative, traumatic, initiatory. In contemporary fiction, one has but to look at such works as Fitzgerald's *Tender Is the Night,* Thomas Mann's *Death in Venice,* or Hemingway's *A Farewell to Arms* to see instances of the reversion to archetypal baptism. In Fitzgerald's story, Nicole Diver finds youth and life again—rebirth is both the archetypal and the Christian image—while swimming in a grotto under a full moon. Aschenbach, in Mann's novel, dies on a beach as he watches the "pale and lovely Summoner" beckoning to him from a sandbar in the ocean. Frederick Henry, in Hemingway's narrative, marks his separation from the Italian army and his rebirth as an individual—a reversal of the usual pattern—by swimming the Tagliamento.

Hemingway, among modern authors, has been especially fond of the renascence-by-water motif. It occurs many times throughout his work, from the early Nick Adams stories to *The Old Man and the Sea.* And in almost every instance it is accompanied by obvious womb symbolism, as in the novel *Across the River and into the Trees,* where Cantwell makes love to Renata in a gondola on a Venetian canal. The sheer repetition of the water-womb imagery in these narratives lends it the force of sacramental enactment. Similar examples could be multiplied by the score; it wants no special talent to discover them.

Nor does the reversion to archetype apply only in the case of water. It extends all the way to the ancient Greek concept of the quaternal elements that were supposed to constitute all matter—earth, air, and fire, as well as water. Fire especially. The whole idea of "baptism by fire" is part of it. From Stephen Crane's *Red Badge of Courage,* the novel about a boy who becomes a man under the pressure of war, an entire genre has developed about the person (he need not be a soldier, or even a man, for that matter) who is purged, matured, or reborn through a battlefield experience. Whether it is from fear to assurance, as in the case of Henry Fleming, or from ignorance to enlightenment, or from selfishness to altruism, or whatever, the direction is essentially the same—from chaos to order—as is intended, in the abstract at least, by the Christian sacraments.

How tame and unimaginative the traditional sacramentalism of the Church must appear to the casual observer! Few Christians seem vitally affected by the fact of their baptisms, and few appreciate at all the sense of great *drama* in the sacrament of communion. Few who, because of the words of institution, regard the latter act as involving somehow the memory, realize even then the real meaning of biblical *anamnesis*—that it is the reconstitution of an event by celebrating it. Thus, most of us miss the impact that the act of communion has in the present, and are largely unable to practice the real presence of Christ at the meal. And very few Christians, ministers as well as laymen, have ever seemed to me to be very much aware of the eschatological significance of the Supper, of the way in which both past and present are gathered up into the eternal banquet of the redeemed. The dynamic is gone. The form remains, but it does not excite and challenge the moral will, because it is only a perfunctory observance. Nothing happens in the Supper. This is the trouble with it—nothing happens! This is the insight of that searing parody in *Brave New World:* communion does not take place. The participants receive the elements, they sing and dance and cross themselves, but they never get out of themselves and beyond their finitude into union either with the divinity or with the other members present. They seek solidarity, but cannot achieve it.

What is left to the individual today if communion no longer represents a real solidarity? What indeed but to push the attempt at communion back to more archetypal methods of finding it? This is the reason, in contemporary fiction, for the variety of acts by which characters seek the ecstatic union with integers larger than themselves. All the wars that protagonists ever join, all the causes they espouse, all the things they ever hate, all the evils that ever entertain them, are confused attempts to get back together, to be part of something again, to find union. Therefore the centaur-leaps and nipping of buds from garlanding boughs by Eugene Gant in Wolfe's *Look Homeward, Angel;* therefore his searching under the stone, the leaf, the door; therefore his mesmerism by the classics: he is trying to find union with the mythological, with the transtemporal and transmoral and even transspatial, to get beyond himself into a whole new dimension. Therefore the Brahmanism of Eliot's earlier poetry, his mosaic from the world religions: he was trying to win through to the transreligious, the religion to embrace all religions. Therefore Larry Darrell's restive search in Maugham's *The Razor's Edge,* culminating in the mystical moment in the sunrise by an Indian lake: he is seeking the hypersensory, the fire, the flame, the burning vision which will transmute him into more than Larry Darrell, into a peaceful and contented part of the cosmos. Therefore the rash of minor novels dealing with Zen Buddhism, offering the reader a specious means of escaping the confinement of his narrow Western way of life: be silent and know that you are an infinitesimal part of all life. As the sparks fly upward, man has an inevitable urge to get beyond himself to the peace and fullness —even relatively speaking—of some larger unity. He longs to know the mystical excitement that Catherine Earnshaw felt when she cried, "I am Heathcliff!"

Tied up with the idea of union and reunion is the subject of ritualism. The penchant for ritual is, of course, innate in man; it is part of the collective unconscious that Jung has reminded us of. And it has always, as far as we can tell, had some connection with the search for communion. It is the mimetic drama by which man accomplishes his self-transcendence. It is the desire for rebirth, refreshment, or reinvigoration crystallized into pantomime. Therefore it is not surprising that a rise of natural sacramentalism in recent years has been accompanied by a corresponding resurgence of the primitive type of ritualism.

I have in mind particularly two authors who reflect most completely this recrudescence of ritualism—Melville and Hemingway. Many others might be cited—I wish especially that space were permitted to speak of the dark rituals with the Holy Grail in Charles Williams' novel *War in Heaven*—but these two must suffice. Melville I have chosen because he is representative of the tumultuous years at the beginning of the modern era, when Nietzsche and Dostoevski and Tolstoi and Poe and Hawthorne were all alive; and Hemingway because he was of our own century, and because he was, as Granville Hicks has said, "pre-eminently the novelist of the years between the wars."

The thing to bear in mind in the case of each writer is that the unusual outcropping of ritualism is part and parcel of an atavism to pre-Christian sacramentalism.

First, let us look at *Moby-Dick,* Melville's greatest novel.

The controlling symbol of the novel is of course the white whale, which, many critics agree, probably represents God, or, as James Baird has observed more carefully, "the ambiguity of God." [7] The very whiteness of the mammal is ambiguous, and contributes to the haunting *otherness* of the image. Baird says that the whale of Melville's tale is not the whale of Jonah—although the sermon by Father Mapple before the whalers' voyage would seem to set it in the context of the Jonah adventure—but the leviathan of the Book of Job. In a sense, this is true. The entire epic might be described as a narrative sermon on the text of Job 41:1, "Canst thou draw out leviathan with an hook?" But there is another sense in which the white whale is something beyond either Jonah's great fish or Job's leviathan, something intensely numinous in itself, almost as if it were the center of strange

[7] *Ishmael,* p. 318.

magnetic forces. This is not true of the biblical whales, which are merely creatures of the Omnipotent. Melville's Moby Dick is something more than they: he is otherworldly, and is for good reason named "the most striking nonanthropomorphous God-symbol from serious religious art in the recent history of the Christian world." [8]

Baird suggests the thesis, though he does not pursue it, that Moby Dick's whiteness is related to the liturgical employment of white during the Paschal feast, and thereby sets the story of the "Pequod" within the context of Catholic ritual. Actually, the ill-fated journey begins on Christmas Day, the day of the Incarnation; and it begins in a whaleman's chapel in New *Bedford,* a New World seaport equivalent of Bethlehem, with a sermon about Jonah, who, seeking "to flee worldside from God," finds that he has run right into him. It is an eastward journey into the seas that sweep upon lands thought to contain mysterious ways and ancient wisdom.

As the "Pequod" nears Japan, the symbolism of ritual begins to intensify almost by geometrical proportions. A cetological chapter is devoted to the subject of "ambergris," and the reader can almost imagine a censer swinging arcs of perfume down the nave that leads to the sanctuary. Is it nothing, asks Melville, "that the incorruption of this most fragrant ambergris should be found in the heart of such decay?" There follows the dramatic account of the Ecuadorian doubloon which Ahab nails to the mainmast as a prize to the man who "raises" Moby Dick:

> Now this doubloon was of purest, virgin gold, raked somewhere out of the heart of gorgeous hills, whence, east and west, over golden sands, the head-waters of many a Pactolus flows. And though now nailed amidst all the rustiness of iron bolts and the verdigris of copper spikes, yet, untouchable and immaculate to any foulness, it still preserved its Quito glow. Nor, though placed amongst a ruthless crew and every hour passed by ruthless hands, and through the livelong nights shrouded with thick darkness which might cover any pilfering approach, neverthless every sunrise found the doubloon where the sunset last left it. For it was set apart and sanctified to one awe-striking end; and however wanton in their sailor ways, one and all, the mariners revered it as the white whale's talisman.[9]

[8] *Ibid.,* p. 319.
[9] *Moby-Dick,* ch. 99.

The imagery here is unmistakable: it is of Christ nailed to the cross: it is Christ who is "virgin" and "immaculate to any foulness," who is nailed "amidst all the rustiness of iron bolts and the verdigris of copper spikes," who is transfixed "amongst a ruthless crew," who is "set apart and sanctified," who has not lost the "glow" of the mint, who is "the white whale's talisman." And, if there be the least doubt of it, we have but to read further for the description of the images on the coin: a flame (the Spirit of Pentecost), a tower (the Cross), a crowing cock (Peter's denial). There is a sense in which the doubloon is Jung's mandala figure, the concentration of life, the summary, the essence of all that is, captured in a shining circle, epitomizing man's deepest unconscious drives. It holds all secrets, or derives from all secrets. As Ahab says, "This round gold is but the image of the rounded globe, which, like a magician's glass, to each and every man in turn but mirrors back his own mysterious self." [10] To Ahab, the tower, the volcanic flame, the proud cock are all Ahab. Pip, the insane little seer, calls it "the ship's navel," which all the men are on fire to unscrew. "But, unscrew your navel," he says, "and what's the consequence? Then again, if it stays here, that is ugly, too, for when aught's nailed to the mast it's a sign that things grow desperate." [11] The navel image is extremely interesting in the light of the ship symbol itself—a boatload of men of widely varied origins, all traveling together on the primeval sea. They are really one body, and the navel is the umbilical point, the common vestige of their creation. It is Christ, the second Adam, who links us thus to our created state. Melville's intention that the coin represent a Christian symbol is only the more emphasized by the fact that Queequeg, the pagan harpooner, stands to look at it and thinks it is "an old button off some king's trowers." And there it stands throughout the chase, the cross in the middle of the vessel.

As the ship continues eastward, we are presented next with a baptism. Ahab commands the ship's vulcan to fashion him a special harpoon for the white whale, and when it is made he calls for a special tempering of the metal. "No, no—no water for that; I want it of the

[10] *Ibid.*
[11] *Ibid.*

true death-temper. Ahoy, there! Tashtego, Queequeg, Daggoo! What say ye, pagans! Will ye give me as much blood as will cover this barb?" [12] Three dark heads nod yes, and Ahab, who is himself of "the dark side of the earth," administers the puncturing of heathen flesh and the tempering of the harpoon, howling deliriously as the blood sizzles on the scorching iron, *"Ego non baptizo te in nomine patris, sed in nomine diaboli!"* Every word so. It is a black baptism.

The sea and winds become threatening and ominous as the ship draws nearer and nearer the whale. But the vessel pitches on into the vortex. Ahab becomes more possessed than ever. He dashes his "heavenly quadrant" to the deck and tramples it, and makes his own compass when the old one goes awry during a storm. He ceases to go below deck. The clothes that the night wets, the next day's sunshine dries. He no longer trims his beard, which grows gnarled and twisted like the roots of trees upturned. His monomania becomes daily more excessive, more wild, until it is totally devouring.

A terrible storm comes upon the ship from the direction in which they are headed. "Here!" cries Starbuck, seizing Stubb by the shoulder and pointing towards the weather bow, "markest thou not that the gale comes from the eastward, the very course Ahab is to run for Moby Dick? the very course he swung to this day noon?" [13] The gale is more than fierce: it is supernatural. At the height of the storm, Starbuck cries to Ahab to look to the tops of the masts. "All the yard-arms were tipped with a pallid fire; and touched at each tri-pointed lightning-rod-end with three tapering white flames, each of the three tall masts was silently burning in that sulphurous air, like three gigantic wax tapers before an altar." [14] Below, the upturned faces of the crew gleam in pale phosphorescence "like a faraway constellation of stars," and Queequeg's tattooing, lit up by the preternatural light, burns "like Satanic blue flames on his body." Ahab calls it a good omen. The white fire seems suddenly redoubled in energy. Ahab apostrophizes it: "Oh! thou clear spirit of clear fire, whom on these seas I as Persian once did worship, till in the sacramental act so burned by thee, that to

[12] *Ibid.,* ch. 93.
[13] *Ibid.,* ch. 99.
[14] *Ibid.*

this hour I bear the scar; I now know thee, thou clear spirit, and I now know that thy right worship is defiance. . . . Oh, thou clear spirit, of thy fire thou madest me, and like a true child of fire, I breathe it back to thee." [15]

There is no doubt now, if indeed there had been before, that the ship is plunging defiantly into the heart of spiritual reality. The gale itself, if we but recall the Greek word *pneuma,* is spirit as well as wind. Ahab leads his men, commands them, drives them, into the holy of holies, represented by the whale.

The moment of the ship's actual entry into the holy of holies may be marked as the instant when a red-billed seahawk snatches Ahab's hat from his head. Ahab has mounted the perch to watch for the whale; he is oblivious, as he scans the horizon, of the swift circlings of the scavenger bird as it darts at him. It spirals upward and downward and eddies around his head. Suddenly the long, hooked bill takes hold of the hat, and the sable wings carry the bird away. It is not an uncommon experience among sailors, reports Melville; but "now almost the least heedful eye seemed to see some sort of cunning meaning in almost every sight." The spirals and eddies anticipate those of Yeats's poetry, and could here be symbolic for the gyre of being, the centrality of energy and power that is being approached.

The whale is sighted, but the first attempt at capture fails. Ahab's peg leg is shattered, and the Parsee is caught in the line and drowned. Starbuck tries to persuade Ahab that the good angels are mobbing him with warnings, but to no avail; his soul's a centipede, and he will go on.

The final chase is divided into three days—a not insignificant touch—and it is on the third day that the ship closes once more with the white whale and the white whale sinks it, sending all the whalers like Lilliputians toward the deep. All, that is, but Ishmael, who is thrown free and floats toward the vortex of the sunken vessel. "When I reached it," he writes afterwards,

> it had subsided to a creamy pool. Round and round, then, and ever contracting towards the button-like black bubble at the axis of that slowly wheeling circle, like another Ixion I did revolve. Till, gaining that vital

[15] *Ibid.*

centre, the black bubble upward burst; and now, liberated by reason of its cunning spring, and, owing to its great buoyancy, rising with great force, the coffin lifebuoy shot lengthwise from the sea, fell over, and floated by my side.[16]

A rapture has taken place, and only the raconteur is left.

This is truly one of the most "infinite" novels in American literature—perhaps *the* great American novel, as some have proposed. Malcolm Cowley, in *The Literary Situation,* had a great deal of fun spoofing the amount of critical ink that has been spilled over it. But the multivalence of Melville's symbolism invites varied criticism. The novel is the story of Adam, of Prometheus, of the Miltonic Satan, of Faust, raising himself in impious pride against the fire and spirit of the God who created him and yet exists as a challenge and a limitation to his own being. Within this framework the implications and possibilities of interpretation are legion.

But one thing is sure: for all Melville's titanic questioning of the Christian theology of his day, he still employs a semblance of Christian ritual in describing the approach to the whale. Sermon, incense, crucifix, baptism, altar candles, and burgeoning intensity, all undergirded by a majesty of style and vocabulary reminiscent of nothing so much as of Shakespeare and the King James Version of the Bible—this seems at first glance completely Christian. As we have seen in closer investigation, though, it is only the form of Christian ritual that is preserved, the name, the species. The content of the ritual in every instance is primitive and vast and archetypal, embedded in nature and not in revelation. The Christian forms are used only as keyholes through which are viewed sacraments of wider and more natural origin, expanding far beyond the more historical Christian sacraments. The sacramentalism of the Church has grown too neat and precise and rational for the souls of men darkly tempestuous like Ahab.

We turn now to Hemingway, whose *Old Man and the Sea* constitutes, in my opinion, the *Moby-Dick* of our time, with one man against the great fish instead of a boatload of men, but without the privilege of Ahab's grandiose death as an ending. Hemingway has had perhaps more influence on modern writing than any other author in the English-

[16] *Ibid.,* Epilogue.

speaking world—more even than Faulkner, whom some critics consider to be a better novelist. And it is therefore extremely significant when we note that the emphasis on sacramentalism has taken an even more primitive turn in his novels than it did in those of Melville.

Randall Stewart, in *American Literature and Christian Doctrine,* speaks of the strong ritualistic aspect of all Hemingway's work and then adds, "One might almost substitute 'sacramental' for 'ritualistic,' remembering the 'Catechism' of the *Book of Common Prayer,* where 'sacrament' is defined as 'an outward and visible sign of an inward and spiritual grace.' "[17] I may be wrong, but I believe Stewart is confusing two meanings of the word "grace" here. Grace for Hemingway was always a humanistic thing, a kind of quietness and self-control and dignity under pressure. "Taking it" was the phrase he sometimes used to describe it. It never meant what the Prayerbook means by it. But if, on the other hand, we may speak of a neosacramentalism, there is some truth in the statement. Hemingway *was* concerned with grace, albeit of the secular variety, and ritual was involved in the manifestations of that "grace," both in his own life and in the lives of his fictional characters. As I have observed elsewhere, Hemingway's agnosticism did not lead, any more than did that of Sartre or Camus, to a total moral collapse. On the contrary, each of these men has been almost inordinately concerned with ethical behavior. Almost in inverse proportion to their lack of theism, they have developed an obsession with *the way one acts.* It is all that is left to them. One must concentrate on form or he sinks into oblivion, into the nothingness that in their view constantly threatens human existence. And form, when observed for such serious ends, becomes ritual—ritual designed to demonstrate the inward human grace.

This is represented almost allegorically in Hemingway's short story "A Clean, Well-Lighted Place," which I mentioned in an earlier chapter. The light-and-dark symbolism of the story is palpable and haunting. The old man who is drinking in the bar doesn't want to go off into the night—the night that is crouched there, waiting for him like an animal. In the bar there is communion; outside is the threat of nihilation, of Tiamat and original chaos. He knows he will be

[17] P. 134.

turned out when closing time comes. Nevertheless, he drinks carefully, never spilling. Even drunk, he doesn't spill. It is a remarkable sign of "grace" in an old man. And Stewart calls the bartenders "ministering priests" at the ritual.

Stewart notes also the ritualism of "Big Two-Hearted River," Hemingway's story-in-two-parts about Nick Adams' fishing expedition in the Michigan woods. The major emphasis of the story is on the form with which things are done: the fishing spot must be perfect, the camp must be laid out correctly, the coffee must be made by a precise formula. In Part Two of the story, Nick demonstrates the proper way to fish. Once he even leaves the stream for a while and crawls up on the bank to smoke a cigarette, lest he rush his sensations. The whole story is a diary of form.

This passion for the form in which things are done was all-consuming with Hemingway, both in his personal life and in his writing. It is demonstrated not only in these stories pointed out by Stewart, but in the episode of the "messy" fisherman who loses Harry Morgan's tackle in *To Have and Have Not;* in Pilar's memories of lovemaking in Valencia in *For Whom the Bell Tolls;* in the kudu-hunting competition between Karl and Papa in *Green Hills of Africa;* in the classic fishing expedition of Santiago in *The Old Man and the Sea;* in Cantwell's sensitivity to "the code" in *Across the River and into the Trees;* and in all the wonderful literature about bullfighting, where Hemingway has written probably with more feeling for the aesthetics of the Spanish sport than any Spanish author has ever done.

Perhaps it is in these chronicles of bullfighting especially that Hemingway's obsession with form is crystallized into ritual, or into a kind of pagan sacramentalism. It is the proper place for it, in a way, because there is some ancient and primitive mystery about the bull. He is still the descendant of the sacred animal of the Dionysians and the Maenads, of the hecatomb and the holocaust and the taurobolium. The matadors do the work of the priests, handling the animals, "sculpturing" their passes, while the crowds look on. In *The Dangerous Summer* Hemingway described one matador with serenity and purity of style by saying of him that he "fought his bulls as though he were serving Mass in a dream." The climactic moment of the service comes, of course, when the *torero,* the high priest, sights down his saber and plunges the long silver death into the beast. All present are caught up in the rapture of a mystery. There is a kind of communion among them—or among the *aficionados,* at least—as the great hairy god falters, topples in the ring that is an altar. They feel purged, cleansed, renewed.

The sacrament Hemingway describes is much more virile than the average Protestant communion service. It is a matter of life or death for the priest—and, vicariously, for the laity as well. The spectator cannot remain merely a spectator; he is drawn instinctively, irresistibly, into real participation in the drama. And somehow the boredom that cloys life seems to break and crack over the bullring, and a glimpse of the numinous appears.

For the early Christians, the sacraments throbbed with drama. The candidate for baptism was immersed in a pool or a river. Sometimes he was stripped naked, lest demons hide in his clothes. It really seemed like a burial and a resurrection. Nor was the Lord's Supper less exciting. For most of those who received it, probably in secret for fear of imprisonment and death, it recounted in miniscule the death and victory of Christ in their behalf. Eating the bread and drinking the wine—his flesh and his blood—internalized and reified the event for each of them individually and personally. What they did had about it none of what Baird calls "the pallor of inertia," so common where the Christian sacraments are observed today.

But it is the fact of the widespread failure of the sacraments of the Church to be real and meaningful to contemporary man that must account, at least in part, for the resurgence of such primitive sacramentalism as we have just been reviewing. When the contrived symbol expires or fails, an atavism occurs. There is a reversion to the archetypal pattern from which the later symbol is derived. Even though Christ is *creator mundi* and *Adam secundus,* so that he himself is basically the prototype for all sacramentalism, there is a return to that stage of sacramentalism considered archetypal in the historical consciousness of the race. This means a recrudescence of pre-Incarnation sacramentalism.

What has happened may be described by the figure formed by two intersecting lines, *AB* and *CD:*

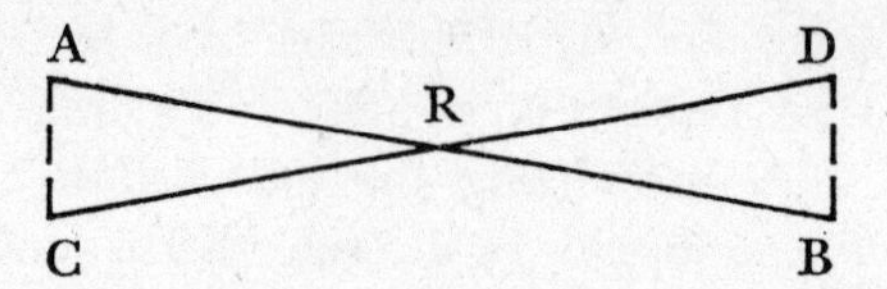

AC represents the era of pagan sacramentalism, when every stream and stone and tree was thought to be the habitation of a god or demon, or at least contained what the Polynesians called *mana,* a supernatural power residual in certain natural objects. Christ, whose work of redemption extends to nature as well as to men, transmuted certain items of natural sacramentalism (which of course already had a cultic significance for the Jews) into meaningful symbols for the Christian community. Even then, however, in the early Christian era, we recall the relative "openness" of the sacramental mind, the unwillingness to restrict sacramentalism to the specific elements of the Christian sacraments. The whole phenomenological world was to the first disciples ubiquitously capable of becoming the bearer of the numinous. The Gospel of Matthew, for instance, mentions that men were healed by touching the hem of Christ's garment, and the book of Acts speaks of little flags of cloth that were sent out from Paul to cast disease and devils out of the afflicted.

As history moved toward the point of intersection (*R*), the Church gradually narrowed its sacramental consciousness, or "refined" the categorization of the sacraments, until the specific number of ecclesiastical sacraments was fixed by Peter Lombard and Thomas Aquinas at seven. These were baptism, confirmation, penance, communion, ordination, marriage, and extreme unction. During the Reformation, represented by the point of intersection, the Protestants reduced that number to two—baptism and communion—for which they quoted scriptural warrants and promises. In the long years of orthodoxy that followed, there was rigorous controversy over the letter and meaning of the two "Protestant" sacraments, until it might almost be said that the very life had been macerated out of them and they came to represent, for most Protestant Christians, mere esoteric confessionaries, intellectual shadows of what had once been dynamic realities. Perhaps the point of intersection in our diagram should represent the theoretical moment when Protestantism entered this period of desiccated sacramentalism.

But as the Church and its sacraments became less and less relevant to human life, men began, in their essential need for sacrament, to revert to primitivism, and, along with it, to primitive sacramentalism. The history of modern primitivism really began in the so-called Age of Enlightenment, when ecclesiasticism was at its nadir. In western Europe it issued in the cult of the "natural" man. Rousseauism and the doctrine of the noble savage colored literature and philosophy until the deaths of Goethe and Wordsworth, and reached even beyond them to the *nouveau-paradise* literature of Robert Louis Stevenson and Somerset Maugham and James Michener. Possibly it is even responsible for what Edmund Fuller calls the "new compassion" in modern literature—a feeling of tenderness for harlots and perverts and sadists and criminals of all sorts. Society and environment are the scapegoats—man never rises to the words *mea culpa.*

The result is that the Church, with its diminished relationship to the world, and its sacraments, with their even more diminished relationship, appear intolerably narrow and confining in the face of a new primitivism that asserts once again the basic sacramental nature of all real relationships. The Christian sacraments have become, so to speak, desacralized, while natural sacramentalism has regained something of sacral significance. In other words, we are now on the way to auxiliary line *DB* in our diagram, with a sacramentalism almost as open-ended and all-embracing as it was in the primitive era before the coming of Christ. Such a conclusion, it seems to me, is verifiable on sociological as well as literary grounds.

H. T. Kerr, in his little book on *Mystery and Meaning in the Christian Faith,* has pointed out a connection between the failure of the Church's sacraments and the failure of traditional form in the arts. In both instances, he says, there is a rebellion being staged against too much emphasis on the rational and not enough on the irrational. We tend to think that it will all come right again, that these innovations are only temporary departures from tradition. "But this judgment surely is a superficial one," says Kerr,

> for behind these contemporary forms there lurks a basic protest against the inadequacies of previous structures to do full justice to the manifold levels of reality which the contemporary artist is most eager to explore and expose.

In this, as I see it, the present-day artistic interpreter is taking seriously—perhaps more seriously than those of us who might be expected to—the tension between mystery and meaning which—he is convinced—is of the very stuff of life. This is *not* just a fad or the transition from traditional structures to contemporary structures. *This is a protest against structure itself.* . . . As such, it appears to be irrational, illogical, unsystematic, in other words, *meaningless.*[18]

This may indeed be the stage we have reached in the development of Protestant sacramental thought—a stage where we fail "to do full justice to the manifold levels of reality" involved in the Christian sacraments. Our dilemma is that the Church has tended to intellectualize the mystery out of its sacraments, while the contemporary world, on the other hand, has substituted a broad, amorphous kind of sacramentalism which has very little meaning and no power to save. The severance is disastrous to redemptive activity: the world has a baptism unable to produce new men and a Lord's Supper for which there has been no Incarnation; and the Church, by ignoring the mystery that alone has the power of converting our natures, is actually left with the same weak sacraments as the world, only more narrowly interpreted.

As for which sacramentalism men will choose, when it is only a question of scope and not of depth of reality, the answer is obvious: it is the one reflected by the majority of contemporary writers—the broader sacramentalism of nature. And for the Christian who is sensitive to the real value of a proper sacrament, this is an unbearable outcome, because, as P. T. Forsyth has said, "Grace is not the superlative of nature. The Cross is more than the epitome of human sorrow, or the acme of noble sacrifice. The meaning in nature is more aesthetic than moral, more general than personal; and she has no word for the guilty or remorseful soul." [19]

The Church, then, has a serious responsibility in our day to rethink the whole question of its sacraments. A mere renewal of liturgical uses is not enough; it must be accompanied by a total reinvigoration of understanding of the sacramental principle itself, of the nature and meaning of "channels of grace." Laymen and even ministers must be

[18] (Toronto: Ryerson Press, 1958), p. 17.

[19] *The Church and the Sacraments,* p. 281.

led to rediscover the sense of the mystery and infinity that lie just beneath the surface of these outwardly simple and ingenuous acts.

And the sacramentalism of the literary artist may be of help in the task. Amos Wilder, speaking of how much better the artists outside the camp know modern man than we on the inside, and how their work rebukes our inadequacy, says:

> It is at this point that the *Christian* artists of our time can enter into their labor and reap the benefits. We recognize that a painter like Rouault or poets like Eliot and Auden can speak out of the same depth and with an adequate rhetoric today because they have learned from secular art. Thus the Christian artist learns how to speak so that modern man can know himself directly addressed when he hears the Gospel today.[20]

The sensitivity of writers like Melville and Hemingway to the basic need of man for a sacramental entrance into the greater mysteries of life may well be a starting point for us toward the recovery of the true meaning of baptism and the Lord's Supper and may also provide us with something of a rhetoric with which to give adequate expression to the recovery. Indeed, we may even refer to this as a "baptism" into holy use of an insight that has come to us from outside the Church.

[20] "Art and Theological Meaning," p. 46.

6

Earthen Vessels

NEAR THE END OF HEINRICH ZADOR'S "HEAR THE WORD," A NOVEL ABOUT Elijah and Elisha, Elisha makes this confession to a younger prophet:

> We know so little about the Lord. I have lived for him and know so little. He is within me. I feel his power, his guiding hand, I know the restlessness he puts within me, the constraint and the revelation—but not his secret, the ultimate truth of his being, which remains his mystery. How could I? I can only form my own picture of him, and surely he is the source of every such picture, since he created everything including me. He is everything that I am and can do, and yet is no part of me. He is within me and yet inaccessibly high above me, for I am his creature and he is the creator. He speaks, but with a different voice from mine. He is the word that is not spoken by any lips, without beginning or end.[1]

This is a high conception of the ministry of the Word. Several times in the novel Elisha has tried to retreat from his calling and has implored God to release him. I am not worthy, he has urged again and again. But always that old familiar restlessness has come, the restlessness that precedes some new revelation of the power and mystery of the Word, and he has become the vessel of that treasure that is beyond price. The tension of which he speaks here is the same as that to which Karl Barth has given voice for all servants of the Word: "As

[1] (New York: McGraw-Hill Book Co., 1962), pp. 282-83.

ministers we ought to speak of God. We are human, however, and so cannot speak of God. We ought therefore to recognize both our obligation and our inability and by that very recognition give God the glory." [2]

Surely this is no late, Protestant development in the idea of Christian preaching. Zador is Jewish, and his concept of the prophetic ministry, if we may accept the supporting testimony of current theologies of the Old Testament, is strongly Hebraic. It was part of the heritage of early Christianity. And it was Paul himself who said, "We have this treasure in earthen vessels, that the excellency of the power may be of God, and not of us" (II Cor. 4:7). Earthen vessels—"crackable pottery," translates someone. How fully conscious Paul always was of this is betrayed by the very style of his prose, with its now turgid, now rapid flow of words, its sudden jumps and surprising acrobatics, its affirmations and rebuttals pairing off against each other, its amazing grammatical and psychological contortions that work grief to the theological student trying to translate them. I like very much what Joseph Sittler has said about it:

> Preaching dare not put into unbroken propositions what the tormented peace of simultaneous existence in nature and grace can utter only in broken sentences. What God has riven asunder let no preacher too suavely join together. When we find, as we regularly do, that Paul stops the forward rush of active-voice statements to crack the integral structure of the affirmation with a joyous and devout regrounding of everything he is saying in the ultimacy of the passive voice, then we are obliged to stop with him. The salvatory power of the Word of God is eloquent precisely at the embarrassed halt. Where grammar cracks, grace erupts.[3]

The doctrine of the ministry has not rolled along on a straight course from the Old Testament prophets to Paul to Barth, however. It crashed and split upon the same rock the doctrine of the sacraments foundered upon: the objective-subjective controversy. When the Council of Arles in 314 upheld the opinion of Augustine against the Donatists, that the sacraments, once performed, have an indelible char-

[2] *The Word of God and the Word of Man,* tr. Douglas Horton (New York: Harper & Row, 1957), p. 186.

[3] *The Ecology of Faith* (Philadelphia: Muhlenberg Press, 1961), pp. 56-57.

acter regardless of the personal qualities of the administrator, it unwittingly paved the way for an understanding of the ministry later in the Middle Ages as an objective type of office. Ordination itself was considered a sacrament, so that the consecration of a man to the office was tantamount to *insuring* his ministerial status for the rest of his life, regardless of his behavior.

In the highest sense in which it may be interpreted, no one would disagree with this. God calls the minister, and no one but God would therefore dare to uncall him, or send him back. And presumably God does not uncall his servants. Moreover, there is no minister who is really worthy to be a bearer of God's Word, and therefore it is merely a matter of degree if the question of moral standards is ever raised against one. God alone justifies, and who is able to call into question his will?

But in the course of human life, with its day-in, day-out emphasis on the practical, few doctrines are ever consistently interpreted in the highest sense. The doctrine of the ministry has fared no better than other doctrines. Every time there was a decline in the spiritual life of the Middle Ages, it fell another notch lower. Gradually the concept of the minister gave way from one of function to one of status. There were occasional resurgences of power and vigor—notably in the various monastic revivals and in the early work of the mendicant orders. But by the end of the Middle Ages, when Dante was writing the *Commedia* and Chaucer the *Canterbury Tales,* the ministry was, in general, hopelessly corrupt, lascivious, ignorant, and unspiritual.

Who can forget Dante's picture of the priests who strain their wits to make a show in preaching and leave the gospel in silence, who go forth with jests and grimaces and are satisfied if they can make the crowds guffaw, and who grow so fat upon their incomes that they must travel on two palfreys rather than one; or Chaucer's portraits of a monk who is a rich hunter, a friar who is a lecher, and a pardoner who sells pigs' bones for ancient relics!

It was against such abuses that the Reformation offered a corrective. "Does ordaining such babbling priests make one a bishop?" asked Luther. "Or blessing churches and bells? Or confirming boys? Certainly not. Any deacon or layman could do as much. The ministry of the Word makes the priest and the bishop." [4] "We are all priests," he insisted, "and there is no difference between us." [5]

Luther did not, however, jettison the idea of ordination; instead, he returned to it something of its pre-Augustinian meaning, as the Church's sanction upon an individual's profession of a call and entry into the ministry of the Word. The ministry of the Word—the verbalized Word—was to be the minister's first responsibility. After this came the administration of the two sacraments, baptism and the Lord's Supper, and the care of souls. Once again the priesthood was functional and not just institutional.

But correctives are always misunderstood and misapplied by succeeding generations, and the Reformed doctrine of the ministry was no exception. While Catholicism, on one hand, despite its own reformative efforts, continued to perpetuate the status-concept of the ministry, Protestantism, on the other hand, forgot the *context* of Luther's quarrel with Romanism and developed his beginning into an overly functional, completely nonsacramental doctrine of the ministry. The tangent by which he corrected the abuse was made the norm. The result was that for four centuries afterwards the majority of Protestant ministers were to lack a proper sense of their true authority and were to flounder miserably in the storms raised against Christianity by deism, higher criticism, evolution, and the physical sciences.

It remained for P. T. Forsyth in the twentieth century to remind Protestantism that "the ministry is a prophetic and sacramental office; it is not a secretarial, it is not merely presidential. It is sacramental and not merely functional. It is the outward and visible agent of the inward gospel Grace. It is more sacramental than the elements. It is a living host, produced by a conversion that goes deeper than transubstantiation." [6]

Novels featuring Roman Catholic priests continue to exhibit strongly the sacramental side of the ministry. The celebration of the Eucharist is given a far more important place than preaching. In Edwin O'Connor's recent novel *The Edge of Sadness,* for instance, Father

[4] *Works of Martin Luther* (Philadelphia Edition), II, 282.
[5] *Ibid.,* p. 283.
[6] *The Church and the Sacraments,* p. 133.

Hugh Kennedy speaks at some length about the lack of rapport between him and his parishioners when he is preaching a sermon. "And yet," he adds, as if to dismiss the whole question, "the saving thing is that it all couldn't matter less. The sermons, I mean. Granted that a good sermon is better than a bad one, what really counts—what *only* counts—is of course the Mass itself, and the people do come to that." [7] Luther would have been enraged!

It is Graham Greene, though, who has dealt most frequently with the subject. His priests are always sacramental figures, and in two respects: first, the indelibility of their ordination is always insisted upon, even when they become morally unfit for the office; and, second, they sacrifice themselves in some way for those to whom they minister. In *The Potting Shed,* for example, Father Callifer has continued to hear confession and give communion during the entire thirty years since he lost his own faith. When his housekeeper reproaches him by saying that his parishioners have a right to a priest with faith, he replies,

> Faith. They want a play-actor. They want snow-white hair, high collars, clean vestments (who pays the cleaner?—not their sixpence), and they want a voice that's never husky with the boredom of saying the same words day after day. All right. Let them write to the Bishop. Do you think I want to get up every morning at six in time to make my meditation before Mass? Meditation on what? The reason why I'm going on with this slave-labour? They give prisoners useless tasks, don't they, digging pits and filling them up again? Like mine.[8]

As it turns out, however, it is his faith that he has sacrificed. Thirty years earlier, when his nephew James was lying in a deathlike coma, he offered God his most precious possession—his faith—if the boy would only come back to life. Unlikely as it was, that is just what happened. The boy revived, and the uncle lost his faith.

A far more powerful treatment of the indelibility theme is Greene's novel *The Power and the Glory,* whose central figure is a "whiskey priest" who never prays and who long ago ceased to be a celibate. In spite of his debauchery, though, he still feels the validity of the Host

[7] (Boston: Little, Brown & Company, 1961), p. 18.

[8] (New York: The Viking Press, 1961), pp. 85-86. Used by permission of the publisher and Graham Greene.

when he celebrates communion. Once, he comes upon a native woman whose child has been murdered by an American renegade and yields to her importunity to pray for the child, even though the words mean less than nothing to him. "He could feel no meaning any longer in prayers like these—the Host was different: to lay that between a dying man's lips was to lay God. That was a fact—something you could touch." [9]

This depraved priest finally proves worthy of sainthood by risking his life—and losing it—to perform the last rites for a criminal who is supposed to be dying. No matter how unworthy he has seemed, at the last moment he fulfills the requirements of the sacerdotal office and himself becomes a sacrament. It was the repetition of this theme, of the paradox of humiliation and grace, in story after story of Greene's that led R. W. B. Lewis to speak of his "fertile vision of the almost comical paradoxes of potential sainthood in our bedraggled time." [10] It is Augustine's doctrine of the indelible priesthood, only with a new and interesting twist.[11]

When we turn, on the other hand, to literature about the Protestant cleric, we are met immediately by an extremely subjective, non-sacramental view of the ministry—almost the opposite of the view we find in Greene. This minister stands in relation to the priest almost as the Protestant concept of the Lord's Supper stands over against the Roman idea of transubstantiation in the Eucharist: what he does must be inwardly and spiritually appropriated by the people or it is of no effect.

It is not a question of a man's ceasing to be a minister when he proves to be a poor preacher or a neglectful pastor, or, for that matter, even an immoral person; there is a kind of unofficial indelibility about his ordination that most Protestants are tacitly agreed upon, so that he is really marked for life as a man of the cloth even though his ministry may have expired or failed.

[9] P. 205.

[10] *The Picaresque Saint* (Philadelphia: J. B. Lippincott Co., Keystone Books, 1961), p. 274.

[11] Greene may have attempted to show the other side of the coin in *A Burnt-Out Case,* in which there is a character who deserted the priesthood after six years in seminary.

It is instead a question of the minister's success or defeat within the prescribed boundaries of what is generally deemed a true ministry of the Word. He stands or falls with the performance of his function. He *is* function. The Catholic priest may fail abysmally; he is still retrieved by the sacramental nature of his office. But the Protestant minister who fails, fails utterly; there is no retrieval.

With this in mind, it is not difficult to trace the path of the criticism of the clergyman in the literature of the past hundred years. Much of it has been of the negative sort, and has revealed an inadequate grasp on the part of society in general—if not indeed on the part of the author in particular—of the real theology of the ministry.

It was about the middle of the nineteenth century when the minister really began to come under fire from "secular" writers. Hawthorne, for example, though not maliciously inclined toward Arthur Dimmesdale in *The Scarlet Letter,* certainly exploded the old Puritan myth of the untainted spiritual leader. His close friend Melville was less kind. Father Mapple, in *Moby-Dick,* was favorably drawn. But *Typee* and *Omoo* were outspoken in their denunciation of the missionaries who were attempting to foist their "grand and glorious Christian religion"—and their corrupt moral practices—upon the "innocent" natives of the South Sea islands.

In England the absorbing topic was the dissipation of faith before the double-wave onslaught of biological evolution and higher criticism of the Bible. The intellectual disturbance of fundamentalism provided the main structure of conflict for many a novel, including Olive Schreiner's *The Story of an African Farm,* William Hale White's *The Autobiography of Mark Rutherford,* Mrs. Humphrey Ward's *Robert Elsmere,* Samuel Butler's *The Way of All Flesh,* and Thomas Hardy's *Jude the Obscure*—disproving somewhat Anthony Trollope's remark that "on our side of the water we deal more with beef and ale, and less with dreams." There had been quite a sea change since the day when Oliver Goldsmith wrote that idyllic little story, *The Vicar of Wakefield.* Parson Primrose—or was it Pollyanna?—had given way to the doubting divine.

Some of these narratives about disenchanted ministers were markedly bitter. Against what, it is not always possible to say—sometimes against society, sometimes against organized religion, sometimes against the ministry—sometimes even against God, or the idea of God, if the writer happened to be an unbeliever. On one hand, they made it sound as if a house of cards had fallen; on the other, as if the collapse were as momentous as that of the walls of Jericho, or of Rome.

Hardy's *Jude the Obscure,* by most odds, was the bitterest of the lot. Its bleak naturalism and Schopenhaurean view of women brought down such a shower of critical bombast on his head that he never wrote another novel. Basically it is the story of Jude Fawley's attempt to get an education for the ministry. He learns Greek and Latin on his own, as Hardy had done, and swears, "I'll be D.D. before I have done!" But fate decrees otherwise. From the moment he is accidentally struck in the head by "the characteristic part of a barrow-pig" while strolling along dreaming of his rise in the Church, he is overruled by some heavy-handed and malevolent providence. He never becomes an archdeacon or even a reverend—not even "a Rather Reverend dissenting gentleman." As he sadly admits after years of pain and toil and doubt, "I am as I was." His will is broken—partly, Hardy makes clear, by the discovery that the Bible is a "human" document—and he dies in wretched despair.

Jude was really Hardy's favorite child, the son of his old age, and Hardy was protesting against his being put on the altar. The plot of the novel is obviously wooden, and the heavy hand that manipulates the tragedy is really that of the author, not of destiny. But it is still a powerful story, with pathos to move any reader.

The erosion of faith by intellectual doubt figured prominently also in an American novel published the year after *Jude,* Harold Frederic's *The Damnation of Theron Ware,* though Ware's downfall hardly measured up to Jude's. Ware is a minister but "thinly sure" of his matters of faith anyway, and it does not take much to change the climate of his theological opinions. When he encounters the new liberal theology of the Hegelian school, he thinks it sophisticated and smart, and submits without a struggle to the reconstruction of his own views. What is more disastrous for his career as a minister is his disgusting moral degeneration. When it becomes impossible for him to continue as a clergyman, he is shuttled off to another state and a job selling real estate, and soon recovers all his vanity and earthly ambitions.

By the twenties and thirties the faith-doubt motif had evidently been given a pretty good working over, and most of the literature about clergymen was beginning to emphasize their moral character—or, more precisely, their lack of it. Lack of spiritual experience and conviction still figured as one of the reasons for improper behavior, but the behavior angle was the one that was played up. It was tangible, and it suited readily the muckraking spirit that was in the air. Everything else was being debunked—why not the ministry too?

There was a rash of "debunking" stories, with characters like the holiness preacher Casy, in Steinbeck's *Grapes of Wrath,* or Semon Dye, in Caldwell's *Journeyman,* at one extreme, and the Reverend Dr. John Jennison Drew, in Lewis' *Babbitt,* at the other.

Some authors wrote regular catalogues, or rogue's galleries, of the ministry. One such catalogue was Thornton Wilder's *Heaven's My Destination,* whose main character, George Brush, meets, in the course of scarcely two hundred pages, a woman evangelist, a poor, itinerant male evangelist, and an old Methodist parson.

Brush was converted under the preaching of the woman evangelist while he was a student at Shiloh Baptist College in South Dakota. He was attracted to the meeting by her picture on the advertisements, was converted on the first night, and did not miss a single meeting for two weeks. On the final night, he came back after everyone else had gone and went to the evangelist's "meditation room" to thank her for what her messages had meant to him. The door was ajar, and no one noticed his approach. What he saw inside stopped him in his tracks: a large older woman was bending over the attractive evangelist with a hypodermic needle in her hand.

Brush meets the second evangelist, the "Rev. Dr. James Bigelow," on a train between Waco, Texas, and Dallas (truly a likely place!). Wilder's description of the meeting is not long, and may be quoted verbatim:

> [Said Bigelow,] "Young man, have you ever thought seriously about the great facts of life and death?"
>
> He [Brush] looked up to see leaning over him a tall unshaven man of fifty, wearing a soiled linen suit. A handkerchief was stuffed into the band of his collar and his cuffs were protected by black cotton guards. He had a white-and-yellow waterfall mustache and black steely eyes.

"Yes," said Brush.

The man removed a newspaper from beside Brush and sat down. "Are you right with God—this very minute?" he asked, putting his arm along the back of the seat in front of him and his nose very close to Brush's face.

"Yes," said Brush, beginning to blush violently, "I try to be."

"Oh, my boy," said the other, with a strong vibrato and an odor of decaying teeth, "you can't answer that question as quickly as that. No one can. Being saved,—oh, my boy!—isn't as easy as being vaccinated. It means wrestling. It means fighting. It means going down on your knees." He took hold of the lapel of Brush's suit and fingered it disparagingly. "I can see that you're still entangled with the world's snares and shows. Boy, do you touch liquor?"

"No."

"Do you use filthy tobacco?"

"No."

The man lowered his voice. "Do you frequent loose women?"

"No," said Brush, expelling the poisoned air from his nose.

"Do you indulge in lascivious thoughts?"

Brush coughed.

"Yes, sir," cried the man. "'Let him who thinketh he stand, beware lest he fall.' The trouble with you is you're puffed-up. You're stiff-necked." [12]

There follows an account of Bigelow's questioning of Brush regarding certain scripture verses, in which Brush comes off poorly because he confuses some prepositions in his recitation of the verses from memory. Bigelow gets so worked up that he rises and begins to harangue the whole car, using Brush as an example of moral cowardice. Soon he is striding up and down the aisle, ranting and shouting in the passengers' faces. At last Brush seizes him, forces him into an inside seat, and talks to him seriously about the foolishness of such antics. When they arrive in Dallas, Brush puts ten dollars in his hand and leaves him.

The meeting with the Methodist preacher occurs near the end of the narrative, when Brush has gone through a harrowing marital experience and has almost lost his faith. He is in a hospital bed, and has no will to mend. He is in a dour mood when he is visited by Dr. Bowie, the pastor of the local Methodist church. "Now a great many people," says Dr. Bowie, "a *great* many, have found it a comfort—what a comfort!—to ask forgiveness of God in the presence of his minister—oh, my boy!—for the things they've done wrong in this life. It lightens the load, my brother." Brush replies that he has broken eight of the

[12] (New York: Harper & Row, 1935), pp. 151-53.

ten commandments and is glad he has. "I made the mistake all my life of thinking that you could get better and better until you were perfect," he says. Dr. Bowie stumbles for words, swallowing his soft palate several times. He tries to lead Brush in "a few . . . words of prayer," but Brush halts him and tells him he is "pretty stupid." The good parson nervously gathers up his questionnaire, hat, raincoat, cane, and Bible, and prepares to decamp, when Brush declares to him that it is one proof that there is no God "that he allows such foolish people to be ministers. I've secretly thought that for a long time, and now I'm glad to be able to say it. All ministers are stupid—do you hear me? —*all*. . . . I mean: all except one." [13]

The single exception Brush has in mind is Father Pasziewski, an old priest with whom he has had but the slightest acquaintance in a boarding house in Oklahoma City, but who has never ceased to be solicitous after Brush's welfare and who has just recently died and sent Brush a silver spoon as a memento. Brush recovers his faith after learning about Father Pasziewski's death, and, soon after, his health. It is a curious thing, this respect for Catholic priests, contrasted with contempt for Protestant ministers. Probably it is a complex matter, with many factors, but part of it is surely the crass ignorance of so many clergymen, especially among the fundamentalist sects.

The classic denunciation of ignorance and hypocrisy in the ministry, though, is Sinclair Lewis' *Elmer Gantry,* which Carlos Baker has called "a kind of 'rake's progress' by an evangelical Baptist preacher." [14] *Gantry* overwhelms the reader again and again with its presentations of the seamy side of clerical life. I have known several young ministers to read it and be so shaken by it that they even considered leaving the ministry. Lewis undoubtedly knew at first hand the deviousness of some unprincipled men of the cloth, and had a sort of personal vendetta against charlatanism in the church. He often attacked ministers from the public platform. For example, he once said of Henry Ward Beecher, the popular pastor of the Plymouth Congregational

[13] *Ibid.,* p. 300.

[14] "The Place of the Bible in American Fiction," in *Religious Perspectives in American Culture,* ed. J. W. Smith and A. L. Jamison (Princeton, N. J.: Princeton University Press, 1961), III, 259.

Church in Brooklyn, that he "was a powerful writer of trash, and all over the land, families got out the carry-all to drive to town and hear him speak on everything from 'The Strange Women' to the cozy theory that a worker who did not rejoice in bringing up five children on a wage of a dollar a day was a drunken gunny-sack." [15] The barbs in this description are the allusions to Beecher's "indiscretion" with the wife of a parishioner and to his $20,000-a-year salary at Plymouth Church.

When one reads *Elmer Gantry* he cannot help thinking that Lewis must have attended a Terwillinger College and a Mizpah Seminary in order to be able to write so convincingly about life in those institutions of "higher learning." Actually, much of the material for each novel he wrote came from careful research. While he was writing *Gantry,* he spent a great deal of time living in the homes of ministers and church people. When it got out that he was chronicling observations for a book, many people invited him in, hoping to see themselves "written up" by a famous author. Many of them did get into *Gantry,* and were infuriated when they saw how they had been portrayed. Lewis' vinegary manner of crusading reached its greatest bitterness in that novel.

In my opinion *Gantry,* and not *Main Street* or *Babbitt,* is really Lewis' masterpiece. Perhaps it is a bit raw (!) and tends too completely to overstate its case; but for sheer concentration and cumulative power it is difficult to match. Its insights into various types of ministerial psychology, its familiarity with the mechanics of religious organization, and its casual juggling of theological vocabulary, both plain and pedantic, are staggering.

The main character of the book, Elmer Gantry, whirls us through a succession of stages in his own evolution that provides us with documentation for a whole panorama of clerical life: from his days at Terwillinger College, where he was a football player known as "Hell-Cat" Gantry; through a feigned conversion and the discovery that his stentorian oratory could spellbind a crowd; through a deplorable career at Mizpah Theological Seminary, from which he was finally expelled for boozing and whoring when he was supposed to be supplying a pulpit for Easter Day; through a stint as salesman for a farm-imple-

[15] Quoted by James McGraw in *Great Evangelical Preachers of Yesterday* (Nashville: Abingdon Press, 1961), p. 100.

ment company; through a formative association with a female evangelist named Sharon Falconer; through a brief apprenticeship to New Thought theosophy; through several small churches in the Methodist denomination; to the full-orbed Dr. Elmer Gantry, illustrious and sensational pastor of the great Wellspring Methodist Church of Zenith, more recently (as the book ends) called to the pastorate of a famous church in New York City and to the chairmanship of the National Association for the Purification of Art and the Press.

Gantry's associations with the opposite sex are never above reproach. As a student at Mizpah, he seduces the daughter of a deacon in his first parish. Later, when he is pastor of the Wellspring Methodist Church in Zenith, she turns up in that city as a housewife, and they continue their affair on Tuesday nights at the church after she has taught a cooking class. As an associate of Sharon Falconer, who was doubtless an image—she was already too much of a caricature to be burlesqued—of Aimee Semple McPherson, he enjoys the attentions of an eccentric woman who feels that she is neither compromising herself nor sinning when she surrenders, as she so frequently does, to the urge of the flesh. Finally, at Wellspring, he ditches the cooking instructor for an attractive new secretary with whom he becomes extremely foolish and intimate; and he nearly loses the whole world he has won when she turns out to be a blackmailer and an account of his amours reaches the front page of the Zenith newspapers. Skillfully got off the hook by a criminal lawyer in his congregation, he resolves never to dally with women again. But then, just as the novel ends, he turns in his pulpit and notices a new pair of ankles in the church choir. The only woman for whom he never manages to conceive a physical desire is his amiable, long-suffering wife Cleo, whom he married because she looked like a good preacher's wife and would make a suitable helpmate for a bishop.

The preaching of the Word has always constituted the primary function of the Protestant ministers. What kind of preacher is Gantry? As we have observed, he first stumbled into the ministry via the back door, as it were, through his discovery that he could hold crowds by his oratory. He is an unabashed sensationalist. His sermons are rah-rah-rah compendiums of suggestiveness, jokes, and shallow but extremely articulate thrusts at whatever happens to be unpopular with his audience, or approvals of whatever happens to be popular, whether in morals, social manners, or theology. There is absolutely no thought content in them. They are invariably "underdeveloped and overexposed." He actually "lifts" his first sermon from a page of the well-known atheist Robert Ingersoll, about love as the morning and evening star; and echoes of this same phrase are heard in every sermon he preaches after that, even after fund-needy Abernathy College bestows an honorary D.D. on him and he goes off to London as a visiting fireman. I have heard undergraduates suggest that, no matter what Gantry was like personally, the people who believed in him actually benefited from his preaching. Perhaps this is an interesting nod in the direction of a sacramental view of the ministry, but I confess that I can hardly see how anyone could profit from this kind of homiletical mishmash.

By contrast with Gantry, there are one or two ministers in the novel for whom Lewis appears to conceive some favor. For example, there is Gantry's unsuccessful classmate Frank Shallard, who labors on for years in meager pastorates despite his own misgivings about the honesty of his profession and the relevance of the symbols of his religion. Finally Shallard becomes the pastor of a sizable Congregational church in Zenith, where, although he is a kind and tender shepherd to his flock, he is able to indulge his honesty about the comparable merits of Christianity among the world religions. But Gantry covets a wealthy member of his church and starts a vicious attack on the orthodoxy of Shallard's beliefs in order to get the member away. To spare the church further embarrassment, Shallard resigns. At last he is free from the restrictions of the church, from orthodoxy in theology, from being looked at by other men as if he were a woman. He becomes secretary of the local Charity Organization Society. After the Scopes trial in Tennessee, he welcomes the chance to travel around the country and speak to clubs on Darwinism and religion. On his first engagement in a western town, however, he is mobbed and literally horsewhipped by a group of "good, orthodox Christians," so that he loses the sight in his badly lacerated eyes and must depend on his wife's earnings for the rest of his life. Lewis does not really respect Shallard as a minister; he uses him simply as a symbol of victimization at the hands of the Church and the Protestant ministry. In his way, Shallard is as unfit for the cloth as Gantry himself.

Lewis did not show the whole picture. But his success in capturing the kaleidoscopic hypocrisies and weaknesses of organized religion in the first half of the twentieth century in America is breathtaking. Even a partial listing of the targets for his satiric wrath in *Elmer Gantry* alone would of necessity include: (*a*) various types of ministers, such as Gantry, the ignorant and vicious showman; Eddie Fislinger, the mealy-mouthed apologist for the faith; Judson Roberts, the square-shouldered, booming-voiced, but secretly doubting Y.M.C.A. speaker; Shallard, the honest liberal who has confused matters of faith and intellect; Jacob Trosper, the stern, isolated-from-the-modern-world Christian educator; and Bishop Toomis, the well-fed, well-traveled, well-greased ecclesiastical politician; (*b*) denominational institutions of so-called "higher learning," where fossilized old churchmen realize that they must "nix" all biology and genuine history and psychology if they are to remain in charge of young minds; (*c*) small country churches, where untutored parishioners and swaggering, ignorant preachers combine to form moral kindergartens; (*d*) the factory-like city churches, with their hybrid institutionalism flowering into university-type Sunday schools, myriads of instruction classes of various kinds, and general plantlike atmosphere; and (*e*) the general decadence of Christianity, as exhibited in the politics and chicanery and sensationalism of its ministers, as well as in the social-climbing and immorality and hypocrisy of everyone else involved in the affairs of the church.

These are sweeping indictments, and if they are irritating it is probably because there is enough truth in them to blanch the cheeks of any Christian. All ministers, chaplains, religious teachers, and theological students should be required to read this book at least once a year; it could not but have a salutary effect upon the Protestant ministry in future decades. As Horton Davies has said,

> It is a sorry verdict on the ministry and the churches, if a tenth of the contention be true. But, true or not, *Elmer Gantry* is a formidable warning against hypocrisy, the cult of personality in the pulpit, and the temptations of mere elocution, and the dangers of a skin-deep and narrow Christian culture and education. It is for every individual reader to determine whether

this is a portrait or a caricature, a scarecrow or a case of "There but for the grace of God go I." [16]

As bitter as *Gantry* is, it is not exactly unwholesome in its effects. Such reflections upon the misdemeanors of certain ministers remind us also of the better image of the true minister of the Word, from whom all the Gantrys are the deviations. It was G. K. Chesterton, who seemed to have the *mot juste* for everything, who said, "Satire may be mad and anarchic, but it presupposes an admitted superiority in certain things over others; it presupposes a standard. When little boys in the street laugh at the fatness of some distinguished journalist, they are unconsciously assuming a standard of Greek sculpture. They are appealing to the marble Apollo." [17] Without the Phillips Brookses and Leslie Weatherheads and thousands of other decent, respectable preachers and pastors, there would be nothing to scorn in Gantry.

Probably there will never be another treatment of the clergy so caustic as Lewis'. There will be no need of it. *Elmer Gantry* is the end-all for such things. But exploring the mind and life of the Protestant minister is such a fascinating business—the possibilities are so limitless!—that there will probably continue to be portraits and character sketches, not to say caricatures, of him as long as there are new novels being written.

One such study that came out of the fifties was Peter de Vries' very funny little novel, *The Mackerel Plaza.* There is no bitterness in this book, as there was in Lewis', and it is not at all a strong novel, for the author lacks the power to sustain a work well begun; but it is nevertheless an interesting view of the life of a minister whose circumstances are quite different from those of Gantry.

Andrew Mackerel, who was known by his seminary classmates as "Holy Mackerel," is minister of an ultra-modernistic church named People's Liberal in Avalon, Connecticut, a well-to-do commuter's haven near New York City. "P.L.," as People's Liberal is affectionately referred to by its constituency, is a split-level church with a large recreation area, a neuropsychiatric wing, and a worship area that by its

[16] *A Mirror of the Ministry in Modern Novels* (New York: Oxford University Press, 1959), p. 34.

[17] *Orthodoxy* (Garden City, N. Y.: Image Books, 1959), p. 42.

diminutive size seems to have been merely an afterthought in the mind of the architect.

Mackerel is just the minister to go with a split-level church. His theology and his concept of the ministry are as contemporary as the building. Because of the muscular style of his public utterances, Molly Callico, his closest friend, calls him "the Hemingway of the pulpit." He considers the God of his particular conception to be "a God free of outmoded theological definitions and palatable to a mind come of age in the era of Relativity." One of his favorite aphorisms is, "It is the final proof of God's omnipotence that he need not exist in order to save us." The first time he says it, in fact, his congregation think it so much better than anything Voltaire said on the subject that they give him an immediate hike in pay and invite him out to more dinners than he can possibly eat.

The novel opens one morning with Mackerel's arising from bed and seeing a new sign that has just been erected in view of his study window. It is a bold, simple statement, in phosphorescent colors, announcing that "Jesus Saves." Scandalized, Mackerel phones the zoning board immediately. The lady at the other end of the line is sympathetic, and admits that it does not help property values much. "Oh, property values!" shouts Mackerel. "Please get that out of your mind, miss. Do you think I own the parsonage I live in? I'm talking about spiritual values. Spiritual and aesthetic ones. How do you expect me to write a sermon with that thing staring me in the face? How do you expect me to turn out anything fit for civilized consumption?" [18]

It happens that the sign has been erected, with a proper permit, by a certain Mr. Turnbull, who is a member of Mackerel's own congregation. Mackerel is dreadfully embarrassed. How could anyone who had sat so faithfully as Turnbull had under his urbane Sunday-morning dissertations possibly come up with anything so gauche as "Jesus Saves"? Mulling it over, he sees how Turnbull could. Turnbull represents "what any minister will tell you is the bane of parish work: somebody who has got religion. It's as embarrassing to a cleric of sensibility as 'poetry lovers' are to a poet, and in much the same way." [19]

[18] P. 8.

[19] *Ibid.*, p. 14.

The denouement of the novel is unusual, to say the least. It consists of Mackerel's losing his faith that God *doesn't* answer prayer. All the churches in the state have been meeting at the governor's request to pray for desperately needed rain. Mackerel has thoroughly pooh-poohed the idea. But, against the Weather Bureau's forecast, which is almost always correct, monotonously correct, the drought is broken by torrential rains on the very night of the prayer meetings. Mackerel goes to bed deeply shaken. "It's not that I resent finding there is a God after all who answers prayers," he says—"it's that my position is no longer tenable. If this is his answer, I'm just not his sort. Because who were at those prayer meetings? All the bores, dullards, and bigots in town—not a person of civilized sensibility was there. If that's the lot he gives aid and comfort to, so be it. But I cannot worship him. I can believe him. But I cannot worship him." [20] For a person of Mackerel's sensibilities, there is but one thing to do. He records: "With the loss of my faith, I threw myself into parish work. It was the only way to forget." [21]

De Vries has laid it on pretty thick, of course. But he has undoubtedly hit close to one large group of clergy—the young sophisticates, usually graduates of Ivy League schools, who condemn the credulity of previous generations and wonder if there is anything at all left from the demolition of fundamentalism in which one can really believe. For some of them, the demolition itself has become a kind of faith, or at least a *modus vivendi.* This is the extreme edge of the nonsacramental interpretation of the nature of the ministry. The very idea of revelation, as opposed to human reason, has become so macerated that not even a possibility of a sacramental type of ministry is left.

I am happy to say that it is not always so bad as it is with the Dr. Bigelows, the Elmer Gantrys, and the Andrew Mackerels. Occasionally an author comes along who writes with a real feeling for the mingled "grandeur and misery" of the men who are called to be servants of the Word. One such author is Conrad Richter, whose novel *A Simple Honorable Man* is one of the finest stories about a clergyman ever printed. Richter's style is crisp and bright and homey. It reminds one

[20] *Ibid.,* p. 188.
[21] *Ibid.,* p. 189.

of the talk of fine, well-bred country people sitting on their porch in the evening. It is somewhat in the manner of the better regionalist writers of the latter half of the nineteenth century—warm, kindly, chatty, down-to-earth—but with more cumulative power.

Richter's clergyman is the Reverend Harry Donner, a Lutheran, who is not called to the ministry until he is in his late thirties. His father-in-law, also a minister, advises him to forget the call: by the time he gets through college and seminary, he will be too old and the churches will not want him. But Harry sees it through. He seems always to be full of some special ingenuousness and zest because he has been called into the ministry from keeping a store. He never loses his "strong tradesman's face." He is always filled with a kind of intoxication when he quotes the verses from Amos, "I was no prophet; neither was I a prophet's son; but I was an herdman and a gatherer of sycamore fruit: And the Lord took me as I followed the flock, and the Lord said unto me, Go, prophesy unto my people Israel." (7:14-15.)

True to his father-in-law's prediction, Harry Donner never pastors a large church. Once, when he has resigned from a rural charge, he goes to preach a trial sermon for a three- or four-thousand member church in Brooklyn that is looking for an assistant minister. The position is his if he wants it, but he turns it down. "I tried my best to accept it, Vallie," he explains to his wife.

> I prayed hard over it but I just couldn't feel the call. The salary would have been wonderful, but the people in the church didn't seem to need me. I felt they could get along very well without me. I didn't talk their language. I saw plenty of people whose language I did speak and they looked as though they needed me. I would have liked to work among them. But they were in the street and I don't think St. Martin's would have liked me to spend my time with non-members any more than St. Peter's did. Besides, how could I go to these people with the Gospel when I knew my own church wouldn't take them in? [22]

His ministry lies in Pennsylvania, in the little hill-cradled towns of hard-drinking, hard-swearing, and hard-working coal miners. Nothing pleases him better than to bring the gospel and build a church house in some little mining-patch community. He collects money to buy a

[22] *A Simple Honorable Man* (New York: Alfred A. Knopf, 1962), p. 223.

home for some miner who has had both arms crushed in a slide, or traverses the mountains to give communion to a dying tunnelman who has always been brusque about spiritual matters. "The words and heart of the Eucharist ceremony had never seemed so rich and moving or yet so mysterious and inscrutable as when he repeated them today to this dying miner propped up in his unpainted Company house on Broad Mountain." [23]

Wiley Drumm, a mining engineer, chides him for being too unselfish and tells him he ought to be in a big city church where he would make a big salary.

> "You've got a fault there, Reverend, a bad one, if you'll excuse me for saying such a thing to you."
>
> "I have many faults," replies the preacher.
>
> "No, not many, Reverend. That's the trouble. But it's enough. It's your mortal sin. It's what holds you back with God and man. Do you know Francis Thompson's poem: 'I fled him down the nights and down the days; I fled him down the arches of the years'? Well, you don't flee him. He doesn't need to follow you. He doesn't need to beg you to go his way. He doesn't need to cross your palm with gold and silver. He can let you starve and do without. He knows you'll stay with him just the same no matter what. Do you follow me, Reverend?"
>
> "No, not yet," Harry Donner says doubtfully.
>
> "Well, can you get it better if I put it another way? I like you, Reverend, but you're too damn good for your own good. Now I don't mean goody-good. You're not that. I don't mean pious and mealy-mouthed. I don't know exactly what I do mean except that you don't look after yourself like the rest of us. When commonsense was handed around, you were left out. If a man asks you for a dollar, you're liable to give him two. If he asks you to listen to his tale of woe, you pray and go to bat for him to boot. You were the same way when you kept store in Unionville. That's how you lost out, giving credit to all these lousy sinners who never paid you. I bet you haven't got a dollar on those back debts since you're here though they see you walking around with your elbows sticking out and your sole leather worn through." [24]

After Harry Donner dies, his sons discuss the way he used to groan at night, as if he were in some kind of agony. One son remembers hear-

[23] *Ibid.*, p. 106.
[24] *Ibid.*, pp. 142-43.

ing it the night the old man stayed with him and his wife: "It sounded like he was praying. You know how he used to break your heart sometimes when he prayed. When I was little, I never believed God could stand up to it." [25] Another son wishes to get to the bottom of the mystery and journeys back to one of the old pastorates to ask a woman with whom his father had once stayed about it. She tells him,

> Well, you come to the right place. We heard him a couple years ago when he stayed with us on his way up to Tim's. He always liked to come here. After he went, Philip and I were talking. I told Philip it sounded to me like he was still doing in his sleep what he done all his life when he was awake, praying for them poor souls he'd seen ailing and suffering in this world. Mind you, he visited a lot of them. It sounded to me like he was eating his heart out that God didn't always answer his prayers over them. It sounded like he was begging God that this oughtn't to be and that oughtn't to be, and he had no right to let all them poor people under the harrow while folks like the Piatts rode rich and free.[26]

Forsyth would have liked this picture of the ministry. It is what he was pleading for in the Protestant church, a ministry "more sacramental than the elements," a "living host, produced by a conversion that goes deeper than transubstantiation." I think Luther would have liked it too, and perhaps even Paul, who was inclined to be rather grudging in his praise of ministers, including himself.

In a memorable Convocation Address at Harvard Divinity School, entitled *But Find the Point Again,* Samuel H. Miller quoted from Melville's description of Father Mapple's pulpit, shaped like a ship's prow, in *Moby-Dick:*

> The pulpit is ever this earth's foremost part. All the rest comes in its rear; the pulpit leads the world. From thence it is the storm of God's quick wrath is first descried, and the bow must bear the earliest brunt. From thence it is the God of breezes fair or foul is first invoked for favorable winds. Yes, the world's a ship on its passage out, and not a voyage complete; and the pulpit is its prow.

Soberly, the speaker admitted: "The truth is that the pulpit, at least now, is certainly not the *prow* of this world, dividing new seas with

[25] *Ibid.,* p. 304.
[26] *Ibid.,* p. 307.

its bold bow. The pulpit does not lead the world either in generating power or in initiating ideas. It is set back now in quieter waters, out of the haste and the traffic where strife is real and decisions must be made." [27]

The world is still on its way out; the passage is not complete. Perhaps our charts are yellowed, and we are less certain even than Melville about where we are going. But the challenge is still present to the minister to make his calling relevant to the chaotic conditions of the times, to put himself once more—or to let God put him once more—in the prow that breaks the dark waters. Said Dr. Miller,

> We come to life as a profession when we stand forth beyond the superficial safety and the limits of praise and blame, to speak the clumsy, daring word which only faith may speak of things unseen but powerful with portent to be, of realities waiting to be born at the far edge of things known, of a realm mysterious with blessing for any who can become like little children, able to leap beyond themselves to a greatness dimly surmized.[28]

He added,

> Yet any man who steps into this kind of pulpit, into this prow where the storms strike first and the dark is thickest, knows right well the terror of his position. The ministry in any age is caught between the offense of God and the offense of the world, between the awful terror of making God plain, of speaking the *verbum dei,* and the terrifying muddle of this world's jumble of circumstances in which human life is crucified. Like a lonely figure, the ministry in our age stands separated from the confident assurance of any infallible or perhaps even divine message easily inherited from the past, and as well from the arrogance of an age which finds all authority in itself.[29]

What this means, if I understand it, is that the ministry must return to its preschizophrenic days, to its view of itself as both objective and subjective, sacramental and secular. What God has joined together, man has put asunder; and grace has, in a manner of speaking, fallen between the stools. The clergyman is not, as he is sometimes presented in Catholic literature, an *ex-opere-operato,* guaran-

[27] (Pamphlet of Convocation Address, September, 1959, Harvard Divinity School, 1959), p. 4.

[28] *Ibid.,* p. 5.

[29] *Ibid.*

teed-not-to-fail sacrament in human form; nor is he, as presented in much Protestant literature, an individual completely devoid of authority and sacramental properties, utterly dependent, for the success of his ministry, upon certain Greek qualities of personal excellence and goodness. The ministry, like the Church, is a gift of God, and therein lies its sacramental nature; but it is also a calling, and therein resides the meaning of its terrible responsibility. To ignore either aspect is to distort it immeasurably.

Perhaps modern literature's portrait of the minister, both Catholic and Protestant, has been more sagacious than we have given it credit for being. Not that it has presented a theologically complete picture of what he ought to be—the evidence is otherwise. But it has, like the little boy who said that the emperor was naked, spoken its piece. It has indicated that the clergy, far from standing like lonely figures in the ship's prow, have tended to be found in far greater abundance on the poop deck. It has helped to specify the negative situation from which the positive may emerge. It has, as it were, held the mirror up to life, that the minister may better see himself as the world sees him. For though we cannot often credit the fiction of our time with knowing what a minister ought to be, we can generously commend it for knowing—and saying—what he ought not to be.

As Chaucer's satirizations of the clergy were coeval with Wyclif and the beginnings of Lollardry, and as Dante's preceded by only a century the initiation of a reform movement that finally culminated in the whole Protestant Reformation, perhaps—we can at least hope and pray—the candid portrait of the decadent minister in so much of contemporary fiction really harbingers a general reformation in the life of the Protestant clergy, and of the rebirth of a genuine theology of the ministry that will redeem our barren, sociological concepts of it.

Meanwhile, we shall do well to join the Chorus of T. S. Eliot's *Murder in the Cathedral* in the words of their closing speech:

> Lord, have mercy upon us.
> Christ, have mercy upon us.
> Lord, have mercy upon us.
> Blessed Thomas, pray for us.[30]

[30] Used by permission of Harcourt, Brace & World, publishers, and Faber & Faber Ltd.

7

"In the Midst of Life"

"In the middle of the journey of our life," Dante began the *Divina Commedia,* "I came to myself in a dark wood where the straight way was lost." He was thirty-five years old—halfway through the span of his biblically allotted three score and ten. He was, quite technically, "in the midst of life." Yet his vision was completely of the afterlife, the "beyond."

How greatly thoughts of what lay beyond death played back upon and influenced life for men in the Middle Ages is in our own time difficult to conceive. Many of them seem almost to have had an eschatological consciousness—a continuous awareness of Last Things that distilled itself into the color and fabric of all they did. It was, perhaps, not of the high quality of the expectation that dominated the thinking of the early Christians, centered upon Christ and a will that he should reign. That this is so is evidenced by the kind of hysteria that swept through the Western nations on the eve of the year 1000, when most people were convinced that the end of the world was imminent. As the church bells tolled midnight, closing the millennium, men shrieked and babbled out their sins and cried for one another's forgiveness and gave away their property; some even died of heart attacks brought on by extreme fright. It was a mad and grotesque hour. But at least the idea of the Day of the Lord, so strong in biblical times, was still a controlling motif in the popular imagination—it had not passed away completely.

Not so completely, at any rate, as in our own day. Contrast with Dante's *Commedia,* for example, the parable of the cave in John Steinbeck's novel *The Wayward Bus.* A dilapidated old bus, traveling from Rebel Corners to Los Angeles, gets mired to its hubcaps in mud on a deserted shortcut some distance from the main road. While the driver goes for help, the passengers take shelter in a nearby cave. Imagine a naïve, stagestruck girl on her way to Hollywood, a pimple-faced boy who is oversexed, a traveling novelty salesman, a family consisting of a shallow-principled businessman, his very proper (and very repressed) wife, and his freethinking co-ed daughter, and, to top it all off, a young lady who has been in the habit of appearing in the altogether at stag dinners, and you have a fairly good idea of the *comédie humaine* that takes place there before the driver gets back. But here is the touch significant to us: over the cave, in a place difficult of access, someone has painted in sprawling black letters the word REPENT. It is still clear against the sandstone cliff. The painter, says the author, had evidently "let himself down with a rope to put up that great word in black paint, and he had gone away rejoicing at how he was spreading God's word in a sinful world." But now only the businessman takes note of the word, and he simply wonders who financed the venture. The others are completely oblivious to it. It is part of a dead language, a language belonging to the premodern age. It is dead because the eschatological consciousness is dead. The people down below, acting out their little drama of frustration and desire, know nothing of *metanoia,* of repentance and conversion. They are out of touch with anything like a doctrine of Last Things. The only time they know is the present or the near-present, and the only aim the gratification of their sensual desires. Thus they proceed, on this stage so heavily fraught with symbols, to carry out their seductions and chicaneries, yielding always to the lower impulses and ephemeral passions. It is a long way from Dante and further still from narratives about the early Christians.

If the cave in Steinbeck's story suggests Plato's famous allegory, the whole situation suggests a Greek view of time and history, as opposed to the Christian view. It is perhaps a generalization to speak too easily of a Greek view of time and a Christian view of time without recognizing that the two have often been conflated in the thinking of both Greeks and Christians,[1] but it is a distinction that is well defended in Oscar Cullmann's classic study, *Christ and Time.* The Hellenistic culture, says Cullmann, regarded time as a kind of cyclical movement in which scenes are always changing but never arriving at any goal. It generally affirmed some version of the Heraclitean doctrine of process, that all things appear to change without really changing and, conversely, that they all change without appearing to change. The Christian view, like that of the Hebrews, on the other hand, was that time and history are not cyclical but rectilinear. They move from a beginning to an end, from creation to fulfillment, from the garden of paradise to the heavenly city. For this reason, says Cullmann, a preoccupation with history stands at the heart of all Christian theology. The emphasis is upon races, nations, peoples, kingdoms, all moving toward some great final cataclysm, with Christ presiding over them all as the Lord of time.

The pilgrims in Steinbeck's novel—I call them pilgrims because the bus trip provides the familiar *Reismotif*—do not react to the exhortation on the cliff because they do not have the sense that all things are moving toward a climactic event under the lordship of Christ. The very fact that Steinbeck's cave is reminiscent of Plato's gives us the feeling that all this has happened before, that history is repeating itself, that the cycle is merely coming round again. The characters themselves must feel it—though certainly none of them knows anything about Plato—because they are unable even to appreciate the novelty of their situation. They complain about its inconveniences and discomfort but do not appear to recognize it as unique. Therefore the word "repent" cannot possibly have any meaning for them. With its implication of *eschaton* and judgment, it is simply alien to their way of thinking. And therefore there is no hope of salvation for them. Conversion is not

[1] Cf. James Barr, *Biblical Words for Time* (London: S.C.M. Press, 1962). In this book and an earlier one (*The Semantics of Biblical Language*), Barr has attempted to provide a corrective to what he considers to be a tendency on the part of some scholars to oversimplification in the extrication of the strands of Greek and Hebrew thought from each other.

a category of the Greek mind.[2] Modification, perhaps, but not conversion. That possibility never occurs to them.

In the Hellenistic scheme of things, time is regarded as antagonistic. It is a bondage of the soul against which man struggles to escape. "Because in Greek thought time is not conceived as an upward sloping line with beginning and end, but rather as a circle," says Cullmann, "the fact that man is bound to time must here be experienced as an enslavement, as a curse." [3] This is not true of the Hebrew-Christian mind, where the emphasis is upon *redeeming* the time; but it is true of the Greek mind, and the emphasis here is upon *escaping* time. Redemption consists mainly in getting beyond time, getting out of it. For the mystery cults, with their ecstatic union with the gods, or for the philosophers, with their teachings about the meditative life, it was all the same: salvation, such as it was, lay beyond or out of time.

This view strongly persists in modern literature. One thinks immediately of such contemporary classics as Joyce's *Ulysses,* Proust's *À la recherche du temps perdu,* Thomas Mann's *Buddenbrooks,* Virginia Woolf's *Orlando,* and Dos Passos' *U.S.A.*, all different, and yet similar in this: that each of them is an attempt to salvage life from the flux of time, to give it some permanence through the ordering factor of the artistic mind. Joyce attempts it by casting a day in the life of Leopold Bloom into the pattern of the original Homeric odyssey. The result, of course, is that the events of Bloom's life are made to seem ludicrously trivial in comparison with their heroic counterparts, and the reader senses the bitterness of Joyce that he should have been born in an age of iron and not of gold. But Bloom and his banal affairs are given at least a minor perpetuity because they are cast in the art form of the Homeric idiom. Proust, Mann, and Woolf all try to conquer time by reconstituting events in the memories of their characters. As the events are recalled and meditated upon, they live again. It soon becomes apparent to the reader that remembered scenes are more real to the characters of these authors than present scenes. They have more per-

[2] Cf. Arthur Darby Nock, *Conversion; the Old and the New in Religion from Alexander the Great to Augustine of Hippo* (Oxford: Clarendon Press, 1933), pp. 1-16.

[3] *Christ and Time: The Primitive Christian Conception of Time and History,* tr. Floyd Filson (Philadelphia: The Westminster Press, 1950), p. 52.

manence; they are extracted from time, so to speak, and are thereby endowed with durability.[4] The same is true of Dos Passos' great trilogy, whose multiple characters and scenes flash by the reader's eye like some impossible phantasmagoria. The only integration seems to be in the method itself. The Camera Eye sections especially seem to range widely and unreasonably, catching mere glimpses of scenes that are thrown on the screen before they can possibly be developed, so that they seem to be a series of line sketches and drawings, not photographs at all, shown entirely too fast for the viewer's comfort or comprehension. At first we are annoyed. "This is formless and irresponsible," we say. "The world of the writer seems to be like that the writers of child psychology textbooks ascribe to the newborn infant: 'a big, blooming, buzzing confusion.'" But the more we read the more we perceive what Dos Passos is trying to do. He is trying to sketch the form behind the formlessness, the river bed beneath the river, the impression of life that is descried in and through the flux. His subject is too vast, his canvas too small, to do it otherwise. He is attempting the impossible: to catch and record the life of a nation in flight. Most of his characters are "lost" in the seismic transitions taking place in the teeming metropolises of post-World War One America. But Dos Passos tries to save the day—and perhaps himself—by writing about it. Writing about it is the only escape.

Art itself, as the Western world knows it, is of Hellenistic origins. It is the attempt of perishable human beings to raise a monument that will stand, beyond the lifetime of man at least, against the erosion of time. Significantly, the greatest periods in the art of the last five hundred years have been those in which the feeling of evanescence was

[4] Cf. Hans Meyerhoff, *Time in Literature* (Berkeley: University of California Press, 1955), p. 113: The frequent, intense effort to recapture the past may be seen as "an attempt to recover oneself by discovering this sense of continuity with and belongingness to something that seems forever lost. This is what Proust is attempting in recording the decline and dissolution of the Guermantes way of life, or Mann in recording the same process of disintegration in the German bourgeois through the history of his own family in the *Buddenbrooks,* or Galsworthy in undertaking a similar task in *The Forsyte Saga,* or Faulkner in trying to reconstruct imaginatively the decline of a whole civilization in the South through the dissolution of the family and social structure. Both the quest and the failure reflect the same need for coming to terms with the loss of that continuity between past and future which was once provided by membership in the family. Both the quest and the failure are summed up in the title of Wolfe's final work: *You Can't Go Home Again.*"

strongest. Shakespeare, for example, was constantly aware of what Marvell called "Time's winged chariot." Especially in the sonnets did he frequently allude to the power of poetry to perpetuate man's fame. Who can soon forget the beauty of Sonnet XVIII, "Shall I compare thee to a summer's day?" with its final couplet,

> So long as men can breathe or eyes can see
> So long lives this and this gives life to thee.

The Romantic poets of the nineteenth century likewise had a febrile sense of mutability, and with it a sympathetic understanding of the motivation for ancient art, as expressed so admirably in such poems as Keats's "On First Seeing the Elgin Marbles" and "Ode on a Grecian Urn."

Nor has the *ars longa, vita brevis* notion perished among the writers of our own time. Consider, for example, the lovely last strophe of W. B. Yeats's "Sailing to Byzantium":

> Once out of nature I shall never take
> My bodily form from any natural thing,
> But such a form as Grecian goldsmiths make
> Of hammered gold and gold enameling
> To keep a drowsy Emperor awake;
> Or set upon a golden bough to sing
> To lords and ladies of Byzantium
> Of what is past, or passing, or to come.[5]

Taken alone, the last line might appear to hint of a linear concept of time; but in context it evidently stands only for the flux of time against which the golden bird represents the permanence of classical art. The bird is, so to speak, above time, and can therefore sing of "what is past, or passing, or to come."

William Faulkner, in his National Book Award address in 1955, defined his usage of the word "artist" as "everyone who has tried to create something which was not here before him, with no other tools and material than the uncommerciable ones of the human spirit; who has tried to carve, no matter how crudely, on the wall of that final ob-

[5] Reprinted with permission of the publishers, The Macmillan Company and the Macmillan Co. of Canada, and Mrs. W. B. Yeats, from *Collected Poems* of W. B. Yeats. Copyright 1928 by The Macmillan Company, renewed 1956 by Georgia Yeats.

livion, in the tongue of the human spirit, 'Kilroy was here.'" The theme of the longevity of art undoubtedly lurks in the thinking, subliminally if not consciously, of anyone who tries to produce a serious piece of creativity.

A novelist who was perhaps even more preternaturally sensitive than Faulkner to the transience of man's life on earth was Thomas Wolfe. Time was Wolfe's essential preoccupation. As Hugh Holman has observed,[6] his philosophy of time had a threefold structure. First, there was ordinary time—"clock time"—in which passing events take place. Second, there was past time, consisting of the events in life and history that have occurred and exist in the present only through the memory. And, finally, there was "time immutable, the time of rivers, mountains, oceans, and the earth." It is against the background of time immutable that the events of ordinary time take place like shadows or dreams that glide across the surface and then are gone.

Wolfe's personae are haunted by the sense of this last kind of time. They try to constitute their objective existence in the universe by recalling the events of their lives and connecting them with all the other events that have ever taken place. The lines with which Wolfe began his first and best book, *Look Homeward, Angel,* are his manifesto about time:

> Each of us is all the sums he has not counted: subtract us into nakedness and night again, and you shall see begin in Crete four thousand years ago the love that ended yesterday in Texas.
>
> The seed of our destruction will blossom in the desert, the alexin of our cure grows by a mountain rock, and our lives are haunted by a Georgia slattern, because a London cutpurse went unhung. Each moment is the fruit of forty thousand years. The minute-winning days, like flies, buzz home to death, and every moment is a window on all time.[7]

This is a key to the undeviating Hellenism of Wolfe's time-concept. The idea of the flow, the flux, the process, is everywhere in his books. His characters are forever searching for "a stone, a leaf, an unfound door," for some hidden exit into the time that is beyond time. The

[6] *Thomas Wolfe* (Minneapolis: University of Minnesota Press, 1960), pp. 34 ff.
[7] P. 3.

diastasis between transience and permanence constitutes the major romanticism of his outlook and explains largely the appeal he has for young minds that are searching, in the swift, kaleidoscopic times of adolescence, for some more enduring state.

For Eugene Gant, the protagonist of *Look Homeward, Angel,* there seemed to be some enviable durability in the stones of his father's monument shop—especially in the angels and the lettered monuments.[8] He was fascinated by them, and thought that they would never perish, but that "when that great skeleton [his father's] lay powdered in earth, in many a tangled undergrowth, in the rank wilderness of forgotten churchyards, these letters would endure." [9] He pitied all the grocers, plumbers, clerks, and clothiers whose work would not endure. "He mourned for all the men who had gone because they had not scored their name upon a rock, blasted their mark upon a cliff, sought out the most imperishable objects of the world and graven there some token, some emblem that utterly they might not be forgotten." [10] The rock and the marking—these were the combination by which man might defy his own evanescence.

It does not seem to me to be an error to say that this very sentiment lies behind all art, of whatever form or medium, in every age. Sculpture, painting, architecture, music, literature, are all efforts to leave something behind that will endure. Men sacrifice themselves for art—in long apprenticeship, in painstaking work, in the traditional penury of the artist's garret—in order to make something that will last. This kind of immolation is an unspoken code among most artists; they believe, quite seriously, that art is worth dying for. It was precisely this idea that Kierkegaard was attacking when he said that some writers cease to be men in order to become books—they sacrifice the primary thing, life, for the secondary, art. Yet all art is based on this theory—that art claims precedence over life—and practically every poem, play, short story, or novel ever adjudged a worthy piece of art is essentially grounded in it. Art for art's sake can easily become more than an aesthetic motto: it can become a religion.

[8] Cf. also Tennessee Williams' *Summer and Smoke,* in which the fountain-statue of an angel dominates the courtyard scene, suggesting the antithesis between permanence and evanescence.

[9] *Look Homeward, Angel,* p. 101.

[10] *Ibid.*

Christianity, on the other hand, insists on the ultimate value of the human soul, and so displaces art as the final goal. This is why old Dr. Johnson was always distrustful of art that was not didactic, and so took Milton to task for mingling so much mythology with the glad tidings in "Ode on the Morning of Christ's Nativity." Christ came that men might have life, not paintings and statues of him to place in the Louvre or the Accademia. Although his teachings were often cast in forms considered aesthetic by the aesthetes of later generations, and although his ministry and death and resurrection have become the subject matter of innumerable works of art, he never spoke a line or enacted a deed that was not intended solely for the redemption and edification of men (which surely *included* the aesthetic side of their nature), and not at all for their "artistic enjoyment." In him is the light of men because he offers life, not art; because he speaks of redeeming the time, not of escaping from it. Art for its own sake therefore represents, in terms of the Christian faith, a decadence and not an excellence, because it signals a cooling of those spiritual passions that in their period of incandescence are interested not in mimesis but in experience.

Wladimir Weidlé, in *The Baptism of Art,* discusses the striking difference between Christian art before Constantine—consisting mainly of wall paintings in the catacombs of Rome and one or two other places, and of reliefs decorating sarcophagi found in Italy and southern Gaul—and Christian art after Constantine. The examples from the earlier period are remarkable for their consuming interest in meaning as opposed to form. "The form, in these carvings and paintings, simply carries their content, and makes no attempt to express or embody it. And this is the result, not of being afraid of art, or puritanically suspicious of 'beauty,' but of sheer indifference to art as such." Indeed, continues Weidlé, "The only interest art could retain for the early Christian was of the kind and degree of importance a modern believer may attach to the way that his Bible is printed or bound." [11]

The late John Baillie put his finger on the utter banality of art for art's sake when he said:

> It is becoming ever clearer to us that what we want in the end is not art for art's sake, which were mere meaningless decoration, but art for the sake

[11] (London: Camelot Press, n.d.), p. 9.

of something not itself which it is humbly serving. . . . Could Gothic architecture, could the *Divina Commedia,* could the prose of our Authorised Version, conceivably have come into being for their own sakes or of their own momentum alone—as mere masterpieces of decorative loveliness? No, when we say "art for art's sake," we think rather of—Swinburne! And about Swinburne I can only feel that he might have been a great poet, if he had ever found anything substantial to say; if, that is, the loveliness of his language had ever been made sincerely subservient to something other and greater than itself.[12]

It is amazing how tangled among Christians themselves have become opinions about art and Christianity. There is a strong tendency among us to allow some vaguely pious identification to be established between godliness and beauty, the latter being a word strangely absent from the vocabularies of Jesus and Paul.

> "Beauty is truth, truth beauty,"—that is all
> Ye know on earth, and all ye need to know.

How often those famous lines from Keats's "Ode on a Grecian Urn" are quoted in sermons and "inspirational" messages—and what rank heresy they represent!

The confusion interferes with that free and simple enjoyment of the Christian life that characterized the primitive Christians. We are forever watchful for opportunities to turn the Christian life itself into a thing of art, a thing with proportion and balance and tone, and the very attitude deprives us of that *élan,* that innocence unconscious of itself, that should be qualities of life in the spirit. As Herbert Farmer has said, "We are like those tiresome people who do genuinely admire the sunset, but when they speak of it, you know at once that, in addition, they admire themselves admiring the sunset; who appreciate music, yet are never fully absorbed in it, but have some attention left over for themselves appreciating music." [13] We are never quite the uncomplicated, untrammeled souls our redemption would make us, for we are forever being diverted—tapped on the shoulder or caught up

[12] *And the Life Everlasting* (New York: Charles Scribner's Sons, 1933), pp. 312-13.

[13] *The Servant of the Word* (London: Nisbet, 1953), p. 110.

at the heels—by that old diehard sense of artistry. Even as new men we are not entirely new, because we yearn to have a hand in the making of ourselves. We cannot be spontaneous in Christ because the hankering lingers in us to be poets, makers, creators. We admire ourselves admiring the Christian faith.

An instance of how far this debasement by art has struck into Christian territory is the attitude of most ministers toward sermons, that they should be works of art. Every year some new treatise on homiletics appears with the title *The Art of Preaching* or *The Art of the Sermon.* Preachers smile coyly and with pride when it is suggested that they are "artists in the pulpit." [14] Of course this is not Christian. Christianity has always relegated art to a functional capacity. The minister may profit from studying the work of the artist, as Jonathan Edwards wished that he might study the novels of Samuel Richardson, but at least partly for the purpose that Edwards had in mind—to clothe his appeals for the faith in more winsome and compelling language. Phillips Brooks, who was no mean preacher, said in his Lyman Beecher lectures that "no man ever yet thought whether he was preaching well without weakening his sermon." [15] The very self-consciousness of art is inappropriate to the art of preaching. Study the sermons of Peter and Stephen and Paul in the New Testament, advised Brooks. They were simple, unpolished, and cogent with vehemence.

> They were tools, and not works of art. To turn a tool into a work of art, to elaborate the shape and chase the surface of the axe with which you are to hew your wood, is bad taste; and to give any impression in a sermon that it has forgotten its purpose and been shaped for anything else than what in the largest extent of those great words might be described as *saving souls,*

[14] Cf. the statement of G. Paul Butler, editor of the annual *Best Sermons,* in a recent article in *Christianity Today* (April 13, 1962, p. 6): "Preaching today is a mature art and our great preachers are artists in the pulpit—the pulpit where God is proclaimed." This way of regarding preachers is by no means new. E. C. Dargan, in his *History of Preaching,* noted that Blackstone, the famous barrister of the time of George III, went to hear every clergyman of note in the city of London, and declared that he heard not a single sermon that might not have been preached by Cicero, or that told him whether the preacher were a follower of Confucius or Mahomet or Christ.

[15] *Eight Lectures on Preaching* (London: S.P.C.K.; Greenwich, Conn.: The Seabury Press, 1959), p. 51.

makes it offensive to a truly good taste and dull to the average man, who feels an incongruity which he cannot define.[16]

I must ask pardon for this *excursus*, but I wished simply to emphasize how very far the confusion between art and life, and redemption-from-time and redemption-in-time, has carried. As Cullman says, whenever the Greek view and the primitive Christian view cross lines, it is the Greek view that wins out and the Christian view that suffers—and this is the case, not only among poets and novelists, but to a large extent among Christian clerics as well.

What I trust is evident is that it is impossible, for artist or minister, to have a Christian doctrine of Last Things together with a Hellenistic view of time as a cycle and a flux against which man's main hope for immortality is in the art he produces. It is the nature of the Greek to establish a *polis* and to produce a civilization in which the arts have their place of great reverence. But it is the nature of the Christian to be a pilgrim and to journey toward a city not made with hands. Art may indeed be a by-product of his journey; but he never conceives of it as a means of escape from the time process, or glorifies it as an end in itself. It too, along with his own life, belongs in the service of God, who is able to redeem it as he redeems time itself.

A writer's view of time has a great deal to do with the way he feels about death, which has always been an important literary subject, and about hell, which has also received significant treatments. Under the Greek view, death and hell are quite different from what they are in the Christian scheme. Death represents the terminus, the cessation, the exit; when man dies, he "escapes" from the time cycle. But it is not equivalent to Nirvana, which is an utter extinction of the senses. There is a kind of afterlife in classical Greek thought, as may be seen in Ulysses' visit to Achilles in *The Odyssey*. Achilles is in a kind of semihell—perhaps more like Dante's purgatory—where his chief frustration is the dissolution of his powers. Hell is a world of shades and half-life. Thus, even with the doctrine of the soul's immortality, the termination of life in this world is a frightful thing to the Greek mind. No Greek could ever utter a jubilant Paulinism like "O death, where

[16] *Ibid.*, p. 112.

is thy sting? O grave, where is thy victory?" He knew too well where the sting and the victory were.

The greatest preoccupation with the subject of death on the modern literary scene is that exhibited by the existentialist writers, who are perhaps generally closer to the Greeks than to any other cultural milieu. The tone of their writings is similar to that of Sophoclean drama; it has that austerity, that starkness, that tautness of the Greek stage. Part of it is the sense of man's aloneness that he never overcomes so long as he remains heroic; he is thrown onto the stage of life naked and alone—*verwerfen* is Heidegger's term for it—and is considered weak and unheroic if he tries to overcome his isolation and abandonment. His aloneness is forever intensified for him by having him constantly face the possibility of his death and utter annihilation.

This seems to be the formula: Take one lonely man. Reveal to him that he is always under the threat of death. Then he is more lonely than ever. He despises the men around him who never seem to be aware of their deaths. They must be cowards who are afraid to face death. Therefore he, the hero, will bravely choose to face his death, and to face it as often as possible. He will stand on bridges and precipices and high places and contemplate the vision of his own body down below. It is a marvelous trick for clearing the head of all false values. Now he goes back to life among the cowards and spits on their tin gods and contemns them for their enslavement to "complicated" life.

The facing of death is hardly alien to the best in Christianity. Consider, for example, the importance in Christian devotional history of Paul's statement, "I die daily" (I Cor. 15:31), or the one, "I am crucified with Christ" (Gal. 2:20). But the attitudes are light-years apart. The existentialist's anticipated death is for his own sake; the Christian's is for his Lord. When Paul wrote, "I am crucified with Christ," he continued with the words, "nevertheless I live; yet not I, but Christ liveth in me." The Christian's "dying" is centered in Christ and his death and resurrection; his idea of death is wholly *other*-conscious, whereas the existentialist's is wholly *self*-conscious. The notion of death among contemporary existentialists is derived chiefly from Heidegger, who conceived of "running forward to death," or anticipating death, as a formative influence on life itself. The anticipation of the end allows the individual to see his life as a whole and to give it aesthetic form. This is a Greek idea of facing death: it throws life back upon itself to make it complete in itself without any reference to immortality. What matters solely is proportion, balance, symmetry, form. Life is regarded as an end in itself.[17] Death is either an escape or a diminution of powers, and, properly faced, exerts a formative influence on life.

The real hell for such a life, consequently, is in the failure to achieve form. Salvation, or quasi-salvation, lies in right behavior. Damnation, as such, is not an eternal threat, because there is no real concept of life beyond death. The doctrine of hell—as punitive but not necessarily as retributive—is, in the main, transferred back into this life, into the here and now. And, in this attenuated version, it is an almost ubiquitous theme in modern writing, amounting, as Nathan Scott has noticed,[18] to a veritable "Myth of Hell."

The archpriest of this new doctrine of hell may well have been the youthful Rimbaud, who wrote in *Une Saison en Enfer,* "I think I am in hell, therefore I am in hell." At least, this appears to be the working motto of many writers in our time. Witness the famous line from Sartre's play *No Exit,* "Hell is—other people," and its converse in Eliot's *The Cocktail Party,* where Edward says,

> What is hell? Hell is oneself,
> Hell is alone, the other figures in it
> Merely projections.[19]

Add to these references Allen Tate's *Seasons of the Soul,* which, though it consciously echoes Dante's *Inferno,* pictures the modern hell merely as a violent world where men do not know what or who they are. It is "Autumn" (Stanza II) that is the hell season, recalling perhaps Faulkner's words, "the season of rain and death." The stanza begins,

[17] Cf. Meyerhoff, *Time in Literature,* p. 78: "Since the decline of religious faith, the aesthetic way of life has become one of the most significant secular responses both to the challenge of death and to the general pessimism pervading the intellectual climate of our age."

[18] *Modern Literature and the Religious Frontier,* p. 74.

[19] From *Complete Poems and Plays,* p. 342. Used by permission of Harcourt, Brace & World, and Faber & Faber Ltd.

It had an autumn smell
And that was how I knew
That I was down a well.[20]

As one critic observed, "The private hell has shrunk to the dimensions of a well."[21]

Among the novelists cited by Scott as evidence of subscription to such a "Myth of Hell" are, besides Faulkner: Sartre, Graham Greene, Robert Penn Warren, and George Orwell. Of the host of names that might be added, none is more prominent than that of Camus. There is a certain Miltonic strain, minus the grandeur, in his rebels. How actual their ameliorated hell seems to them is evident in *The Fall*. It is really a kind of purgatorial hell, a dismal half-life of being and not being, of becoming and yet perishing, in which the real torture of it all lies in the fact that all the meaning there is in life lies in a man's honesty. It is the bleakest life imaginable. The gray clouds are never edged with sunlight; they merely sift down and down until they meet the perennial fog of the Amsterdam landscape—or seascape, it does not matter—and cloy life with a miserable oppression. A darker hell or a brighter heaven is impossible in the world view of such a determined agnostic as Camus. His characters think they are in hell, and therefore, in a manner of speaking, they are.

It must be admitted that the presentation of a truer hell in a novel would be a very difficult thing. It would necessitate passages of apocalypticism, with which the average reader is usually loath to indulge a writer. The reader is not especially to blame; his consciousness has simply not been formed for such things by his cultural environment, as was that of Dante's audience. But the tyranny that he, with his limited spiritual range, exerts over contemporary fiction doubtless accounts for the way many novelists "telescope" the now and the then, the here and the hereafter, so as to present the doctrine of hell as a present reality in this life. I have in mind, for example, the abhorrent features Greene ascribes to the settings of some of his novels—the oppressiveness of the heat, the torpor of the atmosphere,

[20] From *Poems* (New York: Charles Scribner's Sons, 1960), p. 30.

[21] R. K. Meiners, "The End of History: Allen Tate's *Seasons of the Soul*," *The Sewanee Review*, LXX (Winter, 1962), 52.

the rankness of the jungle, the rats and bats and spiders and serpents and vultures, all weighing upon the consciousness of his personae like some inescapable pain they have learned to live with. This is a hell the modern reader can understand—or at least can imagine.

Or take the writings of Joseph Conrad, who preceded Greene in this sort of thing. In *Heart of Darkness* the jungle appears as some kind of demonic region that has the power of completely demoralizing the European mind. Charlie Marlowe, the narrator, suggests the antithesis it stands for: "Perhaps on some quiet night the tremor of far-off drums, sinking, swelling, a tremor vast, faint; a sound weird, appealing, suggestive, and wild—and perhaps with as profound a meaning as the sound of bells in a Christian country." [22] Going up the river into the dark land, says Marlowe, was "like traveling back to the earliest beginnings of the world, when vegetation rioted on the earth and the big trees were kings." [23] The air was heavy and sluggish. Great amphibious mammals sunned along the banks. After a while you were so lost among the wooded islands that "you thought yourself bewitched and cut off forever from everything you had known once—somewhere—far away—in another existence perhaps." [24] As the steamer toiled around some bend, a burst of yells would descend on it, and black bodies would clap and stamp and writhe in incomprehensible frenzy. As Marlowe says,

> The earth seemed unearthly. We are accustomed to look upon the shackled form of a conquered monster, but there—there you could look at a thing monstrous and free. It was unearthly, and the men were—No, they were not inhuman. Well, you know, that was the worst of it—this suspicion of their not being inhuman. It would come slowly to one. They howled and leaped, and spun, and made horrid faces; but what thrilled you was just the thought of their humanity—like yours—the thought of your remote kinship with this wild and passionate uproar.[25]

I have quoted this passage to suggest its similarity to those parts of the *Inferno* where Dante has such a realization about the souls of the

[22] (New York: Signet Classics, 1959), p. 76.
[23] *Ibid.*, pp. 91-92.
[24] *Ibid.*, p. 92.
[25] *Ibid.*, p. 94.

damned. Only here the infernal is of the earth and of the present world. Hell is in the jungle. And it is Mr. Kurtz's vision of it, as an ex-European, that makes him cry out as he is dying, "The horror! The horror!"

Eliot, it will be recalled, set the native's report, "Mistah Kurtz—he dead," as the introductory epigram for "The Hollow Men," which describes "this valley of dying stars" that we have made into our temporary hell. It is all a mammoth conflation, a kind of death in life. The universe in our literature has become flat and two-dimensional. It is architectured to the unspiritual soul of modern man that makes its own damnation out of its own inglorious limitations. For the vertical and rugged terrain of Dante's vision is substituted the foggy monotony of Camus', leveled off as far as the eye can see.

And, if great writers offend, what shall little writers do—the host of poetasters and minor craftsmen? The answer is simple. They will go on writing of war and poverty and squalor and rejection and divorce and greed and sloth and all the other miseries on the face of the earth, and saying, "Why, this is hell, nor are we out of it."

The idea of resurrection is likewise weakened under the influence of the Greek time scheme. Its appearance in current literature is largely as some limited aggrandizement of the individual, such as success in business or arrival at self-understanding or sublimation or some other moment of passage from lower to higher status as a person or as a soul. The future tense is all but forgotten. There is apparently little interest in "what we shall be." What matters is a fuller life here and now, whether as a reinvigorated toreador, an enlightened philosopher, or a newly moral Madison Avenue executive. It is often merely a matter of the elation that a character feels when he makes a good decision, as when Hemingway's Brett Ashley gives up Romero for his own sake. She says, "I feel rather good, you know. I feel rather set up." Later she says, "It's sort of what we have instead of God." [26]

Of those writings in recent years actually dealing with the theme of resurrection, three that I know center attention on the raising of Lazarus of Bethany. They are Lagerkvist's *Barabbas,* O'Neill's *Lazarus Laughed,* and Greene's *The Potting Shed.* The first is a novel, and

[26] *The Sun Also Rises* (New York: Charles Scribner's Sons, 1926), p. 243.

treats the subject only in passing; the other two are plays, and are substantially based on the subject. All are worth looking at, if only to see how difficult it is to write about resurrection in a literal way.

In Lagerkvist's story, Barabbas goes to Bethany to visit the man whom Christ is reported to have raised from the dead. The two men sit opposite each other at the table. Barabbas is struck by the desolate look in the other's face—a look "like a desert." Lazarus speaks slowly, and in a monotone, and gazes out through "pale, lack-lustre eyes." He asks Barabbas if he believes that Christ is the Son of God. Barabbas hesitates a moment, but, under the pressure of that dreadful face, admits that he does not. Lazarus seems not to mind at all. He simply says, "No, there are many who don't. His mother, who was here yesterday, doesn't believe either. But he raised me from the dead because I am to witness for him." [27]

Barabbas inquires about the realm of the dead, and what it is like. "I have experienced nothing," replies the other. "I have merely been dead. And death is nothing." Barabbas continues to press him, but he only repeats, "The realm of the dead isn't anything. It exists, but it isn't anything." [28] Barabbas stares at him—into the empty eyes.

The idea that death is a vacancy, an utter desolation, is, of course, not far from the concept of death expressed by certain parts of the Old Testament. Johannes Pedersen's classic *Israel: Its Life and Culture* bears this out.

But as an instance of resurrection this portrait of Lazarus is hardly a viable one. Death has apparently robbed him of all vitality, and the resurrection has not restored it. Browning's Lazarus, in "An Epistle Containing the Strange Medical Experience of Karshish, the Arab Physician," is at least childlike after his revivification. But this Lazarus is a mere walking shadow, a crater where a man has been. He is hardly convincing as a Christian saint. It is little wonder that when Barabbas dies Lagerkvist can then represent him as saying out into the darkness, as though he were speaking to it, "To thee I deliver up my soul."

[27] From *Barabbas,* by Pär Lagerkvist. Copyright 1951 by Random House, Inc. Reprinted by permission of Random House, and used by permission of Chatto & Windus.

[28] *Ibid.,* p. 63.

The Lazarus of O'Neill's play is quite another fellow. When the curtain goes up on that drama, those who were mourners at Lazarus' tomb are standing around discussing the scene they have witnessed. Jesus has gone away. They recall how Lazarus looked into his face and said "Yes," and how, as the Lord departed, Lazarus stood and laughed softly after him, "like a man in love with God." "Such a laugh I never heard," says the Third Guest. "It made my ears drunk! It was like new wine! And though I was half-dead with fright I found myself laughing, too!" [29]

It soon becomes clear that what Lazarus laughs at is the fact that there is no death. The laughter is contagious, and wherever he goes men begin to laugh with him, forgetting all their earthly cares and chanting exultantly,

> Laugh! Laugh!
> Laugh with Lazarus!
> Fear is no more!
> There is no death! [30]

The rumors about this chortling Jew reach Caesar, and he commands that Lazarus be brought to Rome. When the centurion approaches Lazarus to take him, Lazarus, "as if he were answering not the centurion but the command of his fate from the sky," says "Yes!" and goes off with him, the music and dancing and laughter commencing about them everywhere as they go.

The citizens along the route to Rome worship him as a god. He appears much younger than when he left Bethany. The Athenians take him for Dionysus. "Not the coarse, drunken Dionysus, nor the effeminate God," says O'Neill, "but Dionysus in his middle period, more comprehensive in his symbolism, the soul of the recurring seasons, of living and dying as processes in eternal growth." [31]

But at Rome the members of Caesar's decadent court are thrust into great moral conflict by his presence. Therefore they submit him to torture and at last burn him at the stake in an amphitheater. In that

[29] From *Lazarus Laughed,* by Eugene O'Neill. Copyright 1927 and renewed 1955 by Carlotta Monterey O'Neill. Reprinted by permission of Random House, Inc.

[30] *Ibid.*

[31] *Ibid.,* II, 1.

final scene, they all taunt him to say whether he can still laugh at death. As the fire leaps in the faggots, he begins to laugh. The soldiers cannot help laughing with him. Pompeia, a court strumpet, is drawn irresistibly to him, and throws herself into the flames. Even Caesar is at last convinced, and shouts, "I have lived long enough! I will die with Lazarus! I no longer fear death! I laugh! I laugh at Caesar! I advise you, my brothers, fear not Caesars! Seek Man in the brotherhood of the dust! Caesar is your fear of Man! I counsel you, laugh away your Caesars!" [32]

O'Neill's theme is piquant. The idea of man's yes-saying to the universe, of his laughing with God at the discovery that there is no death, is appealing. It is a sort of flippant, intoxicated version of Carlyle's "everlasting yea." The laughter itself, on stage, tends to become infectious and rings in the mind almost like divine madness.

But there is something not quite right about the whole thing, something that disturbs the Christian consciousness of the audience. We wonder what it is. Certainly the topic of the resurrected life is a Christian topic. The raising of Lazarus is based on a pericope from the New Testament. The symbolism is generally Christian—Lazarus even dies on a stake. When we finally realize what it is that bothers us, we see why it was so intangible. It is just that the whole drama is sub-Christian. It employs Christian motifs, but it is not itself Christian. Death is taken too impertinently as a nonexistent. Christ has not overcome it; he has merely revealed its nakedness. O'Neill's concept of the moral universe here is too monistic; one cannot really say with Lazarus, "There is no death." It is all too unreal, this world in which a man conquers all by laughing at his own fear of death. The dimensions of suffering and grief and pain are not adequately accounted for. The work of Christ is reduced to a mere Gnostic level, on which he has simply opened men's eyes. And Lazarus himself—what is wrong with O'Neill's Lazarus? He usurps the glory of the Savior. He becomes a kind of savior-god, a Dionysian Pied Piper, marching at the head of a band of hysterical followers. The whole thing lacks the proper sense of "He must reign until he has put all things under his feet." It has too much of the Brahmanic about it, too much of the oversoul. The resur-

[32] *Ibid.*, IV, 2.

rection motif of the Christian faith is taken only as a kind of gathering point for a world-religions convocation; its distinctiveness is utterly diminished. There is no more than a suggestion of redemption, and none whatsoever in the sense of an objective atonement. The play is about immortality, not resurrection. The play belongs to the documentation of the mystery religions and not to the literature of the Christian faith.

Greene's *The Potting Shed,* instead of returning to the original Lazarus, deals with a modern-day Lazarus named James Callifer. We do not make the connection between him and the biblical character immediately. At first, Callifer seems like anything but a resurrected person. He is dull, colorless, apathetic—even his wife Sara has left him because he is so completely unimpassioned. He asks her, after the separation, "Sara, what's wrong with me?" "You're not alive," she says. "Sometimes I wanted to make you angry or sorry, to hurt you. But you never felt pain. Why did you marry me? I believe it was curiosity to see if you could feel. You didn't feel." [33]

James tries to recall his youth, to think whether there was anything in it to account for his present lethargy. He becomes dimly aware that something of apparent significance happened once in the potting shed behind the main house, but he cannot bring the event into focus. His family has shut the episode out and refuses to talk about it. Only Anne, his niece, will speak of it, but she does not know exactly what happened. She only knows that it was "something shocking."

At last, James worms part of the truth out of his mother. He had an accident in the potting shed. He slipped and fell, and was unconscious when Mr. Potter, the gardener, found him.

James searches for Mrs. Potter, who is still alive, and gets the whole truth from her. He had hanged himself in that shed, and was *dead* when her husband found him. Her husband had been discharged for saying so. But an uncle, a William Callifer, who had been left alone with the corpse, had somehow brought him back to life.

When James finds the uncle, whom he has not seen since childhood, he is a "whiskey priest" in a run-down presbytery, where he lives in the tedium of hearing the same confessions every day and saying the

[33] *The Potting Shed,* p. 30.

same words over and over again. He does not wish to recall the incident of the potting shed, but James forces him. What he reveals is startling. He loved the unconscious boy dearly, and would have given his life for him to have saved him. But he could only pray. He said, "Let him live, God. I love him. Let him live. I will give you anything if you will let him live." But he was a poor man. What could he give? Only one thing. Therefore he prayed, "Take away what I love most. Take away my faith but let him live." [34]

As if the knowledge of this is all that he has needed, James suddenly comes alive. The spell of suspended animation in him is ended, and he becomes radiant with joy and energy. It is not that he becomes saintly. He says, "I don't even want to pray. Something happened to me, that's all. Like a street accident. I don't want God. I don't love God, but He's there—it's no good pretending; He's in my lungs like air." He speaks to Sara about the old days of their marriage: "Nothing mattered. If I slept with you, what did it matter? We were all going to be as dead as last year's dog. Now, when I look at you, I see someone who will never die forever."

Sara replies that she is not particularly interested in forever: "I don't want eternity, James. I'm bored with eternity, going on and on like a long litany on a wet day."

"It's time that bores us," says James, "interminable time. I move my hand. It moves in space and time. When there's no time there'll be no movement any more. When we think, we think one thing after another. Time, again. When there's no time we shan't think any more."

"A frightening world," she replies.

"I've been there and I'm not frightened."

"But time is all I know."

"Oh, I love time too," he says. "I'm not impatient for eternity. It's the same as when you love a woman. If you are going to see her in a few hours, you love the hours. They have *her* importance." [35]

This, it seems to me, is a great deal more Christian than O'Neill's version of the Lazarus story. I am not even particularly bothered by

[34] *Ibid.*, p. 94.
[35] *Ibid.*, p. 117.

James Callifer's statement that he does not love God. It reminds me of certain passages in the writings of Dietrich Bonhoeffer where that noted theologian speaks so winsomely of the essential "worldliness" of Christianity.

But there is one thing wrong, and it is a major fault. The resurrection of James Callifer is not centered in Jesus Christ. The sacrifice that makes it possible is the faith of a priest—which calls for an unlikely bargain on God's part. The Church, apart from the presence of the priest, has nothing to do with it—James meets no company of the resurrected and has no fellowship in a community of saints. The whole thing is a play about resurrection, about a Christian motif—indeed, *the* Christian motif!—but without a Christian setting. In Paul's writings about resurrection, everything is centered on Christ: the believer is baptized into Christ, dies with Christ, is raised with Christ, lives in Christ, witnesses to Christ. The short of it is that Greene's play is Christian without a Christ, and that, I suspect, should be accounted something of an impossibility, not to say a heresy.

Having looked at these three works, we perhaps ought to raise a question about the real nature of Lazarus' resurrection. The original description of it is in the eleventh chapter of the Fourth Gospel, where it provides the occasion for one of the famous *Ego-eimi* sayings of Jesus—"I am the resurrection and the life"—and doubtless sets the scene for the death and resurrection of the Lord himself. But there are some questions to ask even of the Scriptures. Will not Lazarus have to die again? Has this experience affected him in any way, or has he remained passive through it all? Is he the type of the resurrected man as Paul speaks of him, say, in the book of Romans? The passage is not without its thorns, and one cannot help pondering the legitimacy of using it as an example of God's raising men up.. Surely it is more important for what it says about Jesus—at least, this was the author's intent—than for what it says about Lazarus. Therefore, of the three works we have discussed, it would seem that Lagerkvist's is truer to the spirit of the biblical report. At least the Lazarus in *Barabbas* witnesses to the power of Christ.

But it may be that we have hit here upon the crux of the whole matter—that there is something out of place in the fact that the most conspicuous instances of the resurrection theme in modern fiction are re-creations of the Lazarus narrative and not viable, convincing presentations of real Christians who are engaged in living the resurrected life. Why not more portraits of men who have been qualitatively, spiritually, actually made alive in Christ? The redeemed individual who has been raised up in Christ, who has been given a new life, who goes from day to day with a present joy and a hope of eternal life hereafter, should be a witness to Christ, like Lagerkvist's Lazarus; he should have the sense of values of O'Neill's Lazarus; and he should rejoice in the present moment, like Greene's Callifer, because eternity plays back upon it and gives it significance: but he ought to do all these things together. In other words, the true Christian saint is more than any picture we are able to draw of Lazarus.

We are not given enough Christians in contemporary literature who actually think and act as if they really lived after the occurrence of the resurrection of Christ. Most of them, to use James Stewart's phrase, seem to be "on the wrong side of Easter." The fact of the Resurrection has not entered the picture in such a significant way as to change it for them. It has not truly altered the complexion of suffering or given new meaning to ethics or reoriented personality or suffused existence with joy—either in literature or in life. Of course we cannot expect novels and plays that treat of the lives of saints in heaven in the fullness of the Resurrection. That would be beyond the imaginative powers and descriptive limitations of any artist, whoever he might be. Even Dante's saints in the *Paradiso* are transplanted earth people. But we can expect—and should expect—better portrayals of the man who in Christ is already in this life experiencing the power of the Resurrection and who evidences belief in a resurrection yet to come.

Is there an example of what we might wish to see more of in contemporary writing? I think there is. It is Charles Williams' novel *War in Heaven*,[36] which we shall want to look at rather carefully. Williams was not a popular writer. His books are too difficult for the average taste. They are full of classical and literary allusions, esoteric ideas, even untranslated bits of Latin and Greek. Williams was a scholar, which is a handicap few authors ever overcome. But his pages teem

[36] (New York: Farrar, Straus & Company, Inc., 1949). Used by permission of Farrar, Straus & Company, Faber & Faber Ltd., and David Higham Associates.

with passages of splendid prose—some of the deftest writing ever done in the English language. For delicacy of description, fineness in character drawing, and depth of psychological understanding, he is hard to surpass. And he is perhaps as Christian a writer as may be found in our century.

The most pronounced theme of *War in Heaven,* as the title indicates, is the terrible conflict between good and evil in the universe. It is a theme to which Williams is irresistibly drawn, like some contemporary Zoroaster, in almost every one of his seven novels. Here the forces of good are represented on the human level by Archdeacon Julian Davenant of the parish of Castra Parvulorum, a name now reduced by Grimm's Law to the more British-sounding Fardles; by Kenneth Mornington, a publisher's clerk; and by the Duke of the North Ridings, a young Catholic who indulges himself in the craft of poetry. On the side of evil, ranged against them, are Gregory Persimmons, a retired publisher who has recently purchased an estate at Fardles; Manasseh, a diabolical creature well practiced in the art of necromancy; a Greek chemist named Dmitri, who is factotum to Manasseh; and Sir Giles Tumulty, world traveler, dabbler in the occult, and friend of Gregory—if, indeed, these last could be said to have friends. The stakes of the battle are high: possession of the Holy Grail and the soul of a child named Adrian Rackstraw, who is visiting on the estate of Gregory Persimmons.

Sir Giles, a sort of scholar-historian of such matters, has discovered that one of the communion vessels at the Archdeacon's little church in Fardles is actually the famous chalice from which Christ drank at the Last Supper. The Archdeacon does not realize that it is the legendary vessel until after Gregory Persimmons has managed to steal it. Gregory is a child of darkness, and is interested in the Grail as a venerable relique which he can turn to the service of evil; he perceives that it has been "as near the other centre as anything in this world can get." Somehow he designs to use it as a gate through which to draw into hell the soul of young Adrian Rackstraw, who will be his oblation to the evil powers.

In an awesome scene, Williams describes the Black Mass which Gregory conducts with the Grail as the central artifice. It is placed on a pedestal between two candles and filled to the brim with some strange wine. Gregory, garbed in a white robe marked with esoteric symbols, scatters some herbs and powders about the altar and sprinkles a few hairs into the wine. He draws a wand back and forth in a strange manner before the altar and then sits before it in profound silence. After an hour or so of sitting thus, he begins a dark incantation in which he requests *"animum Adriana cujus nomen scripsi in sanguine meo demitte in sanguine tuo."* He moves the rod in magical symbols upon the wine, from which a faint mist is perceived to rise from time to time. At last he seems to descry the soul of little Adrian through the mists and addresses it. Then the eldritch rite is over, and he rises and replaces the magical implements, sets the Grail inverted on the floor, and retires into deep slumber.

When at last it dawns upon the Archdeacon that the chalice is important in the service of God, as a symbol if not as an artifact, he manages to recapture it from Gregory and to flee with it, in the company of Mornington and the Duke, to the Duke's London residence. There the triumvirate sets up vigil over the precious chalice. While they watch, the Archdeacon, more sensitive to such things than the others, becomes aware that some alien power is trying to dissolve the cup. He admonishes his friends to join battle against the foe. "Pray," he cries, "pray, in the name of God. They are praying against Him tonight." The three men concentrate on the Grail, forming a kind of living shield to ward off the attacks from the evil forces, receiving their own strength from the center formed by the vessel itself. In the moments of greatest intensity, the Grail shudders. Somehow the priest senses that it is the accidental center of Christian power, and yet not it, but something greater than it. "Neither is this Thou," he says, "and yet this also is Thou." At last the alien powers are exhausted, and the cup becomes still. The Christians relax and realize suddenly that they are very, very tired.

But the ministers of evil are not through, and they manage to obtain the chalice again by a ruse. Adrian's mother has succumbed to demonic possession after being treated on a wound with one of Gregory's potions, and Manasseh, the paterfamilias of the wicked company, promises to release her from the possession in exchange for the cup. She is freed, but by some power other than Manasseh's. Though he knows that it was another power that intervened, he accepts the Grail in payment anyway and retreats with it to Dmitri's little chemistry shop.

The Archdeacon is soon after lured to the chemistry shop, where Manasseh, Gregory, and Dmitri bind him and attempt to make a dead man's soul enter into him. At this point, only a *deus ex machina* —or is it really *ex machina?*—can save the good Archdeacon, and it appears in the form of Prester John, the legendary medieval king, who comes amidst the sound of many trumpets, frees the Archdeacon, consigns Dmitri and Manasseh to destruction, and delivers Gregory into the hands of the constabulary as the murderer of the dead man. In an ecstasy of senesthesia, it seems to the Archdeacon that all around him the litany wheels like fire,

> He hath destroyed great nations: for His mercy endureth for ever:
> And overthrown mighty kings: for His mercy endureth for ever.

The war is over; or, at least, this battle.

The final chapter of the book narrates the gathering of the saints in the Archdeacon's little church at Fardles. Even the Duke of the North Ridings is there, suggesting an ecumenical union. It is a lyrical experience, especially for the Archdeacon. At the height of it, they all have a vision of the Lord. "All sound ceased," says Williams; "all things entered into an intense suspension of being; nothing was anywhere at all but He." Then, suddenly, the altar where the Grail has sat is bare, with nothing but the sunlight falling across it—"without violence, without parting, the Grail and its Lord were gone." And, as they all discover when the intensity of the mystical experience has abated, the Archdeacon, in the midst of it, has pleasantly died.

What can one say about this kind of writing? The first inclination, perhaps, is to say that it is unreal, that things simply do not happen this way. Interest in the Grail is residual only among Arthurian scholars and poets of medievalism. Men do not go about trying to steal the souls of children for the devil. Strange powers do not threaten to dissolve metal chalices. People do not try to enjoin the souls of the dead to enter the bodies of the living. Prester John does not make modern appearances. The Lord does not really bring off raptures in church services. But on second sight, one is bound to admit that the things Williams has written about are the real things—real, at least, in comparison with the substance of the average materialistically oriented novel. They are things *beyond mere things.* They are principalities and powers and struggles and lordships. They cannot be handled or tasted or discussed with ease in the average Sunday-school class, but they are as real as whatever it is souls are really made of. And they are the things that count.

Perhaps the most serious criticism of Williams' work is that, despite his acute sensitivity to the profound dualism that underlies even the simplest aspects of life, he offends by casting it too much in the terms of the old mystery and morality plays. The contending powers are, if anything, too naked and apparent. Their "indecent exposure" accounts for the air of unreality in the novels. The Archdeacon, Mornington, and the Duke are fairly credible characters—especially Mornington. But Gregory and Manasseh and Dmitri are not. Like Nero, they are much too obviously antichrist ever to be Antichrist.

But the important thing here is that the Archdeacon really does appear convincing to the reader as one who has been "raised with Christ." Laying aside the implausible parts of the narrative, he seems quite plausibly to be what Williams doubtless intended him to be—a saint. The whole tone and tenor of his life are so measurably affected by the resurrection of Christ and of his own dying and being raised up in him, that the reader senses no discordance whatsoever when, at his death in the little chapel at Fardles, it is implied that he has been taken to be with the Lord.

There are no doubt many men alive like the Archdeacon. He is too well known to us, too easily identified, to be unique. Then why can we not have more representation of his sort in the average novel, where the hero usually bids for our identification with him by being bad or tough or ugly and then becomes the hero by virtue of some good act involving a sudden and perhaps unpremeditated sacrifice on his part?

One thing is sure: not much will remain of contemporary literature that does not have Williams' vision of good and evil as contending powers in the world of human affairs. This vision is what makes great writers. Hawthorne and Melville and Dostoevski are examples in point. The struggle in their novels is more than the sum of the conflicts among the characters; it is a grappling of superhuman forces, of titanic currents that sweep over the souls of men, rolling and tumbling them in some magnetic field that influences them in all they do. It puts issues and outcomes beyond the control of men. The winds that skate and howl through *The Scarlet Letter* and *Moby-Dick* and *The Brothers Karamazov,* though the characters do not know where they come from or where they go, make the storms in men's lives, and they bring the clear skies.

Even literature that knows more of evil than it does of good may be half great—like the works of Thomas Hardy and Robinson Jeffers and Tennessee Williams. But no amount of violence and brutality and so-called "hard facts" can ever make a piece of literature really tough if it has no sense of the pure evil behind them. Norman Mailer's famous *The Naked and the Dead,* for instance, is a veritable catalog of vice and debauchery and destruction, but it is still a soft, muscle-bound work because it has no real sense of the organization of principalities and powers that lies behind the isolated items on the agenda of horror. Or take the punch-happy ephemera of Mickey Spillane. He provides more rage to the page, more out-and-out sadism per chapter, than any writer I know. But compared to Williams he is a sissy, and doesn't know the first thing about real toughness, because all he understands is the phenomenal side, and not the noumenal side, of evil. Like most novelists writing today, he has reduced the scope of the cosmic battle to that of the skirmish between the Id and the Ego.

The trouble is not, of course, in the writers alone. It is in the whole society that produces them. Not even among those of us who consider ourselves to be Christians is the understanding of good and evil profound enough. The more rational and sophisticated we become, the more we try to synthesize, to simplify, to reduce everything to a single level. The first thing to go is either God or the devil. For Ivan Karamazov it was God. For most of us it is the devil. We prefer ranch-style to Gothic. But, as Randall Stewart has reminded us, it is probably impossible to be a Christian and not believe in the devil. That takes some thinking, but I believe it is true. We do not fully belong to Christ unless we appreciate at least partially the character of that from which we have been released and feel some sensitivity for the tension that still exists there for us.

The truth is that most of us don't begin to appreciate the conflict involved in the Incarnation or the measure to which the effects of that conflict have altered the situation for our lives. Our spiritual eyesight is too dim. We seldom experience with any purity of feeling the great things of which Paul wrote in the eighth chapter of Romans—the crescendo chapter—the freedom and the hope and the being in Christ and the conquest over powers and dominions and principalities. We lack the dramatic sense both for the war in our members and for the war that is beyond our members. We miss the sweep and the pageantry and the grandeur of the faith in which we are caught up. If only we had more perception for the battle between God and Satan, between good and evil, moving along always toward its final Armageddon, I feel confident that we would discern greater dimensions in the seemingly insignificant ritual that fills our days, and that the influence of our thinking would be such that even the thousands of paperback novels intended for no higher honor than drugstore consumption would not be so patently shallow and formulistic as is now the case.

As it is, the characters of a novel like Steinbeck's *The Wayward Bus,* with which we began this discussion of Last Things, cannot even begin to be saved, because they have absolutely no understanding of the depth and magnitude and personality of the evil in their lives. They live under the tyranny of the little frustrations, inhibitions, and eccentricities that are its symptoms; they do not begin to suspect that somewhere nonspatially, but nevertheless actually, these things run together and intertwine at a hard core that is the real citadel of evil power, and they cannot guess at the meaning of Christ's words, "I beheld Satan as lightning fall from heaven," and realize that that statement has anything at all to do with their problems. Whatever pathos there is in that third-rate novel is in the terrible ignorance and blindness of those poor, benighted souls who caper about at the mouth of that cave without an inkling of the size of the stage they are playing on or the magnitude of the issues that are involved. They know nothing at all of the real conflict or of its extension into the past and its extension into the future. It is all Id and Ego with them, with maybe a little dash of Superego thrown in. It is a saddening picture. In the midst of life, they are in death.

There is one other thing we must mention before leaving this subject of Last Things, and that is the absence in contemporary literature of any doctrine of the Holy Spirit. The lack of such a doctrine was noted in an earlier chapter, but it is pertinent to our topic here, because the coming of the Spirit is an occurrence to be identified with being in "last days."

In Peter's sermon at Pentecost he interpreted the outpouring of the Spirit, in accord with the prophecy in Joel 2:28-32, as a sign that the "last days" had come. The most casual reading of the book of Acts invariably gives the impression that the two events—"last days" and the coming of the Spirit—were coeval. That the end did not happen to come as soon as the Apostles apparently thought it would does not in any way invalidate their interpretation of the sign. Christ has come, and in his Incarnation in history has established the midpoint of time. Because the Incarnation has already occurred and we look not for another, all days after the coming of the Spirit are "last days." Duration is not the primary matter; the basic time scheme is still the same; and, even today, as Cullmann notes, the Holy Spirit is "nothing else than the anticipation of the end of the present." [37]

Without the gift of the Holy Spirit, there is no eschatological sensibility, no real anticipation of the end. The two are inseparable, in literature or in life.

This again is part of what is missing from Steinbeck's parable of the cave. The reader senses intuitively, from what he knows of such fellows, that the prophetic figure who let himself down the cliff to paint the exhortation of repentance there must have known something of the reign of the Spirit. The chances are he was a member of some pneumatic sect—one of those splinter groups in American Protestantism that Henry Pitt Van Dusen said a few years ago Paul and Peter would belong to if they were alive today. But the other characters—the suave and the glamorous and the clever—because they are so completely in the flesh and not in the spirit, appear pitifully and ridiculously small and petty and trifling.

[37] *Christ and Time,* p. 72.

Nor does Graham Greene, whose play we have examined in this chapter, have much to say about the Holy Spirit, despite the fact that one of the perennial subjects of his serious novels is the theme of sanctification. It seems somewhat ironic that he should neglect the action of the *Spiritus Sanctus* in the process of sanctification. The special twist he gives to the doctrine of sainthood is that his saints are all unlikely candidates for the honor—"picaresque saints," to use R. W. B. Lewis' term for them. It is a splendid Reformation emphasis on the unmerited and unmeritable grace of God. But, unfortunately, the spirit that sanctifies Greene's whiskey priests is more the wind that "bloweth where it listeth" than the Spirit who made himself known in visible signs and in power at Pentecost. It is a kind of whimsical sainthood that is worked out in isolation, at the discretion of the author, in contrast with the sanctification of the early Christians, which was experienced only in the sanctified community that exercised controlling and disciplinary superintendence over its members.

Not even Charles Williams has much to say about the Holy Spirit. It is true that there is something of a sense of community and of sainthood in his novels, but there is little explicit reference to the Spirit who makes both these things possible. This, despite the fact that Williams also wrote a theological book on the Holy Spirit and the Church entitled *The Descent of the Dove*. In his novels he exhibited that reticence about pneumatology that is apparently characteristic of theologians in the established churches.

It is all part of the pattern, whether we are speaking of Last Things, hell, resurrection, or the Holy Spirit. The concerns of the poet or the novelist or the playwright are generally with matters of this life. Death and what lies beyond death are therefore meaningful only as they relate to and inform this mortal existence, only as they are obliquely reflected in the living of these days. The view of time under which most art is produced is the same view under which poetry and drama in the Western world had their start in ancient Greece, and its highest hope for that art is that it will represent life so adequately as to be able, in its standing longer than life, to give it some minor perpetuity. The idea of a Spirit whose coming signals the beginning of the end and whose presence thrusts men into such a state of excitation that they no longer desire monuments and memorials of this life is basically alien to the very production of art. Therefore we are perhaps expecting too much if we expect literature to be thoroughly Christian in this matter of the doctrine of Last Things, for such literature would probably be an anomaly altogether. There simply is little place for an ultimate kind of art in the Pentecostal experience; the one would be static and the other is dynamic. If there is something wistful and plaintive about Steinbeck's *The Wayward Bus,* there is the same quality about Dante's *Commedia.*

8

"The Only Way to Be Cleansed"

I HAVE JUST REREAD T. S. ELIOT'S "THE COCKTAIL PARTY." IT IS REALLY a very remarkable play. Like most of Eliot's works, it is even more rewarding on the second reading than on the first, and more on the third than on the second. One thing I have noticed especially is the way the sense of comedy seems to diminish at each new reading. The wittiness doesn't; it continues to hone itself on the rough areas of the reader's understanding until it becomes cutting sharp. But the comedy just seems to evaporate, and you wonder if it was ever really there at all except in your imagination.

The fact is, *The Cocktail Party* is a comedy only in the sense that Dante's *Commedia* is: that it ends in hope and not in utter despair.

No other poet has influenced Eliot so much as the famous Tuscan. In his essay on "Dante," the St. Louis-born poet placed him even beyond the excellency of Shakespeare, saying that, whereas Shakespeare gives "the greatest width of human passion," Dante provides "the greatest altitude and greatest depth." [1] When in "Ash-Wednesday" Eliot wished to represent the "deeper degrees of degradation and higher degrees of exaltation" in the human soul, he turned to Dante: the second stanza of part two echoes the *Divina Commedia* in almost every line. In other words, Eliot is not a great originating poet. It is perhaps a corollary of his view of "the dissociation of sensibility" that

[1] In *Selected Essays*, p. 265.

the modern author most truly represents his time as he reflects its essential fragmentedness in his macaronic borrowings from all the poets who have helped to shape our culture. From the first, he has been a rewriter, a reviser, a craftsman—skillful, consummately expert in his craft, but nevertheless a craftsman.

I do not make this observation in order to belittle what F. O. Matthiessen has called "the achievement of T. S. Eliot"—it is indeed an achievement, and it has pretty much carried the field in modern poetry. I offer it merely as an introduction to the fact that neither is *The Cocktail Party,* any more than "Ash-Wednesday," a truly original work. It is instead a redaction for our times of Dante's *Commedia,* with an *Inferno,* a *Purgatorio,* and at least hints of a *Paradiso,* of its own.

The topography, however, is considerably changed. In Eliot, everything is an extended flatland and no one ever really gets out of hell, even if he is hopefully on his way to paradise. Eliot has never stopped writing about wastelands and hollow men—these are his perpetual theme. And this is the significance of his rewriting of Dante. There is no hell of concentric circles leading inward and downward (the gyre of unity) to the monster who champs sinners in his teeth. Here hell is a diffusion, a centrifugal force that disperses men's powers and affections and isolates them from one another.

Of the two major themes of *The Cocktail Party*—we shall look at the second a little later—the one that is articulated most fully is the inability of men to communicate with one another in a meaningful way. In Act I, the Unidentified Guest gives the clue to Edward when he says,

> Ah, but we die to each other daily.
> What we know of other people
> Is only our memory of the moments
> During which we knew them. And they have
> changed since then.
> To pretend that they and we are the same
> Is a useful and convenient social convention
> Which must sometimes be broken. We must
> also remember
> That at every meeting we are meeting a stranger.[2]

[2] From *The Complete Poems and Plays,* p. 329. Used by permission of Harcourt, Brace & World and Faber & Faber Ltd.

Celia, the saint of the play, confesses too that

> everyone's alone—or so it seems to me.
> They make noises, and think they are talking to each other;
> They make faces, and think they understand each other.
> And I'm sure that they don't.[3]

Reilly, the psychiatrist who appeared at the first party as the Unidentified Guest, answers Celia's observation with the statement that some people achieve "a good life"—though he hedges at calling it the *best* life—by becoming tolerant of their situation:

> They do not repine;
> Are contented with the morning that separates
> And with the evening that brings together
> For casual talk before the fire
> Two people who know they do not understand each other,
> Breeding children whom they do not understand
> And who will never understand them.[4]

It is the perception of this dreadful state of being incommunicado, of being utterly and finally "out of touch," that prompts Edward to say that hell is oneself. If I may repeat what I said in a previous chapter, these words are a welcome correction of Sartre's oft-reiterated line, "Hell is—other people." Hell is not really other people at all. Hell is being alone, being away, being out of touch. It is the complete sterility of isolation. It is the situation of Quant and Malin, in W. H. Auden's *The Age of Anxiety,* who, having spent the evening together, exchange addresses, promise to look each other up sometime, part, and immediately forget each other's existence. It is what Bernanos' honest curé discovers to the Countess: "Hell is not to love any more, madame. Not to love any more!" [5]

As I have also observed in an earlier chapter, the theme of isolation is one of the most dominant motifs in modern literature. Scott says that it, too, like the idea of hell, has attained to the stature of the

[3] *Ibid.,* p. 360.

[4] *Ibid.,* p. 364.

[5] Georges Bernanos, *The Diary of a Country Priest,* tr. Pamela Morris (New York: Image Books, 1960), p. 127.

mythological. And it is worthy of note how frequently the two myths are related, or even equated. Hell is to be alone, not to understand or be understood, not to love or be loved.

But I have said that there is a second theme in *The Cocktail Party,* and now I must refer to that. It is the theme of atonement—of reconciliation and reunion. It is introduced by Celia. She confesses to Reilly that she is troubled by a sense of sin. It is not a matter of mere morality. She has never felt the sense of sin in connection with anything she has done; and, besides, she was raised to disbelieve in sin. It is instead a feeling of some innate offense, of being guilty for part of the fragmentedness of human relationships. As she explains it in her own words,

> It's not the feeling of anything I've ever *done,*
> Which I might get away from, or of anything in me
> I could get rid of—but of emptiness, of failure
> Towards someone, or something, outside of myself;
> And I feel I must . . . *atone*—is that the word?[6]

It *is* the word, and the second half of the play hinges on it. Reilly sends her to "the sanatorium"—one of the religious orders—and she becomes a missionary nun, working out her salvation among heathen tribes on the Eastern island of Kinkanja. Two years later, word is brought back to her friends—at another cocktail party, appropriately—that she was killed while tending to the ill during a native uprising—apparently "crucified very near an ant-hill."

There are the two controlling symbols set side by side: the anthill, with its superorganization, its detailed efficiency, and its impersonality, and the cross, with its starkness, its offense to the rational world, and its extreme personality. The one for the other. And, miraculously, the news of Celia's death seems to produce a tonic effect on the people at the cocktail party. For the moment, at least, they seem to understand one another better than ever before.

The frequency with which the theme of isolation is repeated in modern literature has been commented upon. Now it is time to note also the frequency with which the theme of atonement appears. In various guises—as redemption, purgation, renewal, restoration, re-

[6] P. 362.

union, and so on—it too, in terms of the number of times it is to be found in contemporary writing, reaches near-mythological proportions.

Consider, for example, the fiction of Kafka. He has written more hauntingly about the isolated consciousness of modern man than perhaps any other author. "Kafkaesque" has entered the language as an adjective to denote strangeness, aloneness, insularity, lack of communication. His story of Gregor Samsa, who becomes an insect and is utterly severed from human relationships, is the classic epitome of the isolation theme. And yet one comes across such a statement as this in a discussion of his novel *The Trial:* "Notwithstanding its unremitting satire on bureaucracy and its reduction to absurdity of the pretentions [*sic*] to justice of various courts and institutions, *The Trial* remains primarily [!] a courageous and harrowing search for a just Redeemer, however far he may be removed from the world of history." [7] This is a valuable key to understanding Kafka's novels. They are not mere accounts of passivity. They are narratives of man's relentless searching for an exodus, for a way out. If Joseph K. accepts death "like a dog" at the end of *The Trial,* it only emphasizes the double frustration of his fruitless search for acquittal.

Kafka's stories express a universal situation. As J. Hillis Miller, Jr., has written, "Each of us has taken a wrong turning, and we wander in endless aberration: 'Every person is lost in himself beyond hope of rescue.' The only difference in Kafka's case is that he knows he is lost, and this is his chance. The discovery of alienation is, perhaps, the only remaining possibility of salvation." [8] This, in the writer Miller considers "the most representative figure in twentieth-century literature."

There are several patterns which the search for atonement or redemption may take. Man may become aware of the malaise in which he lives, and, despairing of complete salvation, accept some token redemption, such as the life of honesty or the life of aesthetics. This pattern is frequently employed by Sartre and Camus and other existentialists. Sometimes the variation is introduced wherein the character finds

[7] William Mueller, *The Prophetic Voice in Modern Fiction* (New York: Association Press, 1959), p. 85.

[8] "Franz Kafka and the Metaphysics of Alienation," in *The Tragic Vision and the Christian Faith,* ed. Nathan Scott, Jr. (New York: Association Press, 1957), p. 286.

purgation and quasi redemption through the crucible of violence, as in Hemingway and Mailer and Spillane. Then there is the pattern of the "religious" man who finds redemption by coming to terms with his own faith, as in the case of several of Greene's characters, of the Savage in Huxley's *Brave New World,* and of Don Wanderhope in Peter de Vries' *The Blood of the Lamb.* And finally there is the pattern of the man who is so overwhelmed by his situation that he can only look for salvation by *escape.* George Kernodle calls this "the most frequent theme in realistic modern drama," [9] and it is also the theme of hundreds of short stories and novels written each year. Often the only conceivable escape is death, so that the character ends by taking his own life in some way, as Willy Loman does in *Death of a Salesman.* There are other patterns, of course, but these are the main ones. In combination or in variation they seem to afford an astonishingly wide range for the imaginative writer. The significant thing is that they are all arrangements of a single theme: man's essential need of redemption.

In a line from Greek drama to Shakespeare to contemporary plays and novels, the idea of catharsis, or purification, has been traditionally associated with a single phenomenon—extreme violence. Oedipus, Macbeth, Willy Stark—it is the same in every age. The price of purgation is always suffering and bloodshed and death. This is the great truth of the Freudian theory of the death instinct as it is elaborated in Karl Menninger's fascinating study *Man Against Himself.* There is in every man a catabolism of the personality as well as an anabolism, a tendency to self-destruction as well as to self-preservation. It is related to his subconscious need to expiate for his sin. In most persons, the life instinct is stronger than the death instinct, and they manage to get through life on partial expiations; in others, the death instinct predominates, and eventually they take their own lives in the attempt to make a complete and final payment. It is the great fact of life. Man must have atonement in order to live. If necessary, he must even die in order to have it.

[9] "Patterns of Belief in Contemporary Drama," in *Spiritual Problems in Contemporary Literature,* ed. Stanley R. Hopper (New York: Harper & Row, 1957), p. 188.

This should say something about the apparent burgeoning of violence in contetmporary writing. I say "apparent" because few modern works really compare with the Elizabethan stage in sheer brutality and goriness. But it is significant enough to have drawn considerable critical attention, and even to have produced one full-length study, by W. M. Frohock, entitled *The Novel of Violence in America.*

Consider the violence in our major poets. Eliot has Apeneck Sweeney conned and clubbed like Agamemnon, then rolled for his money. Edwin Arlington Robinson's Richard Cory,

> one calm summer night,
> went home and put a bullet through his head.[10]

Randall Jarrell's "The Death of the Ball Turret Gunner" concludes with the line,

> When I died they washed me out of the turret
> with a hose.[11]

And who can forget the pain and suffering and death in the poetry of Robinson Jeffers, especially in the tortured tone of "Hurt Hawks" and "Roan Stallion" and "Original Sin"? The last ends with a sort of creedal statement:

> As for me, I would rather
> Be a worm in a wild apple than a son of man.
> But we are what we are, and we might remember
> Not to hate any person, for all are vicious;
> And not to be astonished at any evil, all are deserved;
> And not fear death; it is the only way to be cleansed.[12]

As for the theater, there is still considerable death and murder in drama, though perhaps with more of the latter merely reported on stage than was the case in Shakespeare's time. Two old themes that have been replayed in recent years are the suffering of Job, in Mac-

[10] "Richard Cory," from *The Children of the Night* (New York: Charles Scribner's Sons, 1897).

[11] From *Selected Poems* (New York: Alfred A. Knopf, 1955).

[12] From *The Double Axe and Other Poems,* by Robinson Jeffers. Copyright 1948 by Robinson Jeffers. Reprinted by permission of Random House, Inc.

Leish's *J.B.*, and the slaying of Becket, in Eliot's *Murder in the Cathedral.*

In MacLeish's play Nickles sums up before Mr. Zuss the items that have been reported at various times before the audience: one daughter raped and murdered; another killed by the falling of a building; a son lost in the war; and two other children destroyed in an automobile accident.

J.B. is an interesting experiment, but amounts to a diminution of the exalted power of the King James Version of Job. How superior the older rendering of the antique story is to any modern reconstruction was demonstrated by Orlin Corey's production of *The Book of Job,* which, after a run of several years in an amphitheater in the Kentucky mountains, an appearance at the Brussels' World Fair, and a tour of Canada, played the 1961-62 season off Broadway. Corey himself edited the script, using only the lines from the K.J.V. The costumes *and the make-up* consisted entirely of brightly colored mosaics, giving a sort of cathedral effect to the characters, who were playing against a plain black backdrop. The majesty of story and language linger far longer in the mind from this play than from MacLeish's, which depended a great deal on staging for effect and failed to achieve a truly cumulative effect on the audience.

The intensity of Eliot's *Murder* increases until it explodes naturally in the stabbing of Becket at the end, the death itself dissipating the passions that have been so carefully and steadily built up. It is a masterful piece of craftsmanship. There are few passages in all modern writing so fine as that luridly sensuous catalogue by the Chorus in Part II beginning, "I have smelt them, the death-bringers," and ending with the plea of the women of Canterbury for forgiveness. It is part of the air of the play, part of its essential atmosphere, part of its ever deepening unity. It is basic to the action. In fact, I dare to say that it makes the play and that without it the play would descend an entire measure in its theatrical power.

Turning to the novel, we might adduce any number of instances of the wholesale horror that so dominates the contemporary scene as to make novels without violence seem unrealistically prim and anemic. By quoting from Frank Norris, Theodore Dreiser, John Dos Passos, Erskine Caldwell, Robert Penn Warren, Ernest Hemingway, John

O'Hara, and William Faulkner, to name but a few writers on the American list, we could produce a veritable anatomy of brutality.

In Caldwell's *Trouble in July,* for example, a Negro girl is stripped and burned in turpentine by a lynch mob looking for the rapist of a white girl, and the white girl, when it is learned that she has not been raped at all, is stoned by the vicious mob for having taken them in.

Steinbeck's *Of Mice and Men* depicts an idiot of enormous strength who squeezes mice and dogs and people to death with his bare hands, and who, in an act of mercy, is shot by his friend before a lynch mob can get to him. *Cannery Row* is full of murder and mayhem, and contains an especially brutal scene in which a participant in a fruit pickers' strike pummels the face of a teen-age boy into a bloody, indecipherable mess. *Grapes of Wrath,* the epic of the Okies, likewise contains its share of crimson scenes, including one about strikebreaking in which men's faces and skulls are slashed and crushed by pick handles.

Hemingway's *To Have and Have Not,* in many ways his most unsatisfactory book, has barely begun when we are treated to an old-fashioned, gangland-style machine-gun slaying in which several persons are killed and one gets the whole side of his head blown off. It ends with Harry Morgan's gunning down a boatload of criminals, getting himself shot in the stomach, and drifting into port, hanging onto life by a thread. The author's short stories and other novels are perhaps better known, and they too are full of violence, from the jackknife Caesarean and the Indian's suicide of "Indian Camp" to the broken leg and death of Robert Jordan in *For Whom the Bell Tolls.* And, of course, there is the theater of violence, the bullring. In *Death in the Afternoon,* his great documentary about bullfighting, Hemingway wrote:

> The only place where you could see life and death, *i.e.,* violent death now that the wars were over, was in the bull ring and I wanted very much to go to Spain where I could study it. I was trying to learn to write, commencing with the simplest things, and one of the simplest things of all and the most fundamental is violent death. It has none of the complications of death by disease, or so-called natural death, or the death of a friend or some one you have loved or have hated.[13]

[13] (New York: Charles Scribner's Sons, 1932), p. 2.

Is it necessary to add the comment that Hemingway's own suicide is partially an extension of this paragraph?

And Faulkner must be mentioned, too. His southern landscape, so odoriferous with the perfume of honeysuckle and wisteria, is also redolent of death. As Aunt Jenny says of the name Sartoris in the sonorous passage that concludes the novel by that title, "there is death in the sound of it, and a glamorous fatality, like silver pennons downrushing at sunset, or a dying fall of horns along the road to Roncevaux." In the story, death—violent death—has claimed the noblest son, John, then the patriarch, Bayard, and finally the remaining scion, Bayard, Jr. Each died in a machine traveling at high speed —the old man in an automobile and the two sons in airplanes.

But it is *Sanctuary,* with its murder of an idiot, its corncob rape, its speakeasy funeral, its burning of one man and hanging of another, that bids to be Faulkner's most violent novel. There death is pitched to the level and tempo of a grotesquerie.

Frohock has observed, with proper justification, that at moments there is an absurd disproportion between the stature of Faulkner's characters and the overwhelming horror of the things that happen to them. After examining in some detail *The Sound and the Fury, Sanctuary,* and *Light in August,* he concludes that Faulkner's tragic vision, his fundamental way of seeing people, is more Euripidean than Sophoclean—that is, his characters are more acted upon than acting.

Purely for the sake of illustrating how this penchant for brutality filters down to the trade writers, I mention also the exploitation of the taste for violence to be found among writers in the class of John Faulkner, Dashiell Hammett, and Mickey Spillane. Spillane's Mike Hammer seems to approach the mauling of punks with a grim joy that is not a hair removed from plain sadism. Here is an instance picked at random from a book chosen the same way:

> I clamped down and kicked back. The table went sailing as my feet caught it. I got the knife hand and pulled down hard, and the high yellow landed in a heap on top of me. Just in time I saw the foot coming and pulled my head aside. The coal black missed by inches. I didn't. I let go the knife hand and grabbed the leg. The next moment I was fighting for my life under two sweating Negroes.
>
> But not for long. The knife came out again and this time I got the hand

in a wristlock and twisted. The tendons stretched, and the bones snapped sickeningly. The high yellow let out a scream and dropped the knife. I was on my feet in a flash. The big black buck was up and came charging into me, his head down.

There was no sense to busting my hand on his skull, so I lashed out with my foot and the toe of my shoe caught the guy right in the face. He toppled over sideways, still running, and collapsed against the wall. His lower teeth were protruding through his lip. Two of his incisors were lying beside his nose, plastered there with blood.

The high yellow was holding his broken wrist in one hand, trying to get to his feet. I helped him. My hand hooked in his collar and dragged him up. I took the side of my free hand and smashed it across his nose. The bone shattered and blood poured out. That guy probably was a lady killer in Harlem, but them days were gone forever. He let out a little moan and slumped to the floor. I let him drop.[14]

Perhaps it is unnecessary to quote such material in order to make the point; but the fact remains that the sense of violence is endemic in the whole of modern literature, in the great and the near great, and in the mere tradesmen as well.

In this, as in everything related to the producing of art, we are still debtors to the Greeks, for whom violence was the general expression of the rupture between man and nature. The line still holds, from Sophocles to Shakespeare to Robert Penn Warren: violence bespeaks "the tragic sense of life." Nor has the purpose of introducing violence changed since ancient times. Consciously or unconsciously—how many writers read Aristotle nowadays?—it is to arouse the emotions of pity and fear and to produce a catharsis in the soul of the reader.

Now, in relation to our examination of literature from the Christian perspective, the time has come to say that this fundamental premise of tragic literature is poles apart from the Christian view. How utterly true this is has been convincingly shown by Edmond Cherbonnier in his essay on "Biblical Faith and the Idea of Tragedy." The tragic view, as he observes, springs out of the thesis that "the truth is the whole."

From this quite plausible axiom [he says], the entire theory of tragedy logically evolves. It implies, first, that an adequate philosophy of life must

[14] Mickey Spillane, *I, the Jury* (New York: E. P. Dutton, 1948), ch. 6.

> not only include everything, but must also *affirm* everything. It must not suppress any aspect of reality simply because some particular moral code finds it offensive or ignoble; it must not disparage any human emotion or action simply because some find it unpleasant or shocking. Conversely, it must not prefer other aspects of life simply because they are accounted "beautiful" or "good." This would unduly elevate a mere part at the expense of the whole. In short, if the truth is the whole, then reality is neutral, not partisan. It knows no good or evil, for the "good" is always partisan.[15]

The Christian view, on the other hand, maintains no such neutrality. It holds that God is the good, and that there are therefore certain acts that are good and others that are evil because of their relationship to him, *sub specie aeternitatis*. It speaks of Providence instead of fate, and implies a certain freedom of choice for the man in God's world—he is not under the constraint of an unbending necessity.

Faulkner is an interesting case in point of a writer who is overcome by the confusion born of writing, out of a Christian heritage, of an essentially Hellenistic world. The confusion accounts for his mellow fatalism, for the mixture of Greek and Christian elements in such a passage as this:

> The music went on in the dusk softly; the dusk was peopled with ghosts of glamorous and old disastrous things. And if they were just glamorous enough, there was sure to be a Sartoris in them, and then they were sure to be disastrous. Pawns. But the Player, and the game He plays. . . . He must have a name for His pawns, though. But perhaps Sartoris is the game itself—a game outmoded and played with pawns shaped too late and to an old dead pattern, and of which the Player Himself is a little wearied.[16]

The fundamental Christian note that is missing from the writings of Faulkner and other authors formed by the double tradition of Christianity and Hellenism is that of great *joy*. It is a note that cannot be sounded from within the tragic view of life. It is possible only in a universe that does distinguish between good and evil, that does give preference to the good, and that anticipates both a present and a consummate triumph of the good over the evil.

This anticipation is especially important in determining the extent

[15] In Scott, ed., *The Tragic Vision and the Christian Faith,* p. 26.
[16] *Sartoris,* p. 380.

of the redemptive experience. For the Christian, atonement—felt as forgiveness, cleansing, and restoration—may be received as complete; for the Greek, or gnostic, never as more than partial. It is for this reason that no genuinely Christian tragedy can possibly exist. As Karl Jaspers has said, "Christian salvation opposes tragic knowledge. . . . What is essential to the Christian cannot even emerge in tragedy. . . . Every one of man's basic experiences ceases to be tragic in a Christian context." [17] Even violence itself is deprived of its horror when set within the Christian world view. Its existence is not denied, but its ultimate power over the souls of men is; for, in the Christian view, men are not victims but conquerors.

Of course there are places in contemporary literature where a Christian view of atonement does prevail, and it would be unfair to take no note of them. W. H. Auden, for example, concludes his long poem *The Age of Anxiety* with the reflection that, even as our minds are insisting on their own disorder as their punishment for sin, God is faithful.

> In our anguish we struggle
> To elude Him, to lie to Him, yet His love observes
> His appalling promise.[18]

And something like this may be found also in several of Greene's novels and in Eliot's Christian poems and plays.

And in the novels of Charles Williams. Williams' *Descent into Hell* is pre-eminently concerned with atonement, and especially with the theme of vicarious atonement. It really deserves to be treated here at some length. It is a most remarkable novel, in which the customary demarcations between the living and the dead, the present and the past, the actual and the mythological, are removed, or have at least become fluid, so that the novelist passes from one to the other and back again with an ease that leaves the reader in the grip of a delightful uncanniness.

The action takes place on Battle Hill, an exclusive new subdivision

[17] *Tragedy Is Not Enough*, tr. H. A. T. Reiche, H. T. Moore, K. W. Deutsch (Boston: Beacon Press, 1952), pp. 39-40.

[18] P. 137.

laid out on a historical site thirty miles north of London. But there are times when one is quite sure it must be the one and only hill called Golgotha, the place of the skull. And there are still other times when it seems to be Dante's Mount of Purgation. One thing is certain: It is a hill of battle, of a struggle more deeply knit in the nature of man than topographical facts can suggest; and therefore it is a hill of life and death.

A play is to be given on Battle Hill, written by one Peter Stanhope, a poet in residence there, and enacted by other persons from the Hill. The play is a pastoral, a sort of anachronism for present-day Battle Hill, and most of the cast and the director, an efficient manager named Mrs. Parry, are insensitive to its poetry, its music, and its meaning. But Stanhope is a noted figure in the literary world, and that provides all the motive they require for producing his play. The one person who seems to "feel" Stanhope's poetry is a rather quiet and withdrawn young woman named Pauline Anstruther, who lives on the Hill with her grandmother. As it turns out, she has good reason to appear withdrawn. For years she has been experiencing a psychological phenomenon known by the German term *Doppelgänger*—visitations from her own double. Whether the manifestations are psychogenic or not is a question Williams does not raise; he accepts as important the fact that she does meet her double and is terrified each time it happens. The image has never actually touched her, though it has often seemed to hurry toward her just as she is entering a gate or a doorway. She lives under the constant dread that someday it will overtake her and she will die. Therefore she is reluctant to remain out of doors beyond the twilight hour, and lives an almost cloistered existence with her aged grandmother.

One day Pauline feels intimate enough with Stanhope to confess her terror to him, and she rehearses the whole matter as fully as she can. He proves a sympathetic confidant, and more: he offers to bear her burden for her. He assures her that it may be done and expresses surprise that she has not asked a friend before to carry her fears for her. She is to go her way home in utmost confidence that when she sees the apparation it is he who will fear; she, on the contrary, is to find great exhilaration in the experience.

The actual transference of the fear Williams describes in a chapter entitled "The Doctrine of Substituted Love." Stanhope, still sitting alone in his chair at the rehearsal, conjures up a vision of Pauline's likeness as it approaches her, and simulates the experience of fear and dread. It is not ultimate fear, for he is not really she—but that is the beauty of the arrangement. Says Williams, "The burden was inevitably lighter for him than for her, for the rage of a personal resentment was lacking. He endured her sensitiveness, but not her sin; the substitution there, if indeed there is a substitution, is hidden in the central mystery of Christendom which Christendom itself has never understood, nor can." [19] Pauline, meanwhile, is amazed at the simple joy with which she traverses the distance home; she seems completely incapable of distress, and all nature appears graced with new beauty to her eyes. Excitedly, that evening, she phones Stanhope: the double has not appeared to her. Nor does it ever again. Stanhope has "picked up her parcel." Her life begins to blossom. She becomes less and less withdrawn, even a little extroverted. Her friends note the great change that has come over her, as if she has tapped some new reservoir of assurance and hope.

But the hill that is life to some is death to others. This hill has had long associations with death. The whole eminence of ground seems to lie "like a cape, a rounded headland of earth, thrust into an ocean of death." One victim of the Hill was a workman who had been there during the construction of new homes. He was an alcoholic, and had long been unable to maintain steady employment. Life had become an intolerable necessity, and he could not, the night after he had been fired from his job on the Hill, go home to face a scolding from his wife. Under the globular moon, he slipped back among the skeletons of the houses to hang himself. He found a rope and carried it softly along to a ladder going up the frame of an unfinished house. Williams' description is exquisite:

> The moonlight gently faded, the white rungs grew shadowy; a cloud passed over the sky, and all was obscured. The heavens were kind, and the moon did not, like the sun, wait for a divine sacrifice in order to be darkened. A man served it as well. He rose, and slipped to the foot of his ladder. He went

[19] *Descent into Hell* (New York: Farrar, Straus & Company, 1950), p. 101. Used by permission of Farrar, Straus & Company, Faber & Faber Ltd., and David Higham Associates.

softly up, as the Jesuit priest had gone up his those centuries earlier paying for a loftier cause by a longer catastrophe. He went up as if he mounted on the bones of his body built so carefully for this; he clambered through his skeleton to the place of his skull, and receded, as if almost in a corporal ingression, to the place of propinquent death. He went up his skeleton, past the skeleton frames of the ground floor, of the first floor. At the second the poles of the scaffold stretched upward into the sky. The roof was not on, nor his life built up.[20]

This perichoresis, the mutual indwelling and interpenetration of character, is part of the haunting depth of Williams' novel. The old man is not only himself; he is also Pauline Anstruther's ancestor who died on that very hill as a martyr centuries ago; and he is also the weight-bowed Son of God, mounting the scaffold at Calvary. There is a coinherence involved, a union of humanity more metaphysical, and therefore more complete, than anything John Donne ever dreamed of with his "No man is an islande." It is not traceable always, on every page, for such telescoped narration is impossible to sustain; but one traces the histories of the various characters along lineal paths, and then, suddenly, now and again, the coinherence appears at the intersections where their paths cross.

Another instance of it occurs on the night of old Mrs. Anstruther's death. She has an unshakable presentiment that someone is in need. She calls Pauline, and even though it is in the middle of the night, bids her go to the place on the Hill where she feels that the person is. Pauline goes, and encounters there the ghost of the alcoholic carpenter who committed suicide a few years earlier. He has been restless on the Hill and has decided to return to London after all, to the room where he avoided unpleasantness on that earlier night. He inquires the way to London. Pauline offers him money for train fare, because it is a thirty-mile trip; but he refuses, saying it is just a step, and strides away in the direction she has pointed out. As she watches him go, he stops, and seems to be enduring some terrible agony. She runs to him, and as she runs she hears the faint sound of a trumpet in the distance, "the echo of the trumpet of that day's rehearsal done or of the next day's performance not yet begun, or of a siren that called for the raising or lowering of a bridge." The sound is transmuted into "sight or

[20] *Ibid.*, p. 29.

the fear of sight." She feels a strange terror—as if her whole escape from the *Doppelgänger* has been a trick, an elaborate jest played upon her in order to shut her more finally in a trap of some kind. Even her grandmother seems to be "part of its infinitely complicated steel mechanism, which now shut her in, and was going off." In a moment she would see her twin shape in the road before her. But suddenly, a few yards from the man, she stops and becomes alert. "The trap, if there had been a trap, had opened, and she had come out beyond it. But there was another trap, and this man was in it." He cries aloud, "Lord God!" She asks, "Can I help you?" He only says, "Lord God, I cannot bear the fear of the fire." Suddenly she realizes—it is her ancestor! He is afraid, afraid of the fire. And she knows then what she must do.

> She knew what she must do. But she felt, as she stood, that she could no more do it than he. She could never bear that fear. The knowledge of being burnt alive, of the flames, of the faces, of the prolongation of pain. She knew what she must do. She opened her mouth and could not speak. In front of her, alone in his foul Marian prison, unaware of the secret means the Lord he worshipped was working swiftly for his peace, believing and unbelieving, her ancestor stood centuries off in his spiritual desolation and preluding agony of sweat. He could not see beyond the years the child of his house who strove with herself behind and before him.[21]

The morning is coming. She speaks: "Give it to me, John Struther." He stretches forth his arms again and calls, "Lord, Lord!" They are words of devotion and adoration; they accept and give thanks. Pauline hears the voice, trembling. He falls on his knees and in a roar of triumph cries out, "I have seen the salvation of my God." She smells the burning wood. She hears the voice once more: "I have seen the salvation of my God." The sky over her is red with the glow of the fire. The smell of the smoke enters her nostrils. She inhales, exhales—and it passes.

Later, at her grandmother's funeral, Pauline is struck by the biblical reference to "baptism for the dead." "Why are they then baptized for the dead?"

[21] *Ibid.*, p. 169.

> There, rooted in the heart of the Church at its freshest, was the same strong thrust of interchange. Bear for others; be baptized for others; and, rising as her new vision of the world had done once and again, an even more fiery mystery of exchange rolled through her horizons, turning and glancing on her like the eyed and winged wheels of the prophet. The central mystery of Christendom, the terrible fundamental substitution on which so much learning had been spent and about which so much blood had been shed, showed not as a miraculous exception, but as the root of a universal rule . . . "behold, I show you a mystery," as supernatural as that Sacrifice, as natural as carrying a bag. She flexed her fingers by her side as if she thought of picking one up.[22]

Here, denuded of its shell, is the core of the book: the *descensus ad inferos,* the descent into hell, as a substitutionary measure for the salvation of men's souls, finding its archetype in the Savior's "harrowing of hell" but made real in the participation in it of all the men and women of every age who are ready to bear one another's burdens. It is a supreme answer, a Christian answer, to the nihilism that is so prevalent in the contemporary world where men are, in the words of another author, "innumerable glittering quicksilver globules of individual selves, running hither and thither at random, coalescing, and parting asunder without unity, coherence, or consistency."[23] It may well indeed be spoken of as the central mystery of Christendom. Williams' novel is a unique and forceful presentation of the Christian doctrine of cohesion, of community, of the *communio sanctorum.* What Christ has provided is the necessary prototype, the great Sacrifice; what men must do is to emulate that act of bearing others' burdens. It is "picking up someone else's parcel and bearing it" that saves us all in the end.

But again we must emphasize the fact that Williams is something of a rarity on the literary scene and that he has never been a really popular novelist. A survey of all the writing of our time would probably indicate that few authors write even with the presuppositions behind Williams' stories and that fewer still attempt so courageously to put those presuppositions into writing.

Even in those places where the Incarnation is represented, by sym-

[22] *Ibid.,* pp. 188-89.

[23] From Jean Paul Richter's "Dream of a World Without God," quoted in Helmut Thielicke, *Nihilism,* tr. John Doberstein (New York: Harper & Row, 1961), p. 132.

bol or by direct narrative, nothing is usually made of the atoning work of Christ. Melville's Billy Budd, for example, is undoubtedly a Christ figure. He is like Christ in his perfection, in his innocence, and, at the last, in his death on the mast. Even his "God bless Captain Vere" is a kind of "Father, forgive them" spoken in his dying moments. But, as Baird says, "the element of Christ in the symbol represents Christ the innocent among men, not the suffering Christ of the cross. The agony in Gethsemane, the ascent of Calvary, the cries from the cross have no place here." [24] That is, there is no emphasis on the real work of atonement. Even though Billy is morally an avatar of Christ, there is hardly a suggestion that his presence among the crew is to their welfare, or that his death will serve in any way for their redemption. He is like the typical character in twentieth-century fiction who, says Malcolm Cowley in *The Literary Situation,* is usually a victim rather than a hero or a villain.

Of course there have been those in the history of Christian theology —notably Tertullian and Anselm—who have viewed Christ primarily as a victim in the working out of man's atonement. This view is often called the "satisfaction" theory of atonement, because of its emphasis on Christ's death as a payment for man's sin. But Gustaf Aulén, in his little book *Christus Victor,* says the idea that Christ merely offered a ransom for the souls of men is a misrepresentation of what really happened on Calvary. The New Testament, he says, has a much more dramatic view of the passion of Christ, in which Christ is not really victim but Victor, not conquered but Conqueror. He yielded to the cross in order to storm the very gates of hell and lead captive the powers of sin and death. According to this view, which Aulén calls the "classic" Christian view, atonement is continuously the work of God, who in Christ is reconciling the world unto himself, and not discontinuously, as in any view in which Christ offers a sacrifice to him.

According to H. E. W. Turner, Aulén makes the history of the theory of atonement a bit too categorical, and such sharp divisions between holders of the Christ-victim and the Christ-victor theories are actually unjustified.[25] But Aulén has at least performed a much-

[24] *Ishmael,* p. 221.

[25] Cf. H. E. W. Turner, *The Patristic Doctrine of Redemption* (London: A. R. Mowbray, 1952).

needed service to Christian scholarship by pointing out so clearly the various threads of atonement theology through the years and by restoring to pre-eminence the tone of victory and triumph through Christ's work that was surely characteristic of the redemptive thought of the Apostolic Age.

And it seems to me that even the fiction which contains sacrificial Christ figures, such as Melville's *Billy Budd,* Hemingway's *For Whom the Bell Tolls,* and Ralph Leveridge's *Walk on the Water,* is generally inadequate in its view of the Atonement precisely because this sense of truly victorious redemption is missing. What atonement is found, if it is implied or expressed at all, is almost always of the moral or ethical sort, never of the kind that Aulén claims is classical in Christianity. No matter how many men die or how much violence there is, we seem always to be left asking the question posed by Robert Lowell in "The Death of the Sheriff":

> Who'll atone
> For the unsearchable quicksilver heart
> Where spiders stare their eyes out at their own
> Spitting and knotted likeness?[26]

The whole of it is that because we have no effectual sense of the real work of Christ as atonement, we are left waiting for some new revelation, some novel redemption, some sudden innovation in affairs, that will save us. We seem to feel that the extreme violence which we accept as a hallmark of contemporaneity will force some recrudescence of God's self-revelation for our time. As Nathan Scott has said, ours is "an age of vigil."

What Scott goes on to say is that "nowhere has this aspect of our situation been more affectingly dramatized than in Samuel Beckett's remarkable play *Waiting for Godot.*" [27]

Waiting for Godot has already become something of a classic in our time. It is wonderfully expressive of the bleak and painful landscape of the modern soul. In a sense, it is a pantomime of our despair, a two-dimensional, cardboard stage on which is acted out by a couple of shadows named Estragon and Vladimir the quiet despondency of men

[26] From *Lord Weary's Castle* (New York: Harcourt, Brace & World, 1946), p. 66.
[27] *Modern Literature and the Religious Frontier,* p. 84.

who do not believe even in their belief. There is really no action in the play. It is all a matter of waiting. The two tramps are waiting to meet Godot—an obvious diminutive for the word God. He said he would meet them "by the tree," and it is there that they hold their vigil. Each day at nightfall they decide he is not coming that day, and so retire until time to come back the next day. At last, they attempt to hang themselves with the cord that Estragon has used to hold up his trousers; but the cord breaks, and they stand there a moment in silence, Estragon with his trousers festooned around his feet.

> ESTRAGON: You say we have to come back to-morrow?
> VLADIMIR: Yes.
> *Silence.*
> ESTRAGON: Didi.
> VLADIMIR: Yes.
> ESTRAGON: I can't go on like this.
> VLADIMIR: That's what you think.
> ESTRAGON: If we parted? That might be better for us.
> VLADIMIR: We'll hang ourselves to-morrow. (*Pause.*)
> ESTRAGON: And if he comes?
> VLADIMIR: We'll be saved.
> *Vladimir takes off his hat (Lucky's), peers inside it, feels about inside it, shakes it, knocks on the crown, puts it on again.*
> ESTRAGON: Well? Shall we go?
> VLADIMIR: Pull on your trousers.
> ESTRAGON: You want me to pull off my trousers?
> VLADIMIR: Pull ON your trousers.
> ESTRAGON: (*realizing his trousers are down*). True. *He pulls up his trousers.*
> VLADIMIR: Well? Shall we go?
> ESTRAGON: Yes, let's go.
> *They do not move.*[28]

As Scott says, there is "a kind of great and terrible simplicity" about all this. Even the pauses and inactions are pregnant with eloquence. There is unmistakable pathos in every line, every word, every gesture. It is superlative theater, without a doubt.

But it is not superlative Christian doctrine. For all its Christian sym-

[28] *Waiting for Godot* by Samuel Beckett, Translated from the French by the Author, Copyright © 1954 by Grove Press.

bolism (much of it filtered through Freud!) it is hardly responsible as a Christian play. To be sure, it does pose a spiritual problem, and it involves the audience in a negative mystical quality not entirely unlike the "night of the senses" described by St. John of the Cross and other masters of the devotional life. It satisfies the requirements that Tom F. Driver would ask of the Christian play, viz., "that it arrest the attention of the viewer, that it lead him into an area of thought, emotion or other experience which is broadening for him and which has some relevance to the realities that underlie the Christian faith." [29] But in effect it really neglects the fact that the Incarnation has already occurred and that God has already revealed himself there in Jesus Christ. It belongs to the documentation of the absence of God, not of the presence of God. And therefore we can hardly credit it with being more than sub-Christian.

It is the message of the Christian gospel that there is no longer any need of waiting. "Just as a man can have only one father, is born once and dies once, so he can only believe and know one revelation," says Barth. "He who says revelation says—a revelation which is unique, taking place once for all, irrevocable and unrepeatable." [30] It is this once-for-allness that Beckett's play ignores, at least in part, and that most contemporary writing joins it in forgetting. God has acted in Christ for the reconciliation of the world—and yet that reconciliation is but feebly reflected in most of the literature of our day—even in much of that which purports to deal with so-called spiritual problems. The trouble with so much of the best imaginative prose and poetry being written in our time is the same as that which one critic has diagnosed in *Waiting for Godot:* "it does not realize Christ was born. . . . [that] Godot appeared 20 centuries ago in the form of a child." [31]

[29] "The Church, the Theater and the World," *Dialog,* I, no. 4 (Autumn, 1962), 51. Driver continues: "We do not ask that the play convert the viewer, or that it explain the mysteries of the faith or that it prove to him the validity of the doctrines. We ask only that the play provide the occasion for the viewer's entertaining in his mind and in his feelings Christian ways of looking at life."

[30] From Barth's *Offenbarung, Kirche, Theologie,* as quoted by H. R. MacIntosh in *Types of Modern Theology: Schleiermacher to Barth* (New York: Charles Scribner's Sons, 1937), p. 276.

[31] Fred E. Luchs, "Waiting for Godot," *Christianity Today,* IV (June 6, 1960), 8.

9

The "Christian" Artist

THERE IS PLENTY OF EVIDENCE IN CONTEMPORARY LITERATURE OF CHRISTIANITY's having been in the world these twenty centuries. Whether reading Joyce or Faulkner, Pasternak or Salinger, Ionesco or Eliot, one invariably encounters it. As Weidlé observes, art has always maintained certain invisible links with Christianity: though Shakespeare, Goethe, and Pushkin lived in a world no longer dominated by religion, they were still ruled by consciences formed by crypto-religious forces. Even where faith is least in evidence, it is the demonic that has replaced it, reminding us of the finally indissoluble unity of Christianity and culture. Yeats was right when he said that

> Twenty centuries of stony sleep
> Were vexed to nightmare by a rocking cradle.[1]

Evidence, of course, is not all of one sort. There is one kind in which the merest traces of Christianity must serve to represent the faith itself, somewhat as the tracks discovered by Defoe's Robinson Crusoe put him in mind of a second being on his shipwreck island. This kind of

[1] "The Second Coming." Reprinted with permission of the publishers, The Macmillan Company, and the Macmillan Co. of Canada, and Mrs. W. B. Yeats, from *Collected Poems* by W. B. Yeats. Copyright 1924 by The Macmillan Company, renewal 1952 by Bertha Georgie Yeats.

evidence is not necessarily conclusive, for, as Crusoe suspected, even foot-like depressions in the earth may be made by any manner of creature. The second kind of evidence is the *pars pro toto*—a piece or segment gives rise to rather logical suppositions about the whole. This is generally more dependable than the first kind. Suppose that Crusoe had discovered a leg, say from the knee joint down; he not only would have known for certain what made the prints on his island, but would have been able to conjecture, with reasonable certitude, the size and shape of the person to whom the leg belonged. The third kind of evidence may scarcely be called evidence at all, for it is the kind in which the knower has union with the known, as was the case when Crusoe finally came face to face with Friday. Still, it is evidence, to the senses at least, and must be ranked as such. Needless to say, it is by far the most desirable of all evidences, and ordinarily obviates the necessity of the first two kinds. Crusoe, when he had seen Friday, did not require the proof of the tracks, or of the disjointed leg, to recognize him; the presence of Friday himself canceled the need for lesser proofs. By the same token Thomas, when he beheld the risen Christ, was willing to forego an investigation of the nail prints and the riven side, and confessed, "My Lord and my God."

Evidence of Christianity in modern literature is of all three kinds. There are many works, for instance, in which it consists entirely of a few symbols or oblique references—mere scattered tracks that say Christ has walked this way. In others, there is enough of Christ (for he is Christianity!) to suggest something of the totality of his person and of his influence on human life, and to suggest it with some accuracy. And there are a few works of such blended artistry and devotion as probably to cause some readers to meet Christ in all his fullness there, and to kneel with Thomas and say, "My Lord and my God." As Hans Holthusen has said, "Genius and holiness have never been one and the same thing. Genius wants to make beautiful things or to do great deeds. The saint wants neither beauty nor grandeur. His only concern is self-sacrifice, love for God and for his neighbor. *Between these two extremes spreads the landscape of a Christian culture.*" [2]

[2] "What Is Christian in a Christian Literature?" in *Christian Faith and the Contemporary Arts,* ed. Finley Eversole (Nashville: Abingdon Press, 1962), p. 93. (My italics.)

From the Christian viewpoint, that literature is undoubtedly best which presents most fully the spiritual presence of Christ himself. At its purest, this is to waive the requirements of art in favor of doctrine or devotion and to upset traditional critical judgments. It means, for example, that such a poorly crafted work as James Street's *The High Calling,* which in addition to being poorly crafted is crudely sentimental, even bathetic, ranks by "Christian" standards as high as Henry James's *The Golden Bowl* or Proust's *The Remembrance of Things Past.*[3] Who would dare to suggest that Street replace James and Proust on our library shelves? And yet we are bound to admit that there is a certain something—call it spirit, warmth, witness, hope, or whatever —in Street's book that is more suggestive of primitive Christianity than anything either James or Proust ever wrote. It is what Weidlé has called the "mortification of art"—a disinterest in form and a preoccupation with message.

Here is the dilemma which raises again a question we merely touched on earlier. Are Christianity and art really compatible? Is there such a thing as Christian art, or are the very terms themselves finally anomalous and irreconcilable? Even in the highest periods of religious art—Byzantine, Gothic, and Renaissance—was the result really an embodiment of Christ's presence in the world, or was it considerably less Christian than many of us today, preferring tangibility to faith and taste to dynamics, are willing to admit?

Certainly orthodoxy's tendency to be suspicious of all art is understandable. When Barth says that there is a danger of idolatry inherent in any use of images, he is merely reiterating for our day Calvin's emphasis on the contrast between nature and grace. The human mind always tends to be dependent upon imagery for more than the mediation of grace, and the process of purging symbols is necessarily a constant one. We have seen since Old Testament times—since the golden calf of Aaron—the tendency of men to worship what their hands have made, or at least to worship the muse who led in making it. In the end, even the artist who no longer believes in miracle or sacrament sees something magical or sacred about his art and worships that. "Art for

[3] W. H. Auden's Herod, in *For the Time Being,* predicts that the birth of Christ will cause "the daubs of school children [to be] ranked above the greatest masterpieces."

art's sake" is always a deity-substitute. W. H. Auden, Dylan Thomas, and Christopher Fry, to name but three contemporary poets, have experienced the Christian faith in the heart and along the blood, and what they have written is not unchristian—it is God actively probing them, making sacramental their effort to find words for a mystery plainly too deep for human words. But the moment art becomes art for art's sake—even with them—the moment the poet looks at himself writing poetry—God goes, though the vision stays.

There is a kind of art, then, that is merely the cultural survival of religion, and represents the passing of religious enthusiasm. It is the final stage of the movement from religion to religion-with-art to art-as-religion. "In the realm of art," writes James Baird, "something has been going on in the last century which is wholly unlike any other development in the aesthetic history of the Christian era. Artistic expression originating in the Protestant or 'Protestantly' derived mind has been laboring with the construction of symbols to compensate for a lost sacramentalism. In this act, art has become, in the strictest possible sense, religion." [4] While I agree substantially with Baird, I wonder if it is not possible that this phenomenon is much older than the last century. For example, is it not the meaning of Henry Adams' *Mont-Saint-Michel and Chartres* that the grand cathedrals of Europe are the enduring monuments of a religion that, as a religion, is dead? That they are the glass-and-stone wonders that even in their erection began to replace the religion they were intended to represent? Survivals of inspiration, they may have helped also to deplete the inspiration.

Tillich is surely correct in saying that architecture is "the basic artistic expression"; at least it is the most practical one. And it is therefore a good area in which to test the relationship between art and Christianity. Can the puritanical objection to art be pressed where the church building itself is concerned? Probably so, within limits.

Some time ago, I was invited to become the pastor of a little group of Christians who were then meeting in a rented store front on a busy thoroughfare. With a deacon, I visited the little store on a weekday, when it was being used by a small, greasy man as a guitar-teaching

[4] *Ishmael*, p. 58.

studio. I went home and said to my wife, "I don't know whether I can do it or not. The change"—from the college chapel where I had been preacher—"is too great." But reflection shamed me. Christianity had no cathedrals for three hundred years after Christ. It existed in homes and shops and outdwellings and even in caves. It was dynamic, moving where the people were, carrying the work of Christ into their everyday lives. I accepted the call to the little church. A few weeks later, before I had arrived on the scene, the church had outgrown the store building and moved into a schoolhouse. Now that is too small, and we are making plans for erecting a building of our own. We are glad for the conveniences that such a building will bring. And yet we all live a little in dread of such a move, for we sense that we shall inevitably lose something of the feeling we have now for what Bonhoeffer has called "the essential worldliness of Christianity." Fine church buildings, as a rule, preserve little of this basic worldliness, which is the worldliness of the exile, not that of the settled and established citizen.

The same idea recently came home to me again quite forcefully when D. T. Niles was speaking in the stately chapel of Princeton University on the "pilgrim" nature of the Christian life. That magnificent Gothic chapel was doubtless built in a year when costs were considerably lower than at present; but not even this fact could ameliorate the radical incongruity between cathedral-building and the kind of eschatological Christianity Niles was talking about. Significantly, perhaps, the most abominable church architecture of the past four hundred years has generally been that produced by the sectarians, who of all persuasions are invariably the most pneumatic and eschatological in flavor.

And there is a sense in which what is true of architecture is true also of literature. Our "better" writers are, as a rule, most affected by the traditional churches, and it is therefore not surprising that they should be only moderately concerned about the Spirit and the end of all things. They are more concerned with "religion" than with Christ; that is, more with the deposit that Christ and the Church have made in history than with the living Christ and the living Church. Symbolism is more important to them than the life that produces symbolism. They tend to detach themselves from the event in order to write about it. That is why they are poets and novelists and dramatists and not preachers and evangelists. It is a matter of degree of involvement, a matter of perspective. They understand and evaluate from without, like good sociologists; they possess their material and avoid being possessed. Their relationship to the Christian faith is usually only secondary; were it to become primary, they could not endure the detachment necessary to the production of art, but should declare with Paul, "Woe is me if I preach not the Gospel of our Lord Jesus Christ!"

It will surely be objected that Dante and Milton and other great "Christian" poets have served Christ in the highest fashion. Though I tremble to answer, because of the stature of their names, I am bound to say, not the highest fashion of all. My reason for siding with the puritans here is that artistic productions simply are not the chief end of the Christian faith—they are its aids, its guideposts, its auxiliary issues, sometimes only its centrifugal coolings. We must remember the point made by Weidlé in *The Baptism of Art,* that the primitive Church produced no significant art at all, and was in fact not even concerned to produce any; it was interested only in its message, and matters of form and beauty were given no more than secondary or tertiary consideration.

It is primarily as the faith moves out of some period of incandescence that men begin to speak out of it as artists and not as preachers. In the phases of its strongest missionary zeal, the Church has never erected such cathedrals as Adams has described in his classic book, but has been content to live in the field, as it were, where all campaigns are waged. Considering that every stone in those magnificent edifices was hewn and moved and set by human hands—the feat that overwhelmed the imagination of Adams—they were remarkable testimonies of devotion. But they were, at the same time, evidence that the notion of living in the last days, of putting the sickle to the harvest of men because the time is short, had been dissipated.

Similarly, no man existentially concerned with last things, as Dante was morally and artistically concerned with them, would spend his time writing a *Commedia.* The adverb to describe the way the Christian faith seeks communication to men is "eagerly," not "symmetrically" or "tastefully" or "pleasantly" or any other modifier that may apply more appropriately to art. As P. T. Forsyth has said, "We are not set in such a world as this simply to return its note as artists or esthetes, but to act." [5] The question which the Christian must continually ask about specific works of art is whether they are merely returning the world's own note or acting in behalf of the gospel. (And it is a question that applies to sermons as readily as to poems and paintings.)

But so much for the legitimacy of Christianity's suspiciousness of art. There is something to be said, on the other hand, for the usefulness of the artist to the faith. From very early times the Christian church has exhibited a separatist tendency, an inclination to withdraw from the world and exist as a self-sufficient entity. Paul Lehmann has noted an incipient exclusivism even in the first epistle of John, in its persistent injunction to "love the brethren"—the phrase Lagerkvist used to underscore the isolationism of the Christians in his novel *Barabbas.* While one face the Church has shown has been that of the gross worldliness and imperialistic design of the late medieval papacy, another has been that of retreat and fearfulness at becoming involved with the world. Even in its periods of greatest theological and devotional vigor, the Church has tended to be preoccupied with itself and has lain open to the charge of irrelevance. And it is one merit of art that it plunges the Church back into the midst of life in the world. It keeps open the avenues of sensitivity by which the Church carries on its business with the natural man. As John Dixon has said,[6] the artist deals in the realm of the senses, and he helps to keep the Church alive and "in touch."

We in the Church tend to forget this. We are inclined to become proud of our possession of dogma, and therefore to become calloused in our sensibilities. We are liable to think we have cornered up all revelation and the world must beat a path to our door for our commodity. Our sense of miracle is so cramped that we forget that God will be God and that he will make other bread than ours sacramental when he chooses—especially when we become narrow and prophylactic bearers of grace! But art, if we will allow it to have its say, will not let us forget this. It keeps us committed to "the essential worldliness of Christianity." It keeps our edges pliable and receptive, so that we do

[5] *Positive Preaching and the Modern Mind,* p. 89.

[6] "The Sensibility of the Church and the Sensibility of the Artist," in *Christian Faith and the Contemporary Arts,* p. 81.

not dry up and die of "hardening of the categories." This is what Nathan Scott is pleading for when he speaks of a "theology of the imagination"—a theology that keeps itself alive and vibrant in every generation by combining the truth of revelation with the sensibility of the artist.

If there is such a thing as "the Protestant sin," it is surely the exclusivism with which we endow the rational and verbal aspect of the Word of God. Tom F. Driver, speaking of the quickening of the arts today as a form of witness to the divine mercy in Christ, says,

> The prerequisite of such a development is that the Church shall recognize the validity of nonverbal forms of witness. Obviously the arts are not verbal statements about Christian belief. Neither are they translations of verbal statements into another medium. The arts are visions of states of being. Their function is to move others into a state of being corresponding to their vision. For this reason, their relation to theology and dogma is always less clear than is that of preaching and discursive literature.[7]

Certainly there is no such priority of verbal over sensory communication as Protestantism has asserted. Such a priority is merely a historical accident, a corrective necessitated by medieval abuses and unwittingly made the norm for all time. We are just beginning to recover from the excesses of the Reformation and to regain our perspective—a perspective in which the arts have their place as part of the fullness of man's response to the gracious action of God in Jesus Christ. Catholicism has never lost this sense of the natural that keeps Christianity from becoming docetic and unreal. Catholic writers, as a rule, have a much more abundant power to *feel* than Protestant writers. I think especially of Mauriac as a novelist and Hopkins as a poet: grace performs its assault upon them as an invasion from all nature, not merely through some narrow rubric of dogma. They are like the English metaphysical poets, of whom Eliot said that they felt their thought as immediately as the odor of a rose, so that it actually modified their sensibilities.[8]

Protestantism, itself a correction, needs a corrective at this point.

[7] "The Arts and the Christian Evangel," *The Christian Scholar,* XL (December, 1957), pp. 335-36.

[8] *Selected Essays,* p. 287.

It needs to be reminded that the *whole* man belongs to God and that Christian culture requires genius as well as saintliness. In fact, it needs to be reminded that the saint himself requires the genius if he is not to feed always, like the hyena, on his own intestines. Perhaps the image we should keep before us is that of the companionship between Dante and Vergil. We have all had our pagan guides into thoughts religious and spiritual. They seem now and then to prepare us for a more sensitive realization of God's self-revelation than were otherwise possible. Who does not feel more of the mystery of the Divine Presence in the world after reading a few pages of Rilke's *Notebooks of Malte Laurids Brigge*? Take a single phrase, for example, where he speaks of the pure music made by the soul upon its own hammerclavier as "giving back to the All that which only the All can endure." [9] Who is able to withstand the revelation of such a passage? It probes the heart of mystery and quickens the senses to the edge of esctasy. To repeat a word from Karl Barth, even that doughty Calvinist says that "God may speak to us through a pagan or an atheist, and in that way give us to understand that the boundary between Church and the profane still and repeatedly takes a course quite different from that which we hitherto thought we saw." [10]

And the service of the artist to the Church may be much more practical than this, if we are merely utilitarian minded. John Dixon has expressed it well:

> The artist has much to give to the church. Where its building affirms the irrelevance of the present and the governance of the past, he can recall the life of the church to the community of which it is a part. Where its prayers are flaccid, its services without form, he can give rhythm and shape. He can restore to the church the sense of the Incarnation, the sense of the holiness of the earth, the rootedness of the Christian life in the substance of things as they are. The life of the church must develop its own grace and discipline and rhythm if it is again to shape the consciousness and the sensibility of men. The work of the artist is not the only requisite to the attainment of this goal, but it is a vital part of it.[11]

[9] Tr. M. D. Herter Norton (New York: W. W. Norton, 1949), p. 71.
[10] *Church Dogmatics, I/1,* pp. 60-61.
[11] "Sensibility of the Church," p. 88.

When we speak of the failure of theology in modern literature, then, the accusation is not solely against art, but against the Church as well. Many artists have been guilty of an inadequate appreciation for the Christian faith and of regarding it, in Weidlé's words, merely "as a very rich deposit of useful goods, a sort of dump of finest quality provision of which the artist like a good cook can make highly palatable use." [12] But the Church too has been guilty, of crudeness and blindness and narrowness, and has failed to listen to the artist with the kind of sensitive ear required of an effective mediator of divine grace. In its fearful attempt to preserve the "purity" of the gospel, it has hoarded the gospel and even allowed it, in many instances, simply to stagnate from standing too long in one place. There is a sense in which a *chrétienté pure* is as irrelevant and meaningless as *poésie pure* or art for art's sake.

It is therefore extremely important, to the Church as well as to the arts, that the dialogue between them be pursued with something like a sense of urgency, and that a true entente be recovered as soon as possible. Not in order that we may have a more "decorative" Christian faith—a frosting on our architecture or a cleverness in our hymnology—but for the curing of our dissociation and the fusion of our parts—for the whole man in response to the whole gospel.

Such an entente will require that faith make the man, for the artist is a man before he is an artist. He, the artist, must recognize that his real freedom lies in the necessities of the Christian vision—that *poésie pure* is an absurdity, a contradiction in terms, a case of Swift's spider spinning out of his own entrails. And it will be required of the Church that, having made the man, it set him free—that it trust the man it makes—that it realize that real heresy is more a matter of the disposition than of doctrine. Art is not art if it must submit to "rules" imposed from without. As Jacques Maritain has said, "The virtue of art does not allow the work to be interfered with or immediately ruled by anything other than itself. It insists that it alone shall touch the work in order to bring it into being. In short, art requires that nothing

[12] *The Dilemma of the Arts,* tr. Martin Jarrett-Kerr (London S.C.M. Press, 1948), p. 123.

shall attain the work except through art itself." [13] The only solution then is the one offered by Mauriac in *God and Mammon:* to purify the source itself. In this way the Christian artist will not be forced into a self-contradiction but will be freed to pursue the finest aims of both faith and art.

"Art must first be really despised, must be accounted completely useless," says Philipp-Otto Runge, "before it can again come into its own." [14] Perhaps both art and Christianity have been passing through such a time together. The brave new world of science, technology, and materialism has not been especially kind to either. And maybe with the coming of age of the modern world they are both beginning to come into their own again. Having been chastened and brought near to death, so that the self-confidence of each of them was utterly shaken, they are now being reborn with a new understanding of their mission in the world. On the side of Christianity we have witnessed a recovery of trenchant biblical theology, a renaissance of liturgy, a renewal of the theology of preaching, a revitalization of lay interest, and a worldwide movement toward ecumenical friendship; and on the side of art we have gratefully beheld definite signs of new responsibility in painting, sculpture, music, dance, architecture, poetry, fiction, and drama. And the signs of the times would indicate that they have the good sense to recognize their dependence upon one another in such a period of renewal—Christianity upon art to make it more sensitive, more incarnate in the world of men, and art upon Christianity to provide it with its real meaning and purpose. Weidlé says that such a coalescence is the only future still open to art, "because artistic experience is, deep down, a religious experience, because the world art lives in cannot be made habitable save by religion alone." [15] And even if there are alternatives open to Christianity—which is perhaps debatable—the return of sensibility by way of the arts is certainly one of the most highly desirable of options.

Supposing that the movement toward an entente between Christianity and art continues, with each acting in good faith toward the other,

[13] *The Responsibility of the Artist* (New York: Charles Scribner's Sons, 1960), p. 57.

[14] Quoted by Weidlé in *Dilemma of the Arts,* p. 30.

[15] *Ibid.,* p. 25.

so that we have on one hand a more humanized Church (in the best sense of the word!) and on the other hand a more spiritual conception of the purpose of art, how shall we then identify the Christian artist? Or more explicitly, because we are primarily concerned here with the verbal arts, how shall we identify the Christian writer? Are there any outlines by which we may know him?

Without imposing any "rules" upon him—an imposition forbidden by our desire to behave toward him with fullest respect—it is possible to suggest in a very general way at least two marks of identity in his work.

First, to begin negatively, we shall not set upon such an artist the demand put to Browning's Fra Lippo Lippi, that he "paint souls, not men." What happens when an artist attempts this hazardous course is evidenced again and again in the novels of Charles Williams: the characters often become so noumenal and spectre-like that the average reader cannot even identify the world they belong to. It is a weird kind of docetism, and that is what we are anxious to avoid. Instead, we shall ask that the Christian author write about men in, or juxtaposed to, the redemptive situation—that situation "after the Incarnation," as R. W. B. Lewis has expressed it. Discussing the disappearance of the Judaeo-Christian tradition from the consciousness of most modern authors, Edmund Fuller says, "This is a major reason for the diminishing vision our recent age has had of our kind." [16] How true. Man is never properly man until viewed, potentially or in fact, as the image of God. Let the character of a novel or a drama be a thief, let him be a homosexual, let him be a liar or a murderer or a drunkard: we must deal in the realities of the dust. But let him be seen also as sinner, with the eyes of the crucified Lord upon him, drawing him or forbidding him, sensitizing him or hardening him, redeeming him or damning him. In other words, let it make a difference in his life that Christ has died and been raised and has ascended to the right hand of the Father. Let it make a difference that there was a Pentecost and that ever since, even in the remotest places, there have continued to be Pentecostal experiences. Let him live in a world that, since creation, "groaneth in travail until now." Let him live in such a manner that

[16] *Man in Modern Fiction*, p. 164.

tedium must occasionally give way to *Te Deum*—and vice versa. Let him act upon a stage that has more possibilities than a two-dimensional backdrop and an improvised script and a sleepy-headed director: let his drama have about it the proportions of Paul's letter to the Romans, and his stage directions, the cosmic dimensions of divine foreordination itself. Let him be part of what the Germans call *Heilsgeschichte,* the history of salvation, for Christianity and art both have their roots in history and in transhistory at the same time.

The second suggestion is this: somehow, the writer's presentation of man in the redemptive situation must have about it the kind of totality and coherence that will convince us of the utter reality of such a man in such a situation. The chief criticism of the religious nature of contemporary literature to date is that the appearances of Christian motifs, symbolisms, and points of view have been entirely too scattered and fragmentary really to be called Christian; or that, on the other hand, where these are found to be more consistent, credibility is often overtaxed, and we find ourselves in a world so unreal that we fail to recognize it as our own. The Christian writer, together with the world he writes about, must undergo *in toto* such a baptism as will promise the conversion of both their natures. Symbols of the faith, for instance, must appear as more than enameled flowers upon the surface of a story: they must be seen to have roots proceeding out of the very heart and center of the story-situation, which is somehow involved with the coming of Christ. This is what I mean by totality and coherence. Everything—sacred and secular, pure and obscene, good and evil—must hang together under the overall pressure of a Christian world view.

Here is an artless illustration of what I am trying to say. Early on a Sunday morning, a few summers ago, I was traveling to a distant church for a preaching engagement. I was following a road that wound along the ridgetops of some knobby country in northern Kentucky. The sun had risen just a few minutes earlier, and was glowing an eerie shade of red through the low morning fog. As I rounded a bend in the road and came directly toward a small cattle pond on the summit of a ridge, suddenly the sun appeared to come and stand in that pond as in a bowl, and to assault my consciousness in such a way as to seem, for one mystical second, the fiery core of all existence. It seemed to envelop me, to draw me in and in and in. It overwhelmed the reality of the car, the road, the fence between us—everything. It was as if there were no other thing than it in all the million miles of space. The car's momentum brought me beyond it in a second, and I regained my senses; but not without an emotion of well-being that remained throughout the entire day. Later, as I was reading in Pascal's journal for November 23, 1654, I meditated with new understanding on the word that comprised a whole line of his entry for that day: it was the solitary word FIRE, printed in capital letters.

Somehow, the Christian faith as expressed in literature must appear to the reader like this. It must seem to him to be the structureless structure of absolute reality. It must blind him to all semirealities and pseudorealities, and in so doing regather and reunify his sensibilities in an unfallen order. It must be experienced, not remotely, but directly and immediately, so as to convert his very nature. And yet it must be experienced within the context of the phenomenal world he knows so well, the world of leeks and crabgrass and split-level houses and commuter trains.

It goes without saying, I think, that no artist can communicate such an experience of the Christian faith without first undergoing it himself. It is not a thing to be conjured up and written down at will; it must be felt; it must be believed. It is a matter of what I spoke of earlier as faith's making the man before it makes the artist. This is what Weidlé pointed to when he wrote of religious art in medieval Europe: "The artist worked not merely for the Church but in the Church. He did more than provide for the needs of worship: he took part in it, for the planting of his work was an act of adoration and its growth to maturity was one long prayer." [17] Christianity must modify the sensibility of the artist before he can produce what is truly Christian art. It must permeate him and saturate him until it fairly exudes itself at the periods and commas of his writing.

Graham Greene may have been correct when he said that there is a great difference between writing as a Christian and writing Christian literature. But it ought not to be so. The one should lead to the other; indeed, the one should *be* the other. The converted man, with con-

[17] *Dilemma of the Arts,* p. 11.

verted sensibilities, should behold and write about a world struggling in the grip of redemption. It is a sizable requirement, but not an impossible one. To do more, one need never aspire; for, as Dante said, one cannot "square the circle"—describe the final beatific vision in terms that are incommensurate to the task.

Because Dante is so frequently taken to be the highest example of the Christian artist, it seems only appropriate to make an end with the final lines of the *Commedia:* "To the high fantasy here power failed; but already my desire and will were rolled—even as a wheel that moveth equally—by the Love that moves the sun and the other stars." It is this exhaustion in ecstasy that we would commend to every writer who would become a Christian author.

Index